FROM THREE CENTS A WEEK...

*The Story of
The Prudential Insurance Company
of America*

by William H. A. Carr

Prentice-Hall, Inc., Englewood Cliffs, N.J.

From Three Cents a Week . . .
by William H. A. Carr

Printed in the United States of America
Prentice-Hall International, Inc., London
Prentice-Hall of Australia, Pty. Ltd., Sydney
Prentice-Hall of Canada, Ltd., Toronto
Prentice-Hall of India Private Ltd., New Delhi
Prentice-Hall of Japan, Inc., Tokyo

10 9 8 7 6 5 4 3 2 1

Library of Congress Cataloging in Publication Data

Carr, William H   A
  From three cents a week . . .

  Includes index.
  1. Prudential Insurance Company of America,
Newark, N.J   I.   Title.
HG 8540.P73C37   368'.006'573   75-22086
ISBN 0-13-331611-4

CONTENTS

1/The Two Lives of a Governor

The road was virtually deserted as the Governor's car sped westward towards Bernardsville. A thin sliver of moon lit the road, which was clear and dry. Except for a brief sprinkle two days earlier, there hadn't been any rain for several days. As far as the weather was concerned, the luck of the Irish had held that afternoon for the St. Patrick's Day parades being held all over the country.

Like any prudent politician, New Jersey's Governor Robert B. Meyner had been honoring the Irish that day. In his lapel he still sported the green carnation he had worn that evening at the annual dinner of the Friendly Sons of St. Patrick in West Orange. Now he was going to Charlie Laing's place, and he knew he was going to hear about trouble. Bad trouble. Trouble involving corruption—and a former Governor who was still on the state's payroll.

Charles B. Laing was a senior vice president of the Prudential Insurance Company of America, which was then, in 1954, the second biggest life insurance company in the United States—or, indeed, the world. Little more than a decade later it would move into first place and become one of the three or four largest corporations of any kind, in terms of assets. Laing's association with Meyner had begun four months earlier, as a result of a conversation Meyner had had with Prudential's general counsel, Sylvester Smith.

A few days after his election Meyner had asked Smith, who was an old friend, if he thought that Prudential's then president, Carrol M. Shanks, might be willing to lend a few of his best executives to the state for a short time. Meyner needed the businessmen to advise him on how the state government could be modernized. During his election campaign, Meyner had heard complaints from many voters about the state's hiring practices, the long lines that people had to wait in when doing business with the Division of Motor Vehicles, and the slowness of the Division of Employment Security in processing applications and making payments. Perhaps skilled businessmen could study those opera-

1

tions, among others, and recommend changes that could lead to more efficient and economical procedures.

Shanks had granted the Governor's request immediately. The Prudential head gave the assignment to Laing, with three other Pru officers to assist him: Floyd H. Bragg, Edwin E. Lineberry, and E. Carroll Gerathy. That team, in turn, asked a number of other New Jersey companies to provide executives to work with them. Within a month of his election, six weeks before his inauguration, Meyner had a blue-ribbon, volunteer task force digging into the intricacies of state government.

Bragg's crew began looking into the way the Civil Service system worked. Lineberry and his men took on the job of helping the Division of Motor Vehicles devise methods of processing driver and automobile license applications and car inspections with less delay. And Gerathy's group was instructed to figure out how the state could put money into the hands of the unemployed quickly—as soon as they needed it.

For six years Gerathy had been with Prudential. Before that, he had worked for 15 years for a major pharmaceutical house, McKesson and Robbins, as a cost accountant. Four years after Gerathy went to work at McKesson and Robbins, it was rocked by a scandal that had repercussions throughout the business world: its president, F. Donald Coster, committed suicide after the police learned that he was really Philip Musica, a professional criminal all his life, a man who had served time for bribery and other crimes. It was discovered that Coster-Musica had been systematically looting McKesson and Robbins for more than a decade by means of fictitious purchases and sales, subsidiaries that existed only on paper, and hijackings of the company's shipments carried out by gangsters working in collusion with him. Altogether, Coster-Musica had bilked his own company of about four million dollars, most of which he paid out, towards the end, to blackmailers in a vain attempt to prevent disclosure of his true identity.

Soon after he began studying the Division of Employment Security, Gerathy noticed things, some trivial, others rather substantial, that reminded him uneasily of McKesson and Robbins in the Coster-Musica days. For example, the division's director, Harold G. Hoffman—a popular politician who had been Governor from 1935 to 1938—and a couple of his top aides were so conscientious that they never took vacations. That appeared to be the ultimate in dedication, but Gerathy remembered that Coster-Musica and his close associates always stayed close to their offices, too. After their downfall, it became apparent that they'd felt they had to be on hand at all times to protect their operations from any outsider who might have gotten curious enough to snoop around.

Gerathy found that Hoffman and his closest aides would, if given the opportunity, unwittingly lead the investigators to areas that merited attention. "They kept volunteering favorable information about themselves," Gerathy recalled many years later. "Whenever I heard them talking that way about a particular activity, I knew it was worth looking into."

At the first sign of improprieties, Laing had informed the Governor about Gerathy's early discoveries.

"This is beginning to look ugly," Laing told him. "I feel it's my responsibility to consult with Mr. Shanks."

"I understand," Meyner replied. "As far as I'm concerned, go ahead. Just keep me informed."

The Prudential men then arranged for a conference with their president. After all, they had set out to improve the efficiency of the state government, not to investigate corruption. Would Prudential want its name dragged into a mess like this, even if it were on the side of the angels?

"No," said Harold M. Stewart, the company's executive vice president. "Get the hell out of Trenton. Whatever happens, don't let anyone know that the Prudential is involved."

He was overruled by Shanks.

"The question boils down to this: Can we walk away from this so that the Pru can avoid a political fight?" Shanks said, according to Gerathy's recollection. "The answer is that to walk away now is neither possible nor desirable. We undertook a commitment. Now we have to do what is right, regardless of the consequences."

So the investigators pressed on. Finally, Gerathy met with Laing on March 16 and briefed him fully on what he had uncovered. Laing picked up the telephone and called the Governor.

"We've got to see you," he said, "about the Division of Employment Security."

It had been agreed then that Meyner would join them at Laing's house in Bernardsville after the St. Patrick's Day dinner in West Orange. It was midnight when the Governor's car pulled into the Laing driveway, past trees swaying in the stiff wind. When he left, his breath condensing in the frosty air, it was almost 4:00 A.M.

During those hours, the two men from Prudential laid out the case against Hoffman as they knew it at that time. Trivial records, they reported, had been maintained with great care—the number of pencils consumed each month, for example. But important records were incomplete, "lost," or nonexistent. Hoffman had been keeping $300,000 in state funds in his own bank at South Amboy and almost $2,500,000 in a Trenton bank whose president was a close friend, and neither account was drawing interest for the state. He had used state employees to perform work for himself and for organizations in which he was interested. Specifications for purchases appeared to have been rigged so that only vendors favored by Hoffman could qualify. Exorbitant rentals were being paid for some buildings used by the Division of Employment Security; other buildings had been purchased or constructed without competitive bidding, in violation of state law. State property apparently was being stolen and sold; one such wholesale theft was of 250 slightly used typewriters. A few key men had been receiving substantial payments for overtime which the investigators had reason to suspect had not been earned.

At one point in the conversation, Gerathy challenged the other two men to name "any bad business practice that you can think of"—he was certain he would be able to cite an example that he had uncovered in Hoffman's Division of Employment Security.

"Well, nepotism is certainly a destructive business practice," Laing said, as Meyner listened with interest.

"Yes, it is," Gerathy said, "and we've found many examples of that in Hoffman's division. For example, Hoffman's No. 1 assistant has his own wife and several other relatives on the payroll."

But the three men were talking about more than undesirable business practices. They were talking about betrayal of the public trust. They were talking about crime.

Laing summed up where they stood.

"We think our discoveries have reached the stage where you ought to suspend Hoffman and announce the opening of an official, criminal investigation," he said.

The Governor agreed.

At 9:00 A.M. Meyner was in his office contacting the appropriate state and federal authorities, the latter because the Division of Employment Security was federally funded. The state police were ordered to guard the division's files against tampering. It was not until Hoffman returned his telephone call at 3:00 P.M. that the Governor was able to notify him personally of the charges against him and his suspension. A half hour later, at his regular press conference, Meyner made public the actions he had taken.

Then the storm broke. Although Meyner was a Democrat and Hoffman a Republican, Democratic politicians as well as their G.O.P. counterparts assailed the Governor. Many newspapers throughout the state agreed with the critics that Meyner appeared to be resorting to the lowest political tactics. Only the Newark newspapers, which had been keeping an eye on the study by the businessmen, almost all of whom were Republicans, assumed that the charges probably reflected their work and therefore must be free from the taint of political partisanship.

Almost three months later Hoffman was found dead in a hotel room in New York City, apparently the victim of a heart attack. With renewed fury the attacks on Meyner mounted. At the funeral services for Hoffman, state police had to slip the Governor out a side door to protect him from the anger of the crowd.

The denouement came ten days later. Hoffman's daughter made public the fact that her father, in a letter to be read after his death, had confessed to "one thing which I have done that cannot be condoned." That "one thing" was the embezzlement, over a period of ten years, of more than $300,000 from a bank of which he was treasurer in South Amboy. He had first dipped into the till during his successful campaign for Congress in 1928; after he left the Governor's office at the age of 43 he never again, he said, put funds on deposit at the bank to his own personal use.

But for the last 18 years of his life he had been juggling state funds—perhaps $15,000,000 or more—from bank to bank, account to account, in order to cover up his embezzlement. In the end, the money taken from bank funds had been replaced by dollars that properly belonged to the state.

Like Coster-Musica, Hoffman had been leading a double life.

Another ironic similarity lay in his having paid $150,000 in blackmail to a man whom Hoffman's letter described simply as "a certain state official," unnamed but dead.

Several months later a state official was quoted by a national magazine as saying, "Since this thing came out, just by tightening up the loose practices of the past, we've saved more money than Hoffman stole."

It was, indirectly, a compliment to Prudential and its men. But a more direct comment was made the following year by Governor Meyner. As the Newark *News* reported it:

> Meyner . . . paid tribute last night to the Prudential Insurance Company . . . for its part in uncovering irregularities in the State Division of Employment Security. . . .
>
> The division is now making payments more rapidly and more efficiently at a savings of thousands of dollars annually, the Governor said. . . .
>
> Meyner said that the Prudential has always played an important role in the state's affairs. Shanks, for example, assists in developing fiscal policy for state investments, he pointed out.
>
> The Governor, asserting he has a "warm attachment" for the Prudential, said it is a great enterprise, with its leaders men of integrity dedicated to the interests of the policyholders.

It was true that the Prudential had been a significant factor in public affairs in New Jersey since the latter part of the 19th century, but the Prudential tradition of public service had changed in substance as well as form. Once a Prudential president could run successfully for the Senate, could make political contributions from company funds, could head a corrupt political machine during what a Newark newspaper called "a peculiarly sordid era" of politics. But that was long in the past; for many years Prudential had been building a tradition of disinterested service to the general public welfare.

The change in that field of endeavor was paralleled by other changes which had taken place in the Prudential over the years. Where it had originally been a source of riches and self-aggrandizement for a handful of men, it is now a mutual company, literally a business establishment owned by its customers. In the not-too-distant past it had been a stuffy, priggish, highly regimented organization, even judged by the standards of the time; but in an extraordinarily short time after World War II, it underwent an internal revolution which also altered the nature of its entire industry and strongly affected all business and the national economy. Over the years, sometimes as a result of painful or embarrassing investigations or revelations, it kept setting higher ethical standards for its people, until today it is unlikely that many companies can equal the demands that the Prudential puts on its men and women in terms of business conduct.

But few companies occupy a position of trust comparable to the Prudential's. At the end of 1974, as its centennial year was about to begin, Prudential had assets of $35.8 billion. Its total life insurance sales that year were $30.5 billion. Its books showed life insurance in force —that is, the face value of all the policies issued by Prudential and still in effect—of $218.3 billion. In all three categories, Prudential was the leading company in the life insurance industry.

It is impossible to arrive at a precise figure for the number of individual policyholders. The difficulty is caused by the duplication of persons—one man or woman may be covered by two or three individual life insurance policies, by group life, by group or individual health protection, by a group pension plan or an individually designed retirement program, and by automobile and homeowner's policies written by Pru's property and casualty subsidiary. Some policyholders may scarcely be aware that they are protected by a Prudential policy; this is true, for example, of many who are covered by credit life insurance policies, which protect the families of borrowers from being saddled with their debts in the event of death.

Despite these difficulties, Prudential's statistical experts estimate that about one in every four Americans is protected by Pru. So are great numbers of Canadians.

The vast accumulations of money entrusted to Prudential by these policyholders were helping to move forward the economies of North America. In addition to many Canadian companies, as well as smaller U.S. businesses by the hundreds, Pru had invested in the stocks or bonds of 223 of the companies in the *Fortune* "Five Hundred" lists. It had more farm loans outstanding than any other company; even the California wine served with dinner may come from a vineyard owned by or in mortgage to Prudential. In recent years the company had bought a farm that raised fish, a tugboat, jet aircraft it leased to airlines, and a number of other enterprises or properties not usually associated in the public's mind with a life insurance company.

The Empire State Building belonged to Prudential, and so did other famous structures, including hotels—some bearing names like Hilton, Sheraton, and Regency Hyatt—all symbolizing the productive investment of the company's funds. The same could be said of scores, and sometimes even hundreds, of shopping centers, office buildings, medical facilities, dormitories, and factories, not to speak of thousands of apartment houses and hundreds of thousands of smaller family dwellings. Most of the buildings which Pru has erected for its own use in major cities around the continent have been criticized by architectural authorities as, at best, undistinguished—but almost all have sparked genuine rebirths of vigor, enterprise, and tasteful construction in their respective communities.

In the early part of the company's centennial year, 1975, Prudential was issuing checks at the rate of over 60,000 per day, for an average daily value of approximately $17,519,000, to hundreds of thousands of policyholders and their beneficiaries who received death benefits, health or disability payments, annuity disbursements, matured endowments, surrender values, policy loans, dividends, investment plan distributions, and reinsurance loss payments.

As *Fortune* once said of the Prudential, "It's a kind of universal power plant, vast of maw and spout, breathing in and breathing out. Its function is the collection and redistribution of the people's savings. As the giant mechanism pumps away, there are few U.S. businesses—or few U.S. citizens, in fact—that escape the effect of either its updraft or its downdraft. . . . This aggregate view of Prudential as an economic mechanism does not, of course, do complete justice to the company's character, motivation, and deep-down purpose. Life insurance was a belief before it was a business; it is a missionary effort, largely, that propels the 'pump.' "

The "missionaries"—the men and women of Prudential—were an army of some 60,000 at the time of the centennial, nearly 28,000 of them salesmen or sales management staff, more than any other life insurance company. But "missionaries" is too exalted a term for such great numbers of people. Most Prudential men and women could hardly be described as evangelistic, except perhaps in the religious sense of the word. But Prudential people are remarkable for their pride in their company and the generally high level of their work performance.

Over the years there have been many colorful or intriguing persons in the Pru, some of whom have figured prominently in the company's history. There have been personal feuds and professional controversies. Nepotism was once a problem, until the board of directors did the hard and necessary job of totally outlawing it. One of the organization's finest minds was destroyed, in the end, by alcohol. In the relatively recent past, the man who was more responsible than any other single person for Prudential's preeminence today left the company under a cloud during a furor over conflicts of interest.

In short, the Prudential is a historically continuing mass of human beings, with all their vulnerabilities and virtues, their complexities and contradictions, their logic and their inconsistency.

2/'A Devilish Time'

The Prudential story begins with a tall, lean insurance agent named John Fairfield Dryden, who was to become one of the most significant, if least publicized, figures in the history of American business and a man of some consequence in the world of politics. Over the years, pious myths and reverent legends have tended to obscure the real Dryden, which is particularly unfortunate because he was an uncommon man, and the true story of his life tells a great deal about the strengths—and the weaknesses—of American society in the 19th century.

Dryden was born on August 7, 1839, at Temple Mills (now Temple), Maine, about 40 miles northwest of Augusta. His father, John, had been a "mechanic"—in other words, a skilled laborer—in Holden, Massachusetts, before moving to Maine with his wife, Elizabeth, in the 1830's to take up farming. The younger John, fourth child in the family, was the first boy; another son was born in 1842 but lived only three years. By that time the elder Dryden had given up his attempt to wrench a living from the rocky soil. He was now doing odd jobs and, it is said, was at various times tax assessor and collector, constable, clerk of the school, and highway surveyor. It seems to have been something of a hand-to-mouth existence, so in 1848 the Drydens packed up and left Maine for Massachusetts, settling this time in Worcester, where Dryden found work in a machine shop.

One of the myths about John Fairfield Dryden has it that his father died in 1852, when the boy was 13, and that the privation suffered by the family because of the loss of the breadwinner instilled in the youth a determination to help other families find the means to protect themselves against such distress. It is a touching story, so appealing that it has found its way, over the years, into many Prudential publications and speeches. Apparently every writer and speaker who passed on the story believed it to be true.

However, there is documentary evidence that the elder Dryden did

10

not die until his son was 27 years old. Genealogical records show that the senior Dryden was born in 1788. When the Prudential prepared to issue Ordinary life insurance coverage in 1886, John F. Dryden applied for the first policy, and in his application he stated that his father had died at the age of 78. That would mean the death occurred in 1866—when his son, then 27, was already working as an insurance agent.

Even with the elder Dryden very much alive and contributing to the family's support, there is every reason to believe that they lived in meager fashion. The tradition that has young John working throughout his boyhood is undoubtedly accurate; the family badly needed whatever additional money he could bring in.

Somehow—there is no record of how he managed it—young Dryden managed to scrape up enough money to go to Yale, which he entered in the fall of 1861, when he was 21. In those days, and for another 70 years or more, college was not for poor boys, especially a university like Yale. Always diffident, he must have found Yale a lonely and disheartening place, full of youths from comfortable backgrounds who were preparing to be lawyers, physicians, or clergymen. Not for him the excitement of Tap Day, the comradeship of Skull and Bones or Scroll and Key, the elite student clubs. Even a convivial glass of beer at Mory's was beyond his means.

The young law student lived in a dormitory but took his meals off campus, at 420 Chapel Street in New Haven, where Mrs. Abigail Jennings Fairchild accommodated about 18 or 20 Yale men in her dining room. After the birth of their second daughter, Eliza, Mrs. Fairchild had left her husband, Walter, in Newtown, Connecticut, and moved to New Haven, where the two girls assisted her in the kitchen and waited on tables. That is how John Dryden met the girls and fell in love with the elder, Cynthia.

In the spring of Dryden's third year at Yale, according to the traditional story recounted in Prudential's archives, the two young people eloped. The date and place of the putative wedding do not appear in the records. As one account, based on family sources, put it, "Two weeks later, when the excitement over [the] disappearance [of the young couple] had subsided somewhat, they returned and announced that they had been married." But Cynthia's mother "was a stickler for the conventions," so "the elopement would not do, they must be married again by their own pastor.'' On April 7, 1864, a marriage ceremony was performed by the Reverend S. D. Phelps, minister of the First Baptist Church of New Haven. John was 24; his bride, 23.

That June, Dryden was forced—by ill health, the story has it—to leave the college. It is certainly true that he was never robust. But other factors probably entered into his leaving Yale. In those days, married students were frowned upon. Then, too, Dryden had very little in the way of financial resources to support a wife. And it was soon apparent that his family responsibilities were going to include a baby.

One of his sisters, Hannah, who lived in Ohio, wrote and urged them to move there, so he and Cynthia packed their few belongings and went west. It may be assumed that they lived at Bedford (now a suburb of Cleveland), for it was there that the first of their two children was born, on the day after Christmas in 1864. They named him Forrest Fairfield Dryden.

John had obtained a job working for S. E. Judd, an insurance agent at Hudson, a town not far from Bedford, on the road from Cleveland to Akron. Judd was an agent for the Niagara Fire Insurance Company and for the Aetna Life Insurance Company. Early in 1865 the Drydens moved to Columbus, where an Aetna advertisement soon appeared, signed by ''John F. Dryden, Agent, 107 South High Street.'' It appears that Dryden was on his own as an agent then, but he maintained close and warm relations with Judd. In 1892, when Judd was 80, they were still corresponding.

Later in 1865 Dryden joined forces with a man named Huston to operate an insurance agency together, representing the Travelers Insurance Company as well as the Aetna. Somehow the partnership weathered the postwar depression from the middle of 1865 to the middle of 1866, but when a slight recession occurred in 1867, Dryden and Huston decided they'd had enough, and the partnership was dissolved. When the Drydens headed east—on their way to New York City this time —they left behind some unpaid debts.

Before the end of the year, the Drydens were living in what was then called Belmont Heights in the East New York section of Brooklyn, and John was working out of an insurance agency at 160 Fulton Street in Manhattan, representing the Home Life Insurance Company. Two years later Dryden's business address was 95 Liberty Street in Manhattan, and the family was living at Eighteenth and Fifth Avenue in

Brooklyn, according to a city directory. They moved at least once a year over the next three years—to 75 Dean Street in Brooklyn, then to 253 Warren Street in Brooklyn, and finally to New Jersey. During the last two years of the 1860's Dryden represented the Globe Mutual and, it would seem, the Mutual Life of New York.

During those bleak and restless years of setbacks and shabbiness and frustration, Dryden had been reading everything he could find in print about a controversial new concept called Industrial insurance. For a century or so, the life insurance sold in Great Britain and America had consisted of what is now called Ordinary life—that is, insurance sold on an individual basis in multiples of $1,000, with premiums paid by mail on a monthly or less frequent basis. As an early officer of Pru, statistician Frederick L. Hoffman, later wrote, this was *class* insurance, designed for upper-income people, as opposed to Industrial insurance, which was *mass* insurance—protection for poor, working-class, and lower middle-class families.

Looking back from today's perspective, it is difficult to comprehend how different American society was in the latter part of the last century. In 1874 the average *annual* income of a wage-earner in the U.S. was $424, and that princely sum was for a ten-hour day and a six-day work week. (To make matters worse, the unemployment rate was about ten per cent.) A very small percentage of the American people were rich or quite well off; a larger—but not much larger—portion comprised the small but growing middle class; and the vast majority of the people were poor, even by the standards of their time. It might fairly be said that any American living today whose family arrived on this continent in the 19th century or the first part of the 20th century is the grandchild, or great-grandchild, of people who lived in poverty.

For people in such circumstances, Ordinary life insurance was out of the question. By definition, the poor live hand-to-mouth; they cannot save for an insurance premium or anything else. But such people could be protected by Industrial life insurance, which was so named because it was designed to meet the needs of factory workers, a key problem when England, Canada, and the U.S. were being transformed into industrial nations. Those who argued for Industrial insurance said that it would be offered to the public for as little as three cents a week. The insurance agent would go around once a week to collect the premiums from the policyholders before the money to pay the premiums could be spent on other things. The convenience of this form of payment would add to the attractiveness of the coverage. Moreover, no medical examination would be required for most applicants.

Industrial insurance, as such, began with the founding of the Prudential Assurance Company of Great Britain in 1848. (The British seem to prefer the word *assurance,* and the people of America the word *insurance,* for no good reason that anyone has been able to discover.) The British company met a real and deeply felt social need, made evident in its quick acceptance and rapid growth, which attracted the attention of people all over the world.

For example, Julius Clarke, a Massachusetts insurance commissioner, wrote in 1874:

> In presenting to the Legislature a general view of the different matters of interest and importance relating to insurance which have attracted attention during the last year, reference should be made to the subject of Industrial insurance. . . . Though it does not, like the old friendly societies, guarantee allowances in sickness, yet like them it adjusts the amount of insurance to the premium paid; that is to say, instead of naming certain sums as the premiums for which it will insure the payment of ten, a hundred, or a thousand pounds at death, it offers certain amounts of insurance in return for the payment of small fixed sums each week; such as one penny, twopence, threepence, or fourpence, as the case may be. Like the friendly societies, also, the company sends its collectors from house to house and collects the premiums weekly. . . . The secret of the success of this company may be found in the fact that the ground had been thoroughly prepared for the new system by the old [friendly] societies. The company merely takes advantage of tradition, habits, and ideas that have been the growth of more than a century.

Not everyone, in either Britain or America, shared Clarke's enthusiasm.

The greatest reformer in the history of American insurance, for one—Elizur Wright, often called "the Father of Life Insurance in America"—was bitterly opposed to Industrial insurance. Like many men of real greatness, his errors of judgment were few, but they were massive. Agreeing with other critics of Industrial insurance in the 19th century, Wright's objections included the fear that policies on the lives of infants might lead their parents to murder them for the money. In 1853 the grand jury at the Liverpool Assizes in England had alleged, without offering proof, that the insuring of infants was an incentive to murder them. This theory was a vivid illustration of a common belief among well-bred people a century ago—the assumption that parents who belonged to "the lower classes" were less fond of their offspring than their "betters" might be. It was part of a stereotype of the poor as somehow brutish, stupid, violent, and vicious. In fact, the "infanticide-for-profit" sensation was punctured by several official investigations which found no evidence that such a crime had ever been committed.

Despite the opposition of Wright and some others, before 1874 came to a close the *Insurance Times* was able to carry this announcement.

> The appeal made by Commissioner Clarke, in behalf of the requirements of the industrial classes with respect to life insurance, has met with a prompt response from the capitalists of this city [New York]. Progress has already been made in the organization of a new life company, to be entitled the "Prudential Insurance Company of America," to be conducted on a plan similar to that of the Prudential of London, which has been attended with so much success and benefit to the indigent working classes.

That Prudential was still-born, probably because its backers, whoever they were, could not raise the necessary capital in the depths of the depression that followed the Panic of 1873.

But there would be an American company with the name Prudential very soon now, for John F. Dryden, who had been closely following the Industrial insurance debate in print, had become a passionate advocate of this new concept. He became obsessed with the desire to found a life insurance company on Industrial principles—an absurd ambition on the part of a man who was himself almost penniless at this point in his life.

Not that Dryden's motives were necessarily altruistic. Although it is almost always futile—and unfair—to speculate on another's motives, it seems reasonable to assume that Dryden hoped at least to climb out of penury, and possibly even to make his fortune, through Industrial insurance. As Alexis de Tocqueville had written 30 years earlier, "I never met in America with any citizen so poor as not to cast a glance of hope and envy on the enjoyments of the rich, or whose imagination did not possess itself by anticipation of those good things which fate still obstinately withheld from him." If Dryden dreamed that this new kind of insurance might make him rich, his dream was in the mainstream of American aspirations.

Nevertheless, Dryden knew that Industrial insurance would meet a real social need, if only in enabling people to provide for their own and their families' burials. In 1872 the Labor Commissioner of Massachusetts reported, "There is a class of deposits in our large cities that shows the poverty of working women more than argument could do. This class consists of poor women who save and starve for the sake of having enough to bury them." The slums of the cities were jammed with people living in unsanitary conditions, for the flood tide of immigration was beginning—the annual number of immigrants nearly doubled between 1865 and 1873—and the death rates, especially infant mortality, showed the impact. The death rate among younger children soared by more than 50 per cent from 1871 to 1872, and the impoverished parents of the dead children often could not even give them a burial; many were interred in potter's field. If Industrial insurance did nothing more than provide the means for the poor to bury their own in dignity, it would have accomplished a great deal.

So it really doesn't matter what Dryden's motives were. We do know that he was acutely aware of the pauperized masses in the cities, because he spoke and wrote about their plight often, long after he had become rich. But regardless of his concern or lack of it, what Dryden did ultimately achieved a great social good.

In 1870 Dryden talked a lawyer, H. H. Goodman, into helping him organize a life insurance company which they called the United States Mutual Benefit Company, with offices at 112 Broadway in Manhattan. It was Dryden's intention—he was secretary and Goodman was president—to operate it as an Industrial insurance organization, the first in America. But before it could solicit business, the company had to have a state charter, so Dryden went to Albany and persuaded the legislators to pass a private bill chartering his new company. Within a fortnight, however, the Governor vetoed the bill. Years later Dryden testified, during an investigation, that the Governor had rejected the charter "on the ground that all the powers desired were conferred under the general law." But that was a less than wholly candid explanation. In fact, the Governor said he was opposed to the charter which Dryden and Goodman had drawn up because it gave the company too much power in the handling of funds.

For some reason, Dryden lingered on at 112 Broadway for two more years, still listing himself in the city directory as secretary of the aborted United States Mutual Benefit Company. He must have found increasing difficulties in making ends meet, for the recollections of those who saw him when he first moved to New Jersey in 1873 emphasize his poverty. "These were lean days, indeed, for the Drydens," one Prudential chronicler wrote. "They took up their residence in a modest rooming house" on Lincoln Street. David Maclure, son of the family next door, looked back more than half a century later. "I think I was the first person in Newark to know Mr. John F. Dryden," he said. "I infer that Mr. Dryden at that time was not in opulent circumstances, for I remember that it was his habit to walk to the office . . . which I am quite sure was a matter of economy and not a health requirement."

The office to which Dryden walked was that of the Widows and Orphans Friendly Society. How the society came into being is a matter of some dispute. The traditional story is that Dryden interested Allen L. Bassett in his insurance ideas, and that Bassett provided Dryden with desk space in his basement office in the National State Bank Building at 812 Broad Street, on the corner of Mechanic (now Edison) Street, in which to work while organizing the Widows and Orphans Friendly Society. On its face, that account seems unlikely, for the society did not carry out Dryden's idea of selling Industrial life insurance, but simply sold small Ordinary policies on what amounted to a kind of group basis, the actual policies being issued by the Arlington-Piedmont Company of Virginia.

More credible is the version of one early Prudential historian—and of the Bassett family—that Bassett had already formed the society and hired Dryden to administer the society's affairs. If this story be true, it is probable that Dryden took the job because he was desperate for an income, and also—and even more important for a man of his temperament—because he saw it as an opportunity to jump off into the activity for which he had a true missionary zeal, Industrial insurance. John F. Dryden was 34 then, with a record of failures and defeats behind him, but he still clung stubbornly to hope and to his belief in the success that would attend Industrial insurance.

Regardless of how he became associated with the society, Dryden soon persuaded Bassett that Industrial insurance had a brighter future than a "friendly society." He even had a name for the new organization that he wanted to establish: the Prudential Friendly Society. Most people were familiar with the British Prudential; many of those in the Newark area were immigrants from Britain who had been insured with that company in the old country. Besides, it had been well publicized in the American press. (A number of American companies followed this pattern. For example, the Equitable was founded almost a century after the English company of the same name.)

Together, Bassett and Dryden agreed to enlist the financial backers they would need for a company which actually wrote its own insurance. They could hardly have picked a worse time for such an effort. The country was in the depths of the depression which had followed the Panic of 1873, a depression which would last for more than five years. Many businesses were failing. Suffering was widespread. "There are idle laborers begging for work who may soon be begging for bread without work," one of the Newark newspapers reported. "They may become an unrequiting expense to the city, or a nightly terror to the people." Before this depression was over, there would be serious disorders in a number of cities; and in Pittsburgh, Pennsylvania, and Martinsburg, West Virginia, vandalism, looting, and arson would not be suppressed without the intervention of federal troops.

There is little question that Bassett, a real estate broker whose interests were as much literary as commercial, did not prove as useful as Dryden had hoped. The best thing that he did for the proposed company was to suggest that Dryden call upon Dr. Leslie D. Ward, a physician who also operated a pharmacy at Lafayette and Congress Streets in the Down Neck section of Newark.

The Wards had always been among the leading families of Newark. When the first settlers from Connecticut arrived on the banks of the Passaic River to found the city, a substantial proportion were members of the Ward family; a mural in the Essex County Court House depicts one of them, Josiah, helping a young woman ashore from the boat that brought the colonists. When the Mutual Benefit Life Insurance Company was founded in Newark in 1845, a Ward was among the incorporators, and there has usually been a Ward associated with that company ever since then. With the connections that Dr. Ward had, Dryden might be able to get the support he needed—if he could persuade Dr. Ward of the merits of his case.

"I shall never forget my first experience with . . . Dryden," Dr. Ward once said. "Late in 1874 or early 1875 he called upon me at my office just across the railroad in Newark. I was a practicing physician. I had never heard anything about his Industrial insurance scheme at the time, and when he broached the three-cent policy proposition, I laughed and said that I didn't know anything about it, and that it was useless for him to try to interest me.

"There was something about the man, however, that impressed me, and from the first moment that I saw him I was impressed by his honesty of purpose and strength of character. He spent an hour or more with me going over the details of what I had first thought was a wild, useless scheme. He wanted me to become a subscriber to stock in the project. At that time he was in dire distress. . . . ."

It is easy to imagine just how dire Dryden's distress was at that time. But Dr. Ward, who was himself in somewhat straitened circumstances because of the depression, saved the day for Dryden—and thereby became himself a very rich man.

"After hearing his plan," Dr. Ward said, "and being impressed solely by my confidence in his earnest and honest motives, I told him that I would like to think the matter over and that I would give him my answer the following day. That night I had a talk with [Elias S.] Ward, my brother. He was somewhat impressed, and advised me to subscribe, saying that the amount was small and even if success should not follow, the loss would be insignificant. Whereupon, with an eye to business, I asked him to also become a subscriber. This, however, he would not do. At any rate, I took his advice, and when Mr. Dryden called the next day, I subscribed for $1,000 worth of stock and promised to try to enlist the support of some of my friends."

At last the tide in Dryden's affairs had clearly turned. But even with Dr. Ward's strong assistance, he "had a devilish time," as the physician remembered, raising the $30,000 in pledged capital which had been set as a goal. Although it had been decided that the company could start doing business as soon as $6,000 had been subscribed, "it was like pulling eye teeth" to get that part of the initial funds, according to Dr. Ward.

Most of the investors were elected to the board of directors after the charter and the name of the Widows and Orphans Friendly Society were changed on February 18, 1875. A notice in the Newark *Daily Advertiser* of that date listed 24 persons, including Bassett and Dryden, as directors of the Prudential Friendly Society. Three of the directors —Horace Alling, Aaron Carter, Jr., and James M. Durand—were jewelers and men of considerable wealth. Benjamin Atha was the head of a steel company. Noah F. Blanchard owned a thriving tannery business. Charles G. Campbell had a mirror and picture business. William R. Drake was a bank cashier. Albert O. Headley was a manufacturer of trunks. The clergy was represented by Andrew Hopper, a retired Baptist minister. Alfred Lister's company ground up animal bones, including carloads of buffalo bones from the West, to make fertilizer. William H. Murphy's company, Johnston & Murphy, made the most famous and respected quality shoes and boots in the nation. George Richards was an entrepreneur engaged in railroading and mining. Harness ornamentation was William Robotham's business. Dr. Ward and his lawyer brother Edgar were on the board, and so was a very distant relative, Marcus L. Ward, Jr., whose father had been Governor of the state in the preceding decade. (Marcus Ward's father was one of the founders of the Mutual Benefit Life Insurance Company and was currently on that company's board of directors, and the younger Marcus Ward later served as a Mutual Benefit director, too.) The hat industry was represented on the Prudential board by Henry J. Yates.

"The gentlemen who have the management of this important and humane enterprise are too well known in Newark to require our endorsement," said the Newark *Evening Courier* of November 13. "Their names are a synonym for financial strength and integrity, and our people know that funds entrusted to an organization which is under such control will be guarded with sacred care."

Another newspaper, the Newark *Register,* uttered a rather prescient comment that same day about the Prudential. "One of the most gratifying facts connected with this society is its strength and security," it said, and then it added that the Prudential "may be said to be founded upon a rock." Perhaps some people resented the implied comparison; certainly John Dryden didn't.

In order to conduct the business on an actuarial basis, Dryden in an exchange of correspondence engaged Professor John E. Clark, who taught mathematics at Yale, to prepare life-expectancy tables and to help Dryden determine the rates at which premiums ought to be set. As he began working on the assignment, Clark wrote to Dryden:

"You are aware of the important precautions which this writer suggests should be taken in the administration of such societies. I may, however, recall them briefly.

"1. Care should be taken to secure a sufficient number of members, so that the law of averages upon which the Tables of Contribution and Benefit are based may be applicable.

"2. Proper precautions should be taken to prevent deception on the part of members by appropriate medical supervision where necessary. . . .

"3. The present sickness rates [Dryden planned to insure against illness as well as death] should not be applied to such extra-hazardous occupations as sailors, painters, mining and railway employees.

"4. Care should be taken in all cases in the admission of members.

"5. A distinct account should of course be kept of the receipts and disbursements in each branch of your business. . . .

"6. You should, not very long after you get fairly started, have a proper evaluation made of your liabilities in each department. . . ."

Before closing his letter, the professor reminded Dryden, ". . . At all times, your directors should be impressed with the importance of keeping sacredly the proper reserve on all your policies, so that if your business is successful, as I most sincerely hope it may be, you may secure constantly increasing confidence; and if, in the worst event . . . it should chance to be unsuccessful it may at least not end in dishonor."

Before long Clark learned to his regret and annoyance that the founders of Prudential were not about to spend their reserves—or any other funds—for anything except claims, at least not without prolonged deliberation. In fact, they kept putting off paying the professor's bill for his actuarial services. Money was still very scarce at Prudential, and Dryden wasn't able to remit the fee due to Clark. As weeks lengthened into months, the professor's "reminder" letters grew somewhat acerb.

"Touching upon the payment of $300," he wrote in June, "I shall be very sorry to put you to serious inconvenience, but I have been depending upon it to meet an obligation that I must attend to promptly June 1st. . . ."

A few days later, possibly apprehensive that his earlier tartness might have irritated Dryden and made him less willing to send the money, Clark wrote in a more conciliatory vein, "The payment of $300 can remain until such reasonable time as you can make it without undue inconvenience. . . . I will frankly add, however, without fear of being misunderstood, that I do need it as soon as you can reasonably call upon your friends for their subscriptions. . . ."

A couple of months later, in August, Clark said bluntly that he found himself "seriously embarrassed" by the "protracted postponement" of the payment due him.

On September 17, exasperation seemed to describe his mood: "I have strained my credit thus far to oblige you but I cannot reasonably do it further. . . . While I feel sympathy for you and would not say aught unnecessary to annoy you, it does seem to me that you ought to demand of your immediate associates to come to your rescue in this matter. . . ."

In fact, it was not until the end of September that Dryden even had the basic subscription of stock with which to begin operations: $30,000 in pledges, with 20 per cent of it in cash. A meeting of stockholders was held on October 3, and 10 days later the stockholders, meeting in a room at the Republic Life Assurance and Trust Company, elected their first board of directors. Other directors were added at a meeting later in the month.

After the stockholders' meeting on October 13, the board of directors met and elected Bassett as president; Dryden, secretary; and Isaac Gaston, a bank cashier, as treasurer.

At last the funds and the organization existed for the payment of Clark's long-overdue bill for services rendered. Dryden read to the board the latest message from the angry professor. "Dear Sir," it read, "I have just drawn on you three days after sight for $600, the amount of my account for services. Please honor the draft and oblige. Very truly yours, John E. Clark."

The board voted to honor the draft, and Clark's gratification was no doubt matched only by his astonishment. He began to think better of the Prudential Friendly Society, and he even went along with Dryden's suggestion that he be listed as actuary. "There is no objection to your speaking of me . . . as your 'actuary,' " Clark wrote. "But if you wish to enroll my name in your list of officers I think I should prefer to have you do so as 'consulting actuary.' This title will express cordially my willingness to have my name appear in connection with so honorable and influential a body of gentlemen as your officers must be. . . ."

3/A Voyage to London

The aims of the Prudential Friendly Society, as set down by John F. Dryden, were "to enable people of small means to provide: first, for relief in sickness or accidents; second, for a pension in old age; third, for an adult burial fund; fourth, for an infant burial fund."

So it was ironic that the first policy should be written, not on a person "of small means," but on a prosperous member of Prudential's board of directors, William R. Drake. He was then cashier of the German Bank. (There were so many people of German ancestry in Newark at the time that the Prudential printed some of its policies in that language until 1892.)

At the end of 1875, Prudential had 284 policies in force, largely as a result of talks given by Dryden to men and women in factories owned by men on Prudential's board. But by then Dryden was advertising for agents. A typical notice appeared in one of the Newark newspapers on December 18, 1875:

WANTED!

Canvassers for the Prudential Friendly Society. This first effort in this country to establish a Friendly Society worthy of the patronage of all classes is meeting with a generous response. People in these hard times are more than usually thoughtful in making provision for sickness, accident, old age, and a burial fund, beyond the reach of the exigencies of business. Intelligent ladies and gentlemen can secure good districts by applying to the principal office.
812 Broad Street, State Bank Building.

Among those who responded to the advertisements were a number of women, and women agents were not uncommon for the first quarter century of the Prudential's life. Gradually they disappeared as older women retired, although the women reappeared briefly during World

23

War II. But it was not until the resurgence of the feminist movement toward the end of Pru's first century reawakened sensitivities to such matters that women were again sought out as agents.

One of the earliest agents was Mrs. Julia Babbitt, who started with the Pru on March 6, 1876, and retired in 1912. When her "debit"—the book of Industrial policies for which she collected weekly premiums—was split in two, she insisted that her husband be hired as an agent and given the other part of her debit. Dryden agreed, and Mrs. Babbitt's husband remained with the company for seven years.

"I received 10 per cent on my collections and three times on new business," she recalled after her retirement. "It was the hardest kind of work at first to make headway. The company and its system were brand new and almost wholly unknown. It had no assets to speak of, no debit, no canvassing helps—nothing, in fact, but the wonderful faith and confidence of John F. Dryden and those who believed in him.

"The first week of my connection with the company I earned 10 cents and the first month 45 cents. I was thoroughly discouraged and, with the advice of my husband, resolved to throw up the job. Accordingly, I gathered my books and papers and brought them to the office in the State Bank Building basement and told Mr. Dryden of my resolution. Mr. Dryden talked with me in such a kind, encouraging, and persuading way, urging me to try it again for another month, that I yielded and resumed canvassing. Putting my heart and effort into my work, I was soon . . . rewarded. In a few days I wrote 50 applications. This put me right on my feet.

"When I next saw Mr. Dryden, he said with great feeling and pleasure, 'Now you see what you can do if you make the right try.'

"After that things went along pretty nice and smooth with me."

Visiting their policyholders every week, even for premiums as small as three cents—which was enough for a policy on a one-year-old child of $10—the agents soon became friends, neighbors, relatives, confidants, confessors, marital advisers, job counselors, and just about everything else to many of their clients, and this is true to some extent even today.

Some of the flavor of the work comes through in one of Julia Babbitt's stories about a policyholder who lived on the top floor of a four-story tenement on Colden Street. Every week Mrs. Babbitt climbed the stairs to collect a premium of five cents. One day when Mrs. Babbitt called, the woman refused to pay, saying that she didn't want to break a dollar bill for five cents. Despite Mrs. Babbitt's remonstration, the woman remained adamant; she wasn't going to break that dollar bill, even if the agent *had* trudged wearily up four flights of stairs. So Mrs. Babbitt went away.

"I purposely kept away for several weeks," she recalled. "Finally, one of her neighbors, who was also a policyholder, asked me why I didn't call on Mrs. So-and-So, and told me that she had asked her to tell me to call. I did so. She wanted to know why I hadn't made my usual call. I answered, 'Well, I was waiting until you'd broken that bill.' She laughed and promptly paid up in full.

"She proved a good friend after that, insured her whole family and helped me to get a good deal of business among her relatives and friends."

Mrs. Babbitt said she was rudely treated only once.

"I called at a house in Bank Street," she said. "To the man and woman who were there I told my business. The man grew very angry and shouted at me, 'Get out of here! We don't want any humbug and swindle of that sort. Get out, I say, get out!'

" 'John,' said his wife, 'ain't you ashamed to speak to the woman like that?'

"I spoke up and excused him, saying that he only talked the way he felt. I took the matter good-naturedly and went away.

"Shortly after, while I was passing the same house, the wife saw me and called me in. After apologizing for the way her husband had treated me, she said she believed in the insurance I had to offer and I took her application for 25 cents.

"Not long after I met the hubby and enrolled him for 25 cents.

"This made 50 cents in the house, good staying and paying business. Here was a genuine case where, as the Good Book says, 'A soft answer turneth away wrath.' "

Julia Babbitt was a resourceful woman. She not only arranged for her husband to work as a Prudential agent, but also got a job for her son George as mail boy in the Prudential office. (George later went to college, became a doctor, but was killed when the horse pulling his buggy took fright and ran away, finally overturning the carriage.) The others in the office in the beginning were Bassett; Dryden; Dr. Ward, the medical director; Colonel S. L. Buck, the office manager; and two clerks, David Maclure and George Gaston, who later became a vice president of the Metropolitan Life Insurance Company.

Dryden was regarded with some awe as "an educated gentleman."

Everybody admired his "polite and pleasant manners," his air of "purpose and determination." In later years Maclure remembered Bassett as a "poetic and eloquent" man who would give "glowing encouragement" to prospective agents.

The first sickness claim was received on April 11, 1876. Dr. Ward made an examination and found that Miss Maggie Conover of 101½ Sheffield Street was "wholly incapacitated for her usual occupation."

On the fourth day of the following month the first death claim was brought in—for Industrial Policy No. 724, a three-cent weekly premium policy covering a two-year-old named Joseph F. Smith. His mother, Margaret Smith of 41 Stone Street, signed the claim form with an X and collected $10.

Obviously, the expenses of the business—rent, gas, salaries, commissions, supplies, cost of claims—were outrunning the income in the first months of Prudential's existence. A claim of more than minimal amount was a matter of concern for the people of Prudential. It was the sort of period that was bound to give rise to legendary stories.

One apocryphal account still in circulation at Prudential concerns a policyholder, insured by the company for $500, who was reported to Prudential as being ill with pneumonia and not likely to last the night. As Dr. Ward used to tell the story, Dryden told him about the case and pointed out that a $500 claim at that time might ruin the company.

To save the company, Dr. Ward had to save the patient. So he hurried to the policyholder's house where he found the patient delirious, lying in bed in a cold, shabby room heated only by an inadequate, smoking coal stove. The physician put more coal on the fire, made the patient comfortable, applied the accepted treatment of the time.

"As consulting physician," Dr. Ward liked to say, "I found that it was not only a case of keeping the policyholder alive—which I am delighted to say I succeeded in doing—it was also a matter of keeping the patient's family and myself from freezing to death. The fire in the stove kept going out. I had to 'treat' that fire almost as regularly as I treated the patient. Now, whether in helping to save the life of the policyholder I also saved the life of the company, well, I leave that decision up to your understanding."

It was a good story. It may even have been true. Its authenticity is somewhat tarnished, however, by the fact that Dr. Ward on some occasions identified the policyholder in question as a Mrs. Grover, who lived on Court Street, and at other times as one Caspar Ahmoslechner of 157 Kossuth Street, in the section of Newark that is called "Down Neck" (Court Street is not Down Neck).

By April 1876 the Prudential was so successful that it received the ultimate compliment: a bogus outfit, using the name of the "Prudential Benefit Company," was selling worthless insurance. Two agents of the real Prudential were involved in the fraud, which was exposed by the county prosecutor.

After little more than six months of intensive sales effort—Dryden had already introduced contests and awards as incentives for the sales force—the 5,000th policy was issued, and Prudential appropriated the staggering sum of $34 for a party to celebrate the occasion (although the party was emphatically not of the staggering sort). The festivities, such as they were, took place on June 2, 1876. Bassett, Dryden, Dr. Ward, and the treasurer, Gaston, all made speeches. It may not have been as sparkling an event as some that Prudential has staged in the decades since, but for those who were there it was a night they never forgot.

And of no one was that more true than of John F. Dryden, who could now see his dream of Industrial insurance coming true.

But something was wrong. Halfway into November the Prudential was carrying more than 7,000 policies on its books, but it would finish its first full year of operations at least $1,500 in the red. The company's profitless prosperity was discussed at a meeting of the board of directors on November 23. The directors finally decided that the soundest course of action would be to send somebody over to England in order to compare their operating practices with those of the highly successful British Prudential. At Dr. Ward's suggestion, they agreed to send John Dryden. His total expenses were limited to $250—an inadequate sum, even in those days.

On November 28 Dryden sailed aboard the S.S. *Idaho* for England. He arrived back home on the S.S. *Parthia* on January 7, 1877. First thing the next morning Dryden met in the office with Bassett and Dr. Ward to discuss what he had learned. Before the day was over the directors had all been notified that there would be a board meeting on the evening of January 12.

Dryden told them that he had met personally with Henry Harben, head of the Prudential Assurance Company of England, who had, it seemed, heard of the little Newark company. Harben "cheerfully and cordially'' agreed to answer any of Dryden's questions, and he had instructed his staff to provide Dryden with any blanks, forms, or information he might want.

Then Dryden explained the structure of British Prudential and its methods of operation. In detail he discussed how the English company's practices differed from theirs and how its methods could be adapted to American conditions. Even the bookkeeping system in London was better, and simpler, than that of the Newark company.

Perhaps more important than anything else, Dryden had returned with a new viewpoint on sickness insurance. The British company had stopped writing that coverage because of its ''disastrous experience.'' So now Dryden proposed that the Newark company stop writing sickness insurance on women and issue such policies on men only with extreme caution. (In fact, Pru stopped selling sickness insurance altogether that spring, and it was many years before it got back into that line of insurance.)

Finally Dryden turned to the prospects for their company. British Prudential issued less than 7,000 policies in 1851, he pointed out, but now, a quarter century later, they were writing insurance at the rate of 1,500,000 policies or more a year, and their annual premium income was currently more than $5,000,000 a year.

''Now, then,'' he said, ''this brings us to the practical question, whether we can apply this business to America. Well, we are 40,000,000; in Great Britain they are 30,000,000. I think we have in this country all the elements of a successful business.''

Afterward there was prolonged discussion, and then a motion:

''Mr. President, I move that the report of our secretary be received and placed on file, and that the thanks of this board be tendered to the gentleman for his instructive and intelligent report.''

The motion was unanimously adopted.

As soon as possible, Dryden supervised the revision of the actuarial and rate tables. Clark's tables had been based on Ordinary insurance experience, but the life expectancy of low-income people, the kind who bought Industrial insurance, was different. The rates had to be higher.

The higher rates didn't slow the growth of business. Despite the truly terrible conditions in that year of general distress—when, Dryden said, ''the mass of the people . . . drifted rapidly . . . into poverty and pauperism''—the business of Prudential kept picking up at an accelerating rate.

In keeping with its new feeling of confidence, the board changed the company's name to The Prudential Insurance Company of America. On March 15, 1877, the state legislature approved the change.

Next came expansion outside Newark. After considering a number of communities, Paterson, New Jersey, was decided upon because it was, like Newark, a center of industry with a big market for Industrial insurance. Bassett, the real estate broker, scouted the city and found an office at 114 Ellison Street. While he was in town, he also had a chat with old friends at the First National Bank there.

Before long a letter arrived at Prudential's office in Newark signed by the mayor, the city comptroller, and a good many business leaders of Paterson. It said:

"We the undersigned beg leave to request that you will address a public meeting of citizens interested in this new system of insurance . . . and explain its peculiar features."

On the night of April 12 the meeting was held in the Odd Fellows Hall over Michael Moss's drugstore on Main Street in Paterson. Bassett and Dryden addressed the crowd, which heard to its astonishment that even in those hard times the Pru had sold more than 10,000 Industrial policies to the people of Newark. Soon the company was doing an equally satisfactory business in Paterson.

Within the company, a story was already making the rounds about an actuary employed by the state who had been told to take a look at the operations of the Prudential, which his superiors described as "a peculiar little company which is doing a novel kind of insurance business in Newark."

Despite the rising flood of policy applications and premiums, Bassett was still making only $150 a month; Dryden, $100; Colonel Buck, the office manager, $40. Frugality continued to be the order of the day: discarded envelopes were used for scratch paper, and the clerks were urged to write fine, small characters in order to cut the amount of paper they covered.

And still the business boomed, largely on the strength of word of mouth and a reputation that was being rapidly built for fast, fair claims service. For example, on July 6, 1878, the Paterson *Guardian* reported:

Six policies became due by the death of six persons insured in the Prudential Insurance Company [of] Newark, in one day of last week. They were all paid without delay. The fact that six persons

died in one day—that their friends took their policies to the
company's office and got the money for them, all in 24 hours—is
something which has never been seen in this or any other city of this
country before. The brilliant success of this company is shown
even in the magnitude of its losses. We are informed that the
Prudential is issuing about 500 new policies per week.

That was the year that Prudential outgrew its original quarters in the
basement of the State Bank Building (the building itself was demolished
in 1912 and replaced by a new structure), so the company moved to
quarters in the Centennial Building at 215 Market Street. (This was later
the site of the Newark *News* and, after the *News*'s demise, it housed
some of the operations of the Newark *Star-Ledger*.) In the Centennial
Building the Prudential had three times as much space as in its old
quarters, at two thirds of the old rent.

Not long after the Paterson office was opened, another branch was
established, this time in Jersey City. Within a month there was a third
office, at Elizabeth. Camden was penetrated the following year.

One of the Camden newspapers, welcoming the new insurance company, made a mistake which it corrected the next day with this notice:

A laughable error was made yesterday. The Prudential Insurance Company pays its benefits 24 *hours* after death—not 24 *years*
after.

Other changes were taking place, including refinements of insurance
policies. A suicide clause was added to the adult policy. Other limiting
clauses followed: intoxicant and opiate; military and naval service;
hazardous occupation. An additional insurance clause was added. This
strong new tool for social improvement was being fine-honed.

The first mortgage loans to be made by the Prudential were negotiated
at this time on eight pieces of property near the Pru's original office at
812 Broad Street. They were the germ of an investment program which
would one day be measured in the billions.

Commissions were being increased, too, as the company's financial
position moved from precarious to secure. There was a continuing
problem in finding good agents, but once a man or a woman proved that
he or she could master the job, Dryden tried his best to keep the agent
with the Prudential.

Then as now, agents were gregarious creatures, and at their get-togethers the stories were worth listening to. They told of the new agent who insured a widow and her sizable family, "including Tommy —don't leave out little Tommy." Some time later she told the agent to cancel the policy on Tommy: "He ran away. Poor little Tommy ran away. And with so many cats in this neighborhood, I just know we'll never find him again."

Then there was the woman who was alleged to have stopped an agent on the street and said to him, "When you asked me to take out a policy on my husband, I didn't do it—and, sure enough, he died. Well, I've married again now, and I want a policy on my new husband right away. I wouldn't want to go through a thing like that all over again."

A dying man was said to have begged his physician to keep him alive for two weeks. The reason: "My Prudential policy will be in full force then and my family will collect the whole $500."

When agents got together to swap stories—some of them true—a new spirit could be sensed, a feeling of pride, of being associated with a successful operation. The question on everyone's lips was: How long will it be before Prudential expands outside New Jersey?

At board meetings that had been discussed, too, and there had been general agreement that if the company were going to branch out into New York and Pennsylvania, two of the three adjacent states, it would have to enlarge its staff and its capitalization.

According to the traditional account, Bassett told the directors that he could raise the additional capital easily; but months passed, and there was no apparent progress. Finally, matters came to a head at a special meeting of the board—called, oddly enough, by Bassett—on May 15, 1879. There the personal friction which had marked Bassett's relations with several officers and board members flared into the open. In the minutes of that board meeting, the clash of personalities can be read only between the lines:

> The President stated that he had called the board for the purpose of considering the advisability of extending the business of the company into Philadelphia.
>
> Mr. Whitty stated that in order to get the matter before the board he would move that steps be taken to commence business in Philadelphia but that he himself was opposed to the motion.
>
> The motion was seconded and after remarks by several directors the question was put and unanimously lost.
>
> Mr. Murphy stated that some of the directors felt aggrieved at

certain acts of the President and thought the directors would like to talk the matter over.

On motion Mr. Blanchard, the vice president, took the chair.

Mr. Robotham then presented a preamble of grievances against the president and a resolution calling upon him to resign his office as president.

Mr. Whitty moved that the preamble and resolution be received. The motion was seconded and carried.

Mr. Robotham moved the adoption of the preamble and resolution. The motion was seconded by Mr. Yates.

Remarks were then made by the president and several directors.

Dr. Ward then stated that the president wished him to say that if the preamble and resolution were withdrawn he would resign his office. On motion, action on the preamble and resolution was postponed in order to give the president an opportunity to resign.

Mr. Bassett then handed the following communication to the vice president:

Newark, N.J., May 15, 1879

To the Directors of The Prudential Insurance Company
Gentlemen

I hereby tender my resignation as President of this Company.

I am yours Respfly.
[signed] Allen L. Bassett

On motion of Mr. Robotham the resignation was unanimously accepted and his salary ordered paid until July 1st, 1879.

Adjourned
John F. Dryden Sec.

After leaving the Prudential, Bassett joined a number of officers of the New York Life Insurance Company in trying to form an Industrial insurance company, to be called the Industrial Insurance Company of the United States. But the new company faded into oblivion without ever having even opened its doors. For a year after that, Bassett represented the New York Life in Newark. In 1881 he joined the Metropolitan Life Insurance Company, and from then until his death he represented the Met in northern New Jersey.

4/Winner by One Vote

Although Dryden had conceived the idea for the Prudential, had brought it into being, and headed its day-to-day operations, the board preferred to entrust the ultimate responsibility for the company's affairs to someone who had risked money by investing in it, so Noah F. Blanchard, on the night that Allen Bassett resigned, was moved up to acting president; 12 days later he was confirmed in the permanent title. Because Blanchard was in the business of tanning hides, his clothes reeked of the tannery. "As soon as he entered the premises of Prudential," one early employee said, "you could, without looking up, tell by the smell that the president had arrived; in fact, if the wind were in the right quarter, you could detect that he was on his way."

For two years Blanchard was president, and during that time the great rivalry began between the Prudential and the Metropolitan—a competition long-lived, intense, usually good-natured, but sometimes ferocious. The struggle between the two companies grew out of the Pru's initial success. In 1876 the company sold 4,816 policies with a face value of $443,072; in 1877, 11,226 policies, and the face value of the policies in force had climbed to $1,030,655; and in 1878, 22,808 policies, and the face value of all the policies carried on the Pru's books had almost doubled, to $2,027,888.

Meanwhile the market for Ordinary life insurance, which the other insurance companies were selling, had virtually collapsed under the impact of the severe and seemingly endless depression which followed the Panic of 1873. For example, in 1878 the Metropolitan, which was then 10 years old, sold a mere 984 new policies. "No company destined to survive the catastrophes of 1877 was as hard hit as Metropolitan," Marquis James points out in his history of the Met. Joseph F. Knapp, Metropolitan president, decided that his company could only thrive and grow by taking a new direction. "Knapp intensified his study of the method developed by the Prudential Assurance Company of London and by its Newark namesake," according to James. "For an excessively cautious man with hardly any capital, John F. Dryden was making good progress in New Jersey."

When Knapp committed the Met to Industrial life insurance in 1879, he moved much faster and more aggressively than Dryden and the directors of the Pru had been willing, or financially able, to go. In 60 days the Met had seven superintendents (as the heads of geographic areas were then designated) and 124 agents. A year later the Met hired great numbers of experienced English agents and brought them to the U.S., so that by June of 1880 the Met was selling Industrial life insurance in nine eastern states.

To the dismay of the Pru, Knapp paid the Newark company the somewhat dubious compliment of luring away a couple of its key men. George H. Gaston, who had been one of the Pru's first clerks, was hired by the Met for the then unheard-of wage of $38.46 a week; eventually he became a Met vice president. And Brice Collard, a Pru superintendent "who had learned under Mr. Dryden the answers to at least some of the manifold problems peculiar to the creation of an Industrial field force," as Marquis James puts it, built the Met's agency corps.

As painful as those defections were to the Pru, they did not cause nearly as much emotion as the Met's next move—when in 1881 it appointed Allen Bassett as superintendent of its Newark district. That's when open warfare broke out.

The gage of war was thrown down by Bassett in an announcement that he inserted in the New Jersey newspapers. In it he pointed out that he had resigned the presidency of the Prudential and that the Metropolitan had offered him such inducements to join it that he couldn't resist. After all, he pointed out, "the Metropolitan has $2,000,000 of solid assets as security to policyholders, $375,000 of which is surplus over and beyond all liabilities, present or contingent"—figures far above those of the Pru, of course. But there was still another twist of the knife for Pru in Bassett's notice, for he reminded his readers that the Superintendent of Insurance for New York state had mentioned "in his last official report" that 200,000 Industrial policies had been issued by the Met "during last year alone, more than had ever before been issued by all the companies practicing Industrial insurance in the United States combined, from their inception up to that date." For John Dryden, who had introduced the concept of Industrial life insurance to the U.S., it was the worst of affronts.

In the opinion of the men of Metropolitan, the first blow had been struck by the Pru. Two years before Bassett published his notice, John R. Hegeman, vice president of the Met, had written to Dryden to complain that Pru people were trying to dissuade agents from working for the Met and were spreading the rumor that the New York company was on its last legs.

Despite the bickering between the two companies, business was good for everyone. The Pru was growing as rapidly as its increasing resources and the caution of its directors would permit. By October of 1879 the company had raised enough money to move into New York and Philadelphia—a step that was opposed by its rivals and by a few others. A New York newspaper, for example, said:

> It may be known to some of our readers that a small, one-horse insurance company, with its headquarters at Newark, New Jersey, is actually endeavoring to scoop in a harvest of victims in this city and state. With the grandiloquence which naturally arises from ignorance and presumption, it baptized itself the Prudential, after the great industrial assurance society of that name in England. Then it hung out its shingle, published a wonderful prospectus, and on the 31st day of July 1879 its agents crossed the Hudson River and invaded this city like a microscopic pestilence of an army of worms or hornets. . . .

Nevertheless, the Pru soon found itself with a big and ever-increasing business in New York, and in Pennsylvania, too. The Pru was even getting some modern conveniences, like a telephone which had been installed in 1880. But it was not until well into the 1880's that Dryden would consent to the purchase of a typewriter. He had the idea that carbon copies of letters would not be valid evidence in a court of law because they lacked a signature, so he persisted for some time in requiring the use of a letter press to copy correspondence.

The agents were doing well, too. Partly because of the competition for agents by the Met, John Hancock, and other insurance companies, the Pru raised its agents' commissions sharply. And still it made money.

But in the spring of 1881 Noah Blanchard fell ill. He died on May 11.

A new president had to be elected. The logical person was John F. Dryden, but many of those on the board of directors still thought of him as the somewhat shabby though respectable fellow who had gone from one businessman to another in Newark, trying to raise money for his concept of Industrial insurance. His idea was a success now, and so was he, but some of the directors regarded him somewhat patronizingly, in the belief that his contribution to the venture had been less important than theirs.

That was the background of Elias Wilkinson's attempt to get William Murphy elected as president.

But Dryden's first and staunchest friend among the directors—Dr. Leslie D. Ward—thought that it was high time to elect Dryden, who had been secretary from the beginning and was already recognized as the foremost authority on Industrial insurance in the U.S.

"Wilkinson was extremely bitter," Dr. Ward said many years later, recalling the board meeting of May 13, 1881. "We became quite heated in our discussions on the subject."

When it became clear that Murphy could not win election, Wilkinson put forward the name of another early investor, George Moore, but Dr. Ward refused to switch his support from Dryden to Moore.

"I insisted that Mr. Moore had no interest in the business and a comparatively small amount invested and that he had no qualifications whatever for the office and that my friendship for Mr. Dryden would not permit me to do such a thing," said Dr. Ward. "Finally, the meeting was held, and Mr. Dryden was elected on the narrow margin of one vote."

One vote. It didn't demonstrate great confidence by the board, but it was enough to elect Dryden. And those who voted for him and held on to their stock never had any reason to regret their vote.

Dryden had the honor, but he still was unable to enjoy much in the way of material rewards. Dr. Ward recorded this picture of Dryden's life about that time:

"He lived around in cheap boarding-houses; his health was poor. I was their family physician, and I can remember well rosy-cheeked Susie Dryden and little Forrest when they were small children, living in a small house on Walnut Street. Mr. Dryden's health was such that he had to live out of Newark in the summertime, and it was accordingly arranged to have him, with his family, go to Schooley's Mountain.

"At the time Mr. Dryden was getting $1,200 a year. He drew that amount for some time after he became president of the company. When matters got a little more prosperous, however, it was decided that he should have some kind of conveyance, so as to keep him out in the open air as much as possible. I remember that I undertook the assignment of purchasing a horse and vehicle for them. I went to the Old Bull stable and purchased a little pacing bay mare at a cost, I believe, of $100 or $125, and then went down on Market Street and bought a secondhand low phaeton, the combined rig making one of the most fantastic outfits you ever saw."

Besides coping with his fragile health and his still woefully limited salary, Dryden now had to fret about the warfare with the Met. Both sides were guilty of behavior that violated even the lax rules of business competition that were commonly subscribed to in those days. On December 30, 1881, a New York newspaper, the *Star*, published an article about the Prudential which indicated that a number of the initial investors and board members had sold their stock because they didn't think the company was being properly run. A day or two later the *Star*, obviously in answer to protests from the Pru, published a second article reporting that it had interviewed the investors in question. They told the newspaper that they had never made the statements attributed to them in the first article, which had been based on an anonymous press release. Reporting on the affair, which it called "A Case of Bushwhacking," the New York *Chronicle* said:

> The circumstances surrounding this affair are such as to indicate that Allen Bassett, formerly president of the Prudential and for some time past an agent of a rival corporation, inspired the original publication in the *Star* or was privy thereto. This gentleman claims that he, and not Mr. Dryden, would have been chosen president of the company after the death of Noah F. Blanchard, had Charles G. Campbell been present at the meeting of directors. Mr. Campbell, on the contrary, distinctly states that he "never heard before that the question was mooted of electing Bassett president."

The *Chronicle* explained that it had

> given so much space to this matter because, first, we thoroughly believe in the present management of the Prudential, in its intelli-

gence, its integrity, and its ability; and second, because we thoroughly disbelieve in, and have an inexpressible contempt for, ambuscades and skulking as means and methods of business competition.

That was one for the Pru. But a few months later, in May 1882, the shoe was on the other foot, and it pinched. This time the incident involved Leon T. Blanchard and J. H. Crankshaw, who were, respectively, the superintendents for the Pru and the Met in Philadelphia. An article in a Camden newspaper accused Crankshaw of having been expelled for drunkenness from a church where he was a preacher, of defrauding the public, and of cheating the agents who worked under him. In its next issue the Camden newspaper printed a full retraction of the charges against the Metropolitan superintendent and said its original article was based on facts that "came to us originally from outside sources . . . actuated by malice . . . and interested in a rival organization." Crankshaw swore out a warrant for Blanchard's arrest on libel charges on the basis of what the *Chronicle* called "satisfactory evidence that he procured and paid for the publication of the offensive paragraph, dictated a portion of it, and purchased a considerable number of the papers containing it and distributed them through his agents." The *Chronicle* denounced "the mean and despicable character of the offense," an opinion that could hardly be contested.

The Pru was the victim of the next clash. In Camden—which was obviously being bitterly fought over—a letter from a policyholder was published, denouncing the Prudential for failing to pay the claim on the life of the policyholder's son, who had drowned. The letter warned the public "of the tricks to which they expose themselves by dealing with this company or its agents who . . . have proved themselves utterly unworthy of public confidence. . . ." But it turned out that the letter itself was a fraud; the man whose name was signed to it had not written, seen, or signed it. A Metropolitan official was convicted of libeling the Prudential.

If this sort of thing continued, both companies would have half their field force in jail, and the reputation of both companies and of the life insurance industry as a whole would suffer. Something had to be done, and John F. Collins decided he was the person to do it. Collins had recently been transferred from Philadelphia to New York City, where he was superintendent. With Dryden's permission, Collins set up a "peace conference" in New York with Knapp and Hegeman of the Met, both of whom he knew. Dryden and the Metropolitan men agreed that the savage blows their field forces were exchanging helped no one and harmed the entire industry. From now on, each side would restrain its agents and superintendents. The shooting war was ended. Over the decades that lay ahead, the rivalry would continue, but it would be a cold war.

By the time peace had been achieved with the Met, the Pru had already begun planting the seeds of future trouble. John Dryden hired his son, Forrest F. Dryden, as an office boy in 1880. Inevitably, the time would come when company officials would point to the fact that the lowest wage ever entered in the Pru's books—50 cents—was paid to the president's son. It was usually greeted with the awkwardness that marks any reference to nepotism. There is no reason, in fact, to believe that Dryden or anyone else at the Pru intended to encourage nepotism; people rarely plan things that way. It just happened because no one took precautions to prevent it. But the employment of Forrest Dryden marked the beginning of the infection at the Pru. By 1903, besides the two Drydens, the ranks of the Pru's officers included four Wards and two Blanchards—eight family relationships out of 23 officer posts.

In time, the Pru would overcome that obstacle, too—would master it more completely than possibly any other American company—but before that happened, nepotism would cause critical problems for the company.

The Prudential was growing into the kind of prize any man might want to pass on to his son. By the end of 1885, when it was 10 years old, the company had assets of $1,040,816.39—in a nation still very short of capital, at a time when money had far more value than it would have by the end of the Pru's first century. Business had increased so much by 1883 that the Pru had been forced to move again, this time into a four-story structure called the Jube Building at 880 Broad Street (a site occupied by a tavern in 1974). An Actuarial Department had been established. The company was using so many forms of one kind or another that it had set up its own Printing Department. In 1885 the field force consisted of 34 superintendents, 150 assistant superintendents, 1,200 agents, and 116 inspectors and special agents. The Home Office employed 55 men and 64 women in addition to the officers.

On May 18, 1885, Industrial policy No. 1,000,000 was issued. It covered the life of John F. Dryden.

That fall John B. Lunger, who had been working for the Prudential for five years and was thoroughly imbued with the viewpoint of an Industrial life insurance man, made a rather startling suggestion to John F. Dryden. He said that the Pru ought to begin selling Ordinary life insurance.

Lunger's reasoning was clear and hardly debatable, although one might argue with his conclusions—as a number of Pru officers did. Briefly, it was Lunger's contention that Pru and its economic environment had both changed. The Pru was now well established financially, with a strong field force and an unshakable base among the working men and women of the country; it could afford to expand its services to include more affluent people, as well as those factory workers who were more highly paid, had saved more, and wanted greater protection for themselves and their families. Moreover, the popularity of Industrial insurance had contributed to the general acceptance of the idea of life insurance. Times were better, people were making more money, and they were ready to pay larger sums for insurance that met their needs. As for the lack of a collection feature in Ordinary insurance—well, in some districts where the Pru was very strong, millions of dollars' worth of Ordinary insurance was being sold by other companies to people who were willing to pay by mail on a quarterly or semi-annual basis.

With such arguments, the end was inevitable: on January 18, 1886, the Ordinary insurance branch was established, with Lunger, who was then 25 years old, heading it. Three years later he would be named actuary of the Pru, and then the time would come when he would leave the Pru and become a vice president of Equitable Life.

By the end of 1890, after five years of Ordinary sales, the Pru was selling more than 2,000 Ordinary policies a year, and the face value of its Ordinary policies in force totaled more than $4,000,000.

And still the company grew.

By 1887 it was operating in eight states, as far west as Missouri. By the end of the Eighties the field force numbered more than 3,000, and there were nearly 250 men and women crammed into the Home Office. There was a company publication now, to help build morale. At the Pru's thirteenth anniversary dinner, in 1888, Dryden said he had been thinking about creating a new organization within the company.

"The records show," he said, "that we have 168 persons who have been five years or upward with continuous and honorable service with the company. It has occurred to us that it would be a pleasant thing, an honorable thing, if we could have within the Prudential organization an association based simply on long and continuous service."

So the Prudential Old Guard came into being, open to men and women with at least five years of service. It was named by Dryden after the Imperial Guard created by Napoleon in 1804, his most dependable troop, his stalwarts.

At the beginning of the decade that would be called the Gay Nineties, Dryden decided that it was time the Prudential built a home for itself. The building would be the first specifically designed for the company's needs and desires. As Dryden later wrote, "The idea is to construct a building which shall typify and symbolize the character of the business of the Prudential, exemplify its all-pervading spirit of beneficence and its ingrained love of the Golden Rule."

For an age which still doubted—sometimes with reason—the solvency and stability of insurance companies, tall buildings were intended to convey a feeling of permanence and security. In the words of historian Daniel Boorstin, "The history of the American skyscraper could have been illustrated by monuments to the growing insurance industry. . . ."

According to contemporary statements by Prudential spokesmen, the new Home Office structure, called, appropriately enough, the Prudential Building, was designed by New York architect George Post working from the design of an ancient French chateau of the Loire River valley. That may, indeed, have been his inspiration, but in later years a number of Pru people noted a striking resemblance between their building in Newark and the Home Office of British Prudential in London.

Situated at 761 Broad Street, on the corner of Bank Street, the 11-story skyscraper contained 114,000 square feet; the overall cost came out to $8.22 per square foot. It was, for its day, a marvel of modernity, with steam heat, hot and cold running water, electric wiring throughout, mail chutes, and five hydraulic, piston-driven elevators that shot upward at 500 feet a minute. It had more than 600 doors and 5,000 windows. To build it required 5,000,000 bricks, 12 miles of beams and girders and iron posts, and vast quantities of marble, mahogany, and even stained glass—the last being a feature that made some rooms look truly like temples to Mammon, in the view of some critics.

When the new building was formally opened on December 2, 1892, there was a parade through Newark, featuring, among others, nearly 4,000 Prudential employees, as well as five military bands. A celebration dinner for 2,256 persons was served in Caledonia Park. It was a great day for Newark.

Dryden's great day had come earlier, on the eve of the dedication, when nearly 200 of the most important men of the world of finance and insurance attended a private dinner at Delmonico's in New York. They were pleased to be invited, for the Pru was now a very big business, with one million policyholders in 17 states, and still growing. John Dryden was in very comfortable circumstances now, and well on his way to becoming a rich man—a very rich man.

He had struggled so hard to found and to build his company in order to make money, which is not an ignoble motive for any man, especially one who must provide for a wife and children. But he had also had a genuine vision of helping the working man and woman. In his speech to the gathering at Delmonico's he tried to express some of that.

"Our names," he said, "may be forgotten; those whose brains have planned, whose hands have builded the great structure, may pass into oblivion and be forgotten. . . . The iron pillars which support the structure may topple to the ground. But after we are forgotten and after the building itself is leveled to the dust the principle upon which the Prudential is founded, the immutable principle of the brotherhood of man and that love of family which binds society together—that principle will live, for it is divine and eternal."

What the Prudential still needed was a symbol which would indicate its strength, its dependability as a base on which to plan for the protection of the family. The Prudential Building wouldn't do; it was tried in some advertisements which called the Pru a "Tower of Strength," but somehow they didn't quite reach people.

Then, in 1896, a young New York advertising man named Mortimer Remington, who was with the J. Walter Thompson agency, was introduced by his father-in-law to John F. Dryden, who suggested that Remington try to devise a service mark for the company. Remington succeeded, but the source of his inspiration is a matter of dispute. One story has it that, while riding on a train from Newark to New York, he passed Laurel Hill, a rocky elevation rising out of the Jersey Meadows, and noticed that it looked like the Rock of Gibraltar. According to another version, he came across a picture of Gibraltar in a book in the Astor Library in New York. Copying the picture, he lettered across the face of the Rock the legend: "The Prudential Has the Strength of Gibraltar." The slogan—if the second account is correct—was developed by Remington after reading a book by Nathaniel C. Fowler, Jr., which contained a chapter on life insurance advertising, where there was a reference to life insurance being as "sound as the rock."

Regardless of which version is true, one fact is certain: on August 20, 1896, *Leslie's Weekly* carried the first advertisement that showed the Rock of Gibraltar and carried the words, "The Prudential Has the Strength of Gibraltar."

More than three quarters of a century later, Gibraltar was still recognized everywhere as the symbol of the Prudential, and the slogan was still in use—with a modern twist:

"Own a Piece of the Rock."

5/'A Wrong Thing to Do'

From its beginning the Prudential had been a stock company—that is, a profit-making enterprise owned by shareholders. It made rich men out of those of its founders, investors, and officers who stuck with it. But problems arose, too, as the Pru's assets climbed into the millions.

For one thing, the Prudential's dividends were limited by charter to 10 per cent. Pru shareholders looked about, saw Robber Barons carving new domains out of far less profitable activities, and felt they were being dealt with unjustly.

One way out was to expand the company's stock capitalization. Although only $115,000 had been contributed by stockholders in the Pru's early years, the company kept increasing its capital by transferring funds from its surplus, issuing additional shares on a pro-rata basis to those persons who were already shareholders, until by 1894 the outstanding shares represented a capitalization of $2,000,000. But the capitalization couldn't be expanded indefinitely.

As early as 1880 the company's success had begun to create difficulties. According to the Pru's charter, policyholders were entitled to vote for directors. One day the directors realized with alarm that so many policies had been sold that the policyholders now could outvote the stockholders. The company appealed quietly to its friends in the state legislature, and on March 3 of that year the lawmakers passed a measure called "The Bill of a Hundred Words," taking away the voting rights from policyholders.

In 1898 a powerful group of investors demanded that more money—$3,000,000—be transferred from surplus to capital, so that the stock could be increased. As far as Dryden was concerned, this was going too far. He said that such an action would be dangerous to the company and unfair to the policyholders. Nevertheless, the directors voted the action, subject to ratification at a stockholders' meeting.

As word of the proposed action spread through financial circles, protests began to mount. The insurance commissioners of Ohio and Connecticut were among those who objected. So were Knapp and Hegeman, the two top men at the Metropolitan. In their letter the Met officers pointed out that the proposed action would raise the dividends of Pru's stockholders to "more than 200 per cent on the original investment, while keeping up the high cost to policyholders of Industrial insurance. . . . The gravest sense of duty [impels us] to . . . protest against such an act. You and we have been placed a good many times in the position of defending Industrial insurance against a charge that it was made unduly onerous to the policyholder. . . . We have in reply earnestly expressed our belief that the business was being done as economically as possible . . . that the small amount of dividends paid to stockholders . . . made the companies, in effect, mutual companies . . . that the policyholders could feel certain that . . . [any] extra profit . . . should go to reduce the expense to them."

Those were John Dryden's convictions, too, and the protests helped him by providing an arguing point when he went into the stockholders' meeting. With some difficulty, he persuaded the stockholders to reject the directors' action.

Still the pressure for more money remained unabated. In all fairness to the investors, it must be said that their appetites undoubtedly were whetted by observing how Dryden and his associates were enriching themselves by the effective use of the company's assets. As one newspaper later reported, "Once they had secured the assets, steadily growing from month to month, they turned the money in their keeping to the purchase of interests in the gas works, electric railroads, lighting companies, banks, trust companies, manufactories, and other substantial interests of the state. The Prudential wove a network of money tentacles that stretched from end to end of the state of New Jersey and made its officers the most powerful men in the community, able to dictate to the executives at Trenton, and to make and unmake Governors."

Nevertheless, it would be an injustice to Dryden to suggest that he was unconcerned about the welfare of the policyholder. A critical 1963 study of that period in the history of the life insurance industry, written by Morton Keller, points out, correctly, "As the company became, in size as well as function, an institution of manifest social importance, Dryden the insurance officer took precedence over Dryden the stockholder. . . . The ideology of life insurance made the normal acquisitiveness of stockholders seem alien, out of place." The managers were still the biggest investors, Keller says, "but the managers inevitably were more engaged in business expansion than in earning legally circumscribed dividends or exploiting limited possibilities of stock expansion."

But what was to be done about those angry stockholders who wanted more money? How could they be prevented from harming the company, especially if they should be able to buy enough shares to give them control?

Eventually the time came when John Dryden testified about his thinking at that time, and where it led him.

"For some time," he said, "I had been apprehensive as to the distribution of the stock of the company. The founders of the company, those who were associated with me, and my other co-workers were getting older and dying off, and the stock was passing into the hands of their estate or it was being sold and distributed.

"I saw that the time might come when that would be a very dangerous situation for the policyholders of the company. The company had been my own life work, and I had my pride in it. . . . In addition to that, I was extremely anxious to protect the great mass of policyholders who had shown their confidence by insuring with us."

After discarding one scheme after another, he hit upon the idea of selling a majority of Pru's stock to the Fidelity Trust Company, a Newark bank, and then, in turn, having the Pru purchase a majority of the Fidelity's stock. This somewhat hermaphroditic device would have made both boards of directors self-perpetuating, in effect, but, like most humans, Dryden felt his own motives were noble and couldn't see any reason why anyone else should question them. "This scheme I advertised widely," Dryden said. "It was not done in a corner."

Under Dryden's plan all operations—including annual meetings—would be arranged in such a way that the insurance company would emerge as the senior member of the strange partnership.

Among the many benefits of the idea would be the freedom it would give the Prudential from the frustrating restraints imposed on investments by rulings of the state insurance commissioners. Moreover, those who took part in the deal would reap a profit estimated at $6,000,000 from the sale of their stock. "Dryden's plan," says Keller, "was a significant thrust against the profit limitation that so paradoxically accompanied the expansion of the great life insurance firms.''

Before making the plan public, Dryden had visited Hegeman, who was by then the president of the Metropolitan, and Haley Fiske, who was vice president of the Met, to explain to them what he planned to do. After studying the details for several hours that October evening in 1902, both men wrote to warn him against carrying out the project. Fiske thought that the end sought by Dryden was commendable, but the means would be ''a fruitful subject for litigation.'' Hegeman, who had long since become a close friend of Dryden, for whom he had great respect, spoke more bluntly. He reminded Dryden that for some time ''the peculiar financial performances of sundry corporations'' had tended to ''bring discredit'' on American businessmen. ''The step you now propose savors strongly of reprehensible stock-jobbing methods,'' Hegeman asserted. ''Nor can these views be brushed aside by protestations of good motives.''

Unfortunately, Dryden had already started to put the plan into execution. As soon as he notified the various state insurance commissioners of the Pru's intentions, 12 commissioners announced their opposition. The Massachusetts commissioner declared, ''Such concentration of authority, so far removed from the reach of the individual stockholders, is contrary to public policy.''

Two minority stockholders of the Pru brought suit to block the Pru's purchase of Fidelity stock, and the Court of Chancery granted an injunction to the plaintiffs, telling the Pru's managers tartly that they ''were not elected to revise the laws of New Jersey, or to devise schemes for evading those laws.''

Complicating the whole matter was the fact that half of the scheme had already been executed: the Fidelity had bought its shares of Prudential stock, giving it control. Because of the public outcry, however, the Fidelity sold eight shares of Prudential, just enough to prevent its having a majority. But investigators later found that the interlocking holdings of stock by officers of the bank and the insurance company, plus each company's ownership of minority blocs of the other organization, provided the central group with ''an effective if not a technical control'' over both companies.

At the height of the uproar, one insurance periodical carried an article

which began, "In an interview with Mr. Dryden on last Monday
morning, he declared that the sole motive . . . was the future welfare of
4,500,000 policyholders of the Prudential. Mr. Dryden said these
words with much intensity of feeling. We believe he meant what he
said."

But there were not many people who thought that Dryden's primary
concern had been for the policyholders. His mail and the press were
filled with bitter accusations. After reading one communication that
lashed him more savagely than most, Dryden walked out of his office to
the desk of his personal secretary, George Williams.

"Williams," Dryden said, "I'd like to ask you a question. You've
been reading about the merger plans and the various things they've been
writing up in the papers. I want to know—what's your own personal
opinion of that plan, Williams?"

Williams had been working for Dryden for 23 years, but Dryden had
never sought his opinion—at least, on any matter of such importance
—in all that time.

The secretary hesitated, shuffling the letters on his desk. Finally he
cleared his throat and looked up.

"You want an honest answer, sir?" he asked.

Dryden nodded.

Williams said, "I think it was wrong. I think it was a wrong thing to
do, to start a plan like that, sir."

Without speaking, Dryden turned away, walked into his office, and
closed the door.

The whole affair had been a painful mistake, and perhaps a decisive
one, for John Dryden's life thereafter was marked by setbacks, reverses,
and disappointments.

The only beneficial thing that emerged from the furor was Dryden's
discovery of a lawyer named Richard Vliet Lindabury of the firm of
Lindabury, Depue & Faulks, which had offices in the Prudential Building. Lindabury, representing the minority stockholders of Pru, had
obtained the injunction preventing Dryden from carrying through his
Fidelity scheme as originally planned. Instead of being angry at Lindabury, Dryden decided he wanted a lawyer of such brilliance to
represent him.

It seems odd that Dryden had not already retained Lindabury, for he
was the attorney who most often represented J. P. Morgan's interests in

New Jersey—and elsewhere—and Dryden was very close to Morgan by this time. Of Dutch and English stock, Lindabury had grown up on a farm near Peapack in Somerset County, New Jersey. He had begun his law practice in the little town of Bound Brook, later moving to Elizabeth, which was still not the sort of place from which one might expect a great corporation lawyer to spring. After serving as associate counsel with the famous attorney Joseph H. Choate in a case in which they represented the Singer Sewing Machine Company, Lindabury had come to the attention of Morgan and his associates. His successful defense of the American Tobacco Company, which had been charged by the New Jersey Attorney General with operating in restraint of trade, gave Lindabury national recognition.

To Dryden, Lindabury seemed to be the sort of fellow a man would want to have on his side in a difficult legal fight. And that was the predicament that Dryden was about to find himself in because of one of his business allies.

The ally in question was the Equitable Life, with which Dryden and the Prudential had worked very closely for several years. Four officers of the Equitable Life were on the board of directors of the Fidelity Trust Company. After the death of the Equitable's founder, Henry B. Hyde, in 1899, his controlling bloc of stock was put in trust for his son, James Hazen Hyde, who would come into complete control of the stock and the company in 1906. In the intervening years the company was in the hands of the Hyde trustees, who included young Hyde himself and James W. Alexander, who had been his father's chief assistant.

Alexander resigned as a trustee in 1903 and began to criticize Hyde, who was then 27, for his "public coaches, special trains, elaborate banquets, costly and ostentatious entertainments, accompanied . . . by continuous notoriety of a flippant, trivial, cheap description." The Alexander faction wanted Hyde kept out of the active management of the Equitable. They also wanted the policyholders to participate in the election of directors.

For a couple of years the two factions jockeyed for positions of control. Suddenly in 1905, young Hyde sold his share to Thomas Fortune Ryan, a speculator and Wall Street operator, for $2,500,000, far less than Hyde could have obtained for the stock. Ryan, of course, wanted the company in order to deploy its assets most advantageously.

The fight over the Equitable, occurring about the same time as a series of articles in *Everybody's* magazine, later published in book form under the title *Frenzied Finance,* by Thomas W. Lawson, had considerable impact on the public. The press began raising serious questions about the state of affairs within the life insurance industry. The *Nation,* which was at the time probably the most respected journal of opinion, said, "No greater calamity to the insurance business can be conceived than the invasion of its field by the snatching and grasping methods which marked our railway and industrial company finance of 1901 and 1902."

Policyholders formed committees to demand an investigation of the Equitable. Three or four Wall Street factions which had been struggling for control of that company thought a public examination might serve their purposes. Thomas Fortune Ryan felt that it would strengthen his hold on the company. The press was insistent that the affairs of the insurance companies must be exposed to the light of day.

The great Wall Street lawyer, Paul Cravath, who represented the Equitable, pledged his cooperation—but promised to "see to it that there is also a thorough and impartial investigation of the other companies."

That was the first indication of what lay ahead for the life insurance industry.

On July 20, 1905, the New York state legislature adopted a resolution appointing a committee, headed by State Senator William W. Armstrong, to look into nearly all phases of the life insurance business.

The Armstrong investigation was about to change the life insurance industry and, indirectly, the very constitution of the Prudential.

6 / The Making of a Chief Justice

Chance has a greater effect on the fortunes of men and women than most of us are willing to believe. But opportunity most often comes to the person who has prepared for it, and it can only be exploited by the person who has developed the resources for it.

Example: Charles Evans Hughes.

When State Senator Armstrong set out to find a lawyer to carry out his investigation, his criteria narrowed the choice. The chief inquisitor must be an attorney who had already earned the respect of the bar. He must be relatively young and without long-standing ties to the great life insurance companies, their banking affiliates, and the network of companies connected with them. He must be known as an incorruptible man.

Armstrong asked most of his lawyer friends; none could come up with a name. As politicians often do, Armstrong turned to a newspaper acquaintance, the editor of the New York *Press*. In turn, the editor telephoned one of his friends, Don Seitz, of Joseph Pulitzer's New York *World,* which had been leading the press pack in attacking insurance abuses.

"You are more interested in this than I am," the *Press* editor said to Seitz. "Can you think of anybody?"

"What's the matter with Charley Hughes?" Seitz asked.

And so Hughes, who had recently concluded an official investigation into New York's public utilities, got a cable in the German Alps, where he was relaxing, asking him to come home to head up the insurance inquiry.

"You don't know what this investigation would mean," Hughes told his wife. "It would be the most tremendous job in the United States."

In fact, his conduct of the investigation won the praise of both liberals and conservatives and led to his being elected Governor of New York in November 1906, beating newspaper publisher William Randolph Hearst; Hughes was the only Republican to win state office that year. In 1910 he was appointed an Associate Justice of the U.S. Supreme Court, from which he resigned in 1916 to run for President against Woodrow

Wilson—an election so close that it was not decided until two days after the votes were cast. After serving as Secretary of State and later as a member of the Permanent Court of International Justice at The Hague, he was appointed Chief Justice of the U.S. Supreme Court in 1930, a post in which he served for 11 years.

Most of his major achievements were still ahead of Hughes in the fall of 1905 when, at the age of 43, he opened up the insurance industry to the light of day—but his powers of intellect, character, and temperament were already fully developed. As a result, he carried out an investigation which to this day remains unequaled for speediness, fairness, thoroughness, impartiality, civility, and courage.

He spent only two weeks preparing for the public hearings. That was all the time he needed.

"For the duration of 57 public hearings . . . from September 6 to December 30, 1905," recalled conservative journalist Mark Sullivan in his informal history, *Our Times,*

> Hughes put upon the witness stand a parade of the plumed elite of New York finance, politics, and society. Under the cold questioning of Hughes, "great reputations became great notorieties." His incisive, tenacious, unhurried methods made such an impression on the personalities of finance and insurance that some, terrified at the prospect of being subjected to his even-voiced questioning, unobtrusively departed for destinations unknown, while others found reasons of health for temporary retirement; one of the most conspicuous went to a sanitarium. . . . Without ever heckling a witness, permitting every sweating financier to make such explanation or excuse as he could improvise; without seeming to be a cross-examiner at all, as unemotionally as a teacher finding a mild enthusiasm in leading a child to concede the irrefutable verities of mathematics, with no violence of gesture or words, in a voice that was only saved by its virile timbre from being monotonous, Hughes by the sheer clarity and power of his mind made every newspaper reader understand what had gone on. As undramatic himself as an adding machine, he brought out such a series of dramatic revelations as had the effect, on the public, of a tumbling cascade of sensations.

Among the abuses that the investigation spotlighted were nepotism and unjustifiably high salaries; disregard of policyholders' rights; officers who chose to be financial promoters and manipulators rather than insurance men; inordinately expensive marketing methods; an alarming decline in dividends to policyholders; innumerable and blatant conflicts of interest; corporate political contributions and other political improprieties; misuse of company funds; and various other acts of corporate misconduct.

Of course, not all the companies proved to be equally guilty. The worst abuses were charged against the "Big Three"—the Mutual Life Insurance Company of New York, the New York Life Insurance Company, and the Equitable Life Assurance Society—which was to be expected, because their size had made them prime targets for unscrupulous financial operators in those fevered days when there were scarcely any restraints on Wall Street.

Not that the smaller companies, which in those days included the Metropolitan and the Prudential, escaped the keen eye of Hughes.

The Metropolitan's interests in various banks, the links between its own investment activities with those of its officers, and its participation in 39 syndicates underwriting bond issues—those were some of the matters that particularly interested Hughes. Met president John R. Hegeman did not help his cause when he testified, "I have never been able to see . . . why . . . a man who was fortunate or unfortunate enough to be a life insurance company president should be shut out of those profits, which an ordinary man should be permitted to participate in." But a life insurance company occupies a special position of trust and responsibility, as the Armstrong Committee and the public well understood.

Of the major insurance companies, the Prudential was the only one that avoided direct participation in bond syndicates, although its affiliate, the Fidelity Trust Company, did take part in syndicates from time to time, and often part of the bonds found their way into the Pru's portfolio. This and other facts about the Prudential were brought out when John F. Dryden appeared on December 12, when the committee was winding up its hearings.

In his grave, deliberate way, Hughes drew out of Dryden, who was nervous at first but soon recovered his composure, the number of Pru officers and employees who were members of Dryden, Ward, or Blanchard families. However, although nepotism was proved, the payment of excessive salaries was not. Dryden's salary had gone from $20,000 in 1889 to $30,000 in 1891, $50,000 in 1893, and $65,000 in 1899. Considering the phenomenal growth of the Pru, and comparable salaries in other companies—usually $100,000 or a good deal more—the Pru could not be accused of showering money on Dryden.

Hughes spent most of his examination of Dryden digging out the facts on two matters: first, the relationships among the Prudential, the Fidelity, the Union Trust Company (a smaller Newark bank which later merged with the Fidelity), and the Public Service Corporation, which Dryden had helped to organize in 1903 to combine most of the smaller public utilities in New Jersey into one large company; and second, the lapse rates and the costs of Industrial insurance.

On the whole, Dryden made a better witness than most of the life insurance company presidents who testified. At least one part of his testimony, however, suggests that Dryden was disingenuous, at best. In answer to a question by Hughes, Dryden told how the policyholders had been deprived of their vote in 1880, and he added, "I regret now [that] it was done."

That expression of regret does not jibe with Dryden's comments to the Republican members of the New Jersey legislature little more than a year later, when he said he believed the elimination of the policyholders' vote to have been "justified." They didn't know enough about the company's business to vote intelligently, he said, and besides, "no policyholder had a right to a single dollar of the surplus."

When the Armstrong investigation was all over, the Prudential had been bruised less than most of the companies. The principal impact of the investigation—besides creating a new awareness of the special responsibilities of life insurance companies—resulted from the passage of corrective laws regulating almost every activity of insurance companies. Indeed, some of the laws were so rigid that they had to be modified in a relatively short time. All of those laws applied to Prudential because it was licensed by and doing business in New York state.

As it happened, the business and political interests identified with Dryden and the Pru were under attack by some newspapers, the muckraking magazines, and reform politicians in New Jersey in 1906, when New York state was passing its corrective legislation. Inevitably, a public clamor arose for a similar investigation by the New Jersey legislature. New Jersey's insurance commissioner opposed an inquiry in his state, arguing that the New York revelations had been "most unfortunate and regrettable," causing "vast harm to the interests of American life insurance" (although Paul Cravath, the distinguished attorney who had represented the Equitable, had praised the Armstrong hearings for their "thoroughness and fairness"). Reluctantly, a legislature controlled by forces friendly to Dryden authorized an investigation to be headed by State Senator Thomas J. Hillery of Morris County.

Compared with the New York hearings, the New Jersey sessions were tame, partly because many of the committee members did not have their heart in it, and to some extent because this inquiry lacked a Charles Evans Hughes to give it life and direction. But the major reason why the New Jersey hearings were so dull was that they focused on the Prudential—and the Pru's transgressions, while real and, in the opinion of the Armstrong Committee, serious, had not been as extreme, as extensive, or as spectacular as those of some of the other companies which, being based in New York, were not drawn into the New Jersey study.

Nevertheless, the New Jersey investigation did result in reform legislation. Because of the Pru's interest in the Fidelity, one new law limited the amount of stock which an insurance company could hold in any other corporation. Dryden's admission that the Pru had contributed $26,000 to the Republican Party in recent years resulted in the outlawing of such gifts. Other new laws provided for greater publicity about insurance company operations, protection of the stake of policyholders in the company's surplus, and the election of some directors who would represent the policyholders.

But laws were not the only result of the Armstrong and other investigations. The insurance companies themselves instituted internal changes in their personnel, corporate policies, and business practices designed to prevent a recrudescence of improprieties. All of the presidents and most of the senior officers of the "Big Three" resigned or were forced out of office. The life insurance companies joined together in industry associations to impose upon themselves standards of ethics and behavior which went far beyond the new requirements of law.

Did the investigations, with their truly shocking revelations, hurt the insurance business?

One might reasonably expect that the investigations would do harm, by shaking the confidence of the people in the insurance industry. But just the reverse occurred. Apparently the public, with that inarticulate wisdom which the people sometimes display, had been deeply suspicious of the industry *before* the Armstrong hearings. The investigations, and the legislation that followed, persuaded the public that the life insurance industry had been cleaned up and could now be trusted.

It is true that the companies were stripped of their investment affiliates and their overwhelming political influence, but they gained more than they lost. As Morton Keller wrote in his scholarly study, "During the next half century the companies found that, paradoxically, the end of power led to new heights of business success. In the long run, the life insurance corporations showed great capacity for growth. After the immediate post-Armstrong years, the large firms—and the business in general—rose to undreamed-of volume and size. The Prudential's $500,000,000 worth of new insurance in 1909, the largest annual business volume for one company at that time, set the pace for the vast scale of life insurance marketing to come."

What is even more remarkable, as Keller points out, is that "antitrust activity has not touched life insurance; and the companies have not had a central place in the concerns of those disturbed by the phenomenon of big business."

Twenty years after the Armstrong investigation, the Association of Life Insurance Presidents asked Charles Evans Hughes to address their annual convention. In his speech he said:

"I am not here to review the past save as I am permitted to congratulate you upon the unparalleled growth and soundness of the life insurance enterprise. [The expansion of the last 20 years] has been achieved with wise conservation in management, without undue expenditures in obtaining business, and with the returns to policyholders that are consistent with safety. I believe there is no safer or better-managed business in our country than yours."

For John Dryden, there were two personal effects of the Armstrong upheaval. One was his resignation from the board of directors of the Public Service Corporation—the first sign that the Prudential-Fidelity-Union Trust-Public Service Corporation group might be breaking up.

The other development was a brief notice from the Prudential, about a month after the hearings ended, to the effect that Dryden had been re-elected president. His salary, the announcement said, would be $30,000. What the notice didn't say was that the Armstrong hearings had caused the board of directors of the Pru to cut Dryden's salary by more than half—by $35,000, to be precise—because of the unfavorable publicity given to the far more generous earnings of *other* life insurance heads.

7 / Mr. D. Goes to Washington

At the beginning of 1902, John F. Dryden must have felt that life was indeed good. He, who had once seemed to be a born loser, was now a rich and powerful man as a result of his own imagination, perseverance, and hard work—like one of the heroes of those juvenile novels by Horatio Alger, Jr., which were so popular just then. Besides heading the great Prudential, he was a director of three Newark banks, two New York banks, the Public Service Corporation, and J. P. Morgan's masterpiece, the United States Steel Corporation. At least eight exclusive clubs were proud to claim him a member. In Newark he had a mansion, and he had just acquired a great home and estate, which he called "Stronghold," at Bernardsville, off in the Somerset Hills. What honor was left to covet?

The U.S. Senate.

It was not an unusual ambition for a man like Dryden in those days when, as Dr. George H. Haynes, a political scientist of the time, wrote, "it [had] become very common, both in conversation and in the press, to refer to the Senate as the 'Rich Men's Club,' the 'Paradise of Millionaires.' " Moreover, the reputation was borne out by the facts; Haynes conducted a study which showed that 20 per cent of the men in the Senate were millionaires, and most of the others were well on their way to that financial level.

The reason for that state of affairs lay in the Constitution. As originally set forth in that document, the Senate was to consist of members chosen by the legislatures in each state. But the state legislatures were notoriously venal; with enough money, almost anyone could be elected to the Senate. Sometimes in a contested election, so much money was passed in bribes on both sides that the result was a stalemate, with no one elected. Such deadlocks occasionally deprived states of any representation in the Senate—there was no U.S. Senator from Delaware, for example, in 1902–1903 for this reason. (The direct, popular election of Senators, which began with ratification of the 17th Amendment in 1913, put an end to scandals of this sort.)

Dryden—with his allies, the McCarter brothers—already controlled the political machine that had a firm grip on New Jersey. All that Dryden needed to satisfy his senatorial ambitions was a vacant Senate seat.

That deficiency was remedied the day after Christmas, 1901, when General William J. Sewell, one of New Jersey's Senators, died.

Candidates for the Senate seat began to declare themselves. Dryden approached the matter differently. Colonel Anthony R. Kuser, who had married Dryden's daughter Susie, "dropped an intimation here and an intimation there that Mr. Dryden would make an admirable Senator," as a veteran Republican political observer, William E. Sackett, wrote. According to Sackett, Dryden "had been for years an active influence in Republican affairs; was the associate and adviser of all engaged in them, and always an open-handed contributor to the funds that made their achievement possible."

Even so, it took 19 ballots in the Republican legislative caucus before Dryden was chosen as the party's nominee. Because the Republicans had overwhelming majorities in both houses of the legislature, his election was then a foregone conclusion. It was hailed by Governor Franklin Murphy, whose father had been one of the original investors and board members in the Prudential.

As a member of the Senate, it cannot be said that Dryden added luster to that body, although he certainly brought no discredit upon it, either. In his first year he made a speech on the subject of the exclusion of the Chinese from America. Three years later he attracted considerable attention by introducing a bill providing for national, rather than state, regulation of insurance; it never got out of committee. The following year he argued in support of President Theodore Roosevelt's plan for a lock canal, as opposed to a sea level route, across the Isthmus of Panama.

All in all, his record didn't add up to much. Professor Haynes, studying the Senate, listed Dryden among the "men whose presence in the Senate finds its chief, if not its sole, explanation in their great wealth"—unlike Senator Nelson Aldrich of Rhode Island, for example, who was both rich and an outstanding political leader.

But Dryden enjoyed Washington—the clubbiness of the Senate, the ceremonial functions, the formal dinners, the deference paid to what the newspapers liked to call the "solons." Besides, he had a colleague in the Senate with whom he could talk his own special kind of business: Morgan G. Bulkeley, the head of the Aetna Life Insurance Company, for which Dryden had worked in Ohio 40 years earlier, had been elected Senator from Connecticut.

However, the temper of the times was against Dryden. While he was Senator he retained all his business interests. During his term of office, the furor over the Prudential-Fidelity arrangement erupted. So did the Armstrong investigation and its New Jersey follow-up.

The newspapers and magazines were full of muckraking articles, and Dryden's visibility as a Senator made him a better target than before. The most respected crusader of all, Lincoln Steffens, wrote a series of articles for *McClure's Magazine* in 1905 entitled, "New Jersey: A Traitor State," which was aimed primarily at Dryden and his business and political allies. "[Dryden's] election caused some surprise and some difficulty," Steffens told a national audience; "his friends had to buy outright several [legislative] votes for him—unbeknown to him, they say—but that will not happen again. The next time he runs for the United States Senate, he will probably go through as the chief visible representative of the system."

It was all that was needed to ignite New Jersey politics. Even at the time of Dryden's election in 1902, there had been questions about the wisdom of choosing a man in his position for a post in which he would have to vote on measures having a direct and immediate effect on his enterprises. Within the Republican Party itself, as political observer Sackett reported, "there arose the inevitable hue and cry against the selection of so conspicuous a corporation chieftain at a time when the people were making war on the corporations."

That had been in 1902, when it appeared that the hold of Dryden's machine was unshakable. "It would have taken a rash prophet indeed," wrote historian Ransom E. Noble, Jr., "to predict that within a decade New Jersey would be a leading progressive state—and under the leadership of the scholarly and conservative president of Princeton University," Woodrow Wilson. But the reform movement, a coalition of anti-Dryden Republicans and Democrats, was growing in size and strength while Dryden commuted between Washington and Newark. The reform group, headed by State Senator Everett Colby, was called the "New Idea" movement.

The New Idea men first surfaced as an organized force in the state legislature, with a proposal aimed at curbing the Public Service Corporation. The ploy was frustrated, but it was only the first of many actions—throughout the state, as well as in the legislature—to build opposition to the Dryden group. The insurgents received editorial support from a number of newspapers, including the Newark *News,* then the state's most influential journal.

The legislature to be elected in 1906 would choose the Senator to go to Washington in the spring of 1907, so the fight centered on the election of the legislators. The day-to-day operations of the Dryden group were directed by Major Carl Lentz, the political boss of Newark.

"It is doubtful if Senator Dryden ever really understood why his candidacy should have aroused so great a commotion as it did," wrote political observer Sackett, who was close to Dryden's group and sympathetic to his cause. "In the successful chief of a world-wide business enterprise, the people saw one of those hideous monopolists at whom [Teddy] Roosevelt was railing."

Roosevelt was not the only one. Senator Robert LaFollette of Wisconsin, one of the best known and most popular political figures in the nation, roared into New Jersey determined to help the New Idea coalition. In six days he made 16 speeches throughout the state, attacking Dryden for having voted against reform legislation in the Senate.

At the same time, stories began to circulate about the manner in which Dryden's election had been secured five years earlier. "Money flowed around the State House and Trenton hotels in a golden stream for anybody who wanted it and could give an excuse for taking it," wrote the political correspondent of the Newark *News* in a reminiscent column.

Some corroboration seemed to be provided by a former Ocean County Assemblyman who gave an affidavit that he had been offered $5,000 and later $10,000 to vote for Dryden for Senator in 1902. The bribe had been offered, he said, by a railroad lobbyist who had since died. A few days later a Morris County Assemblyman testified to a similar experience with the same lobbyist in 1902, but he had only been offered $250. Because the lobbyist was dead, the stories could not be verified, but the wide difference between the size of the bribes in the stories made skeptics reluctant to accept the Assemblymen's versions. The five-year silence of the men after they had allegedly been offered the bribes also cast doubt on their authenticity.

The reformers' hopes were high on primary day, but they were destined to be disappointed on a scale they had never envisioned. They had concentrated their efforts on ten counties, and in every one of the ten the New Idea nominees lost in the Republican primary.

But the general election held a surprise for everybody. The Democrats—only a small minority in the state, but a part of the New Idea movement—were small no longer: they polled a substantial majority over the Republicans in what amounted to a wholesale overturn of political allegiances. Even Dryden's home county, Essex, went Democratic.

Because the Democratic vote was poorly distributed throughout the state, the Republicans retained a majority in the legislature, but a majority of only seven, and the Assembly, the lower chamber, had a Democratic majority. There were more than seven Republicans opposed to Dryden in the legislature, so it was clear that he could not be re-elected. (Indeed, opposition to his re-election was one of the major reasons usually given for the Democratic victory.)

After two hopeless ballots—when the Republican legislators would not even caucus with him—Dryden withdrew from the race, pleading ill health. A bulletin from his physician said Dryden's health was "too delicate" to warrant his subjecting himself to the rigors of further political work.

With Dryden out of the way, the legislators quickly elected a Republican of the Dryden group who was known to be not unsympathetic to the New Idea movement. Later, however, it was learned that the selection of the new Senator had been made at a secret meeting in the Prudential Building in Newark attended by Dryden; his son-in-law, Kuser; two party leaders; and the candidate himself. Bossism had triumphed again, said the Newark *News*.

But not entirely. The Dryden political machine fell to pieces, and it was never put back together—at least not by him or by anyone else connected with the Prudential.

The Dryden foray into politics had resulted in "a peculiarly sordid era," remarked the Newark *Star* several years later. "His failure to secure re-election to the Senate . . . marked the beginning of the end of that mercenary period of Jersey politics."

In the years that have passed since that day of disappointment for Dryden in 1907, many Prudential men and women have participated in politics, in one party or the other, but they have done so not as representatives of Prudential, but as individual citizens, expressing their personal convictions and trying to give shape and substance to their inner vision of the City of Man.

8 / 'Against All Odds'

Despite the distractions of politics, investigations, and disputes with stockholders over distribution of the Prudential's ever-growing surplus, John F. Dryden devoted most of his time during the first decade of the 20th century to supervision of the company's rapidly expanding operations. As he celebrated the company's 25th anniversary, in 1900, he could watch work underway in Newark on four additional buildings being built as part of the Home Office complex—the Main, West, North, and Northwest buildings, all of which were completed and occupied in 1901.

The intricate web of relationships, customs, taboos, privileges, and routines that creates the overall personality of any organization was already well established, and it would endure for nearly half a century, until another leader shook the company to its foundations. Although the years before World War I were a time of change in America —precipitated by the telephone, the typewriter, the automobile, the airplane, and other inventions—within the Prudential life had settled into a style so fixed and firm that it seemed it would always remain so.

There were thousands of clerks—men and women, but the women then as later far out-numbered the men—in the cluster of Prudential buildings in the heart of Newark. They were supervised by managers who wore morning coats, striped trousers, and derby hats and carried walking sticks. A manager was never addressed by his first name. And he ran his division like an autocrat. There was no appeal from his decisions.

Throughout America more and more women were working. At the Pru only single women were employed; when a girl married, she lost her job. Nevertheless, the Pru was considered possibly the best place for a young woman to work in Newark. Women were often told, by their pastors or relatives, "If you *must* work, work for Prudential." The Prudential, it was generally agreed, was respectable.

In retrospect, it seems stiflingly respectable. Women at the Pru were not permitted to wear makeup of any kind. A young woman found wearing rouge or lipstick might be forced to stand up and wash it off in front of the whole department. Short-sleeved blouses and dresses were outlawed, and the hems of skirts were expected to reach to the ankles. The approved blouses had high necks and stiff-standing collars. "Underneath our petticoats," Helen Ahrens remembered many years later, "there were always long black stockings and high-button shoes." While at her desk, each girl wore a white apron.

On the tenth floor of the North Building was a "drying room" where women who had been caught in the rain could go and wait in robes while their skirts and petticoats were made wearable again in a huge clothes dryer. Umbrellas were furnished free to women employees for many years.

The sexes were segregated as much as possible. For a number of years there were separate elevators for men and women. There were separate cafeterias, too; the women ate in the North Building, the men in the Main Building.

Of course, smoking was not permitted for women at any time, but men were not allowed to smoke either, after the starting bell rang in the morning. However, they could chew, and spittoons were provided for those who did.

In the middle of the morning and again in the afternoon there was a brief "recess" period, when every window was opened—even in the coldest weather—to air out the offices, which probably needed airing in that time when deodorants were not yet in common use and most people over-dressed, by modern standards.

In the typical field office, the superintendent, who would later be called a manager, worked at a high, roll-top desk; but the agents were forced to make do with desks of the kind used in schools. In the typical agency there would be one wall telephone.

To help him govern this vast army of agents and clerks, Dryden had developed a general staff capable of making most of the decisions regarding operations. His son, Forrest F. Dryden, was a vice president. John K. Gore, who today is a figure in most histories of computer development, was chief actuary. Richard V. Lindabury, the lawyer who had represented both the Prudential and the Metropolitan during the Armstrong hearings, had refused to give up his private practice to devote full time to the Prudential, but he had joined the board of directors and accepted appointment as chief counsel.

According to tradition, it was Lindabury who first suggested to Dryden that he recruit Edward D. Duffield to organize the Pru's law department in 1906, on the retirement of Edgar Ward. That may be the way it happened, but certainly Dryden, either through his politically active son-in-law, Anthony Kuser, or through his close associates, the McCarter brothers, already knew of Duffield, for he had been a leading figure in Republican politics. (Lindabury, on the other hand, was a Democrat.) Elected to the lower house of the legislature from Essex County, which contains Newark, Duffield had originally been a reformer, but he soon switched sides and supported the Dryden organization. In 1905 the state Attorney General, Robert H. McCarter—brother of Thomas N. McCarter, the head of Public Service, and Uzal McCarter, the head of the Fidelity Trust—appointed Duffield as his top assistant. So when Duffield left his state post to join the Prudential as general solicitor, in 1906, he must have been well known to Dryden.

Another figure of some consequence in the Prudential of those days was Dr. Frederick L. Hoffman, who came to America from Germany at the age of nineteen and eventually became the Pru's chief statistician and a vice president. In every generation of the Pru there seems to have been at least one especially colorful person, and Hoffman filled that role during his 41 years with the company. He was witty, daring, insatiably curious, unorthodox, and high-spirited—sometimes to the annoyance of his more staid colleagues.

At one party, for example, a woman went up to Hoffman and said, "I've often wondered, doctor—what is the difference between a statistician and an actuary?"

"About $25,000 a year, my dear," Hoffman replied.

Most of those present laughed at the joke, but not all. When Louis R. Menagh, an actuary who later became president of the Pru, was 80 years old, he still remembered the incident with anger, although it had occurred more than 35 years earlier.

During his long career with the Pru, Hoffman traveled all over the world, investigating the facts of life and death. From one of his trips, in 1901, he brought back what he called "a Chip" of the Rock of Gibraltar—a 2,000-pound block of stone. Because of his concern for the victims of disease, Hoffman played a significant part in the founding of the American Cancer Society and the National Tuberculosis Association. During the 1920's, when flying was still regarded as extremely hazardous, he traveled by air frequently. His publications fill a considerable length of shelf in the Prudential's museum.

One of his studies reveals a good deal about life in America in the first decade of the century. Covering the four years from 1907 to 1910 inclusively, it found that 103,434 men insured by the Pru died during that time, 58 per cent of them men employed in factories. Of those 15 years of age and older, 21.9 per cent died of tuberculosis; it was the leading cause of death. Apparently the jokes about drinking up profits had a grain of truth to them: bartenders were twice as likely as most men to die of alcohol-related liver diseases, but saloonkeepers succumbed to such liver ailments at a rate double that of the bartenders who worked for them. The disregard for job safety precautions were indicated in two grim figures: among coal miners the principal cause of death was accidents, 22.9 per cent perishing that way; and among railroad brakemen, 63.3 per cent of all deaths occurred as a result of accidents.

In its time, Hoffman's statistical bureau was considered the best in the Western Hemisphere. The dimension of his work indicated how solidly established the Prudential now felt itself to be. And with good reason.

Before the century was a year old, Edward A. Reilly, the Pru's general agent at Philadelphia, had written the company's first $1,000,000 policy—on the life of L. Rodman Wanamaker, the son of Philadelphia department store magnate John Wanamaker. Hearing that the younger Wanamaker intended to take out a life insurance policy, Reilly filled out an application blank in his name and put in the million-dollar face amount. Obtaining an interview through a mutual friend, he put the application before Wanamaker, explained the benefits of whole life coverage on the five-year dividend plan, and walked out an hour later with the signed application. When the time came to pay a claim on the policy 28 years later, the Pru sent out a check for $1,066,525, including dividends, on the same day that proof of death was received.

Before the decade was out, there were Prudential agencies in virtually every state and territory, including Hawaii. And in 1909 the company opened its first Canadian office, in Toronto.

That was the year that one clever agent made what was, for him, a memorable sale. Reading that Dryden would soon be seventy—the cutoff age beyond which no additional insurance could be sold by the

Pru—the agent, William H. Downs, with the encouragement of his superior, Albert C. Joyce, wrote to Dryden suggesting that he might want to buy additional protection. By return mail came a check for $18.20, the first year's premium, and a letter which said, in part:

"I have taken pleasure in signing the [application] not only as evidence of my continued faith in this form of insurance, which time has proved to be so beneficial and essential to the public weal, but as recognition of your forethought and enterprise in bringing the matter to my attention."

Despite Dryden's satisfaction in the achievement of having established his company on a solid basis, there was still a cloud. The stockholders again sued for more of the company's profits. Moreover, their suit, pressed by the Blanchard heirs under the leadership of Leon Blanchard, asked the court to prohibit the Prudential from granting any benefits to policyholders of any nature beyond those specifically stipulated in the policies. Since 1897 the Pru had been distributing millions of dollars in dividends to Industrial insurance policyholders whose contracts did not call for dividend payments. Furthermore, the Pru had been steadily liberalizing the provisions of many of its existing policies. All of this would be outlawed if the Blanchards were successful in their suit.

The court handed down a compromise decision: the Pru easily could and should pay out an additional $2,500,000 in dividends to the stockholders. But the company was to be permitted to continue to make such concessions to the policyholders—beyond contract requirements—as a legal and necessary part of its business activities.

Neither side was willing to accept the compromise. Both sides appealed. Lindabury, that brilliant counsel who had turned down so many judgeships, told Dryden he was certain that the Prudential would win the appeal.

But it was clear that the pressure from the stockholders for a greater share in the profits would never let up unless—

Unless the Prudential became a mutual company, Lindabury told Dryden. Unless the policyholders, the customers, owned the business.

To mutualize the Prudential would present awesome problems. It also would mean surrendering the future share in the profits that Dryden and his heirs might expect to enjoy. But none of that really mattered to John Dryden now. To him, the Prudential was more than a company; it was a cause. He regarded it as his monument. He said to the directors of the company:

"The faith and confidence of three generations are today placed in this institution, and no words of mine can do justice to my sincere desire to impress upon the board of directors the solemn responsibility which rests upon us all, to administer the affairs of the Prudential for the best interests of the vast aggregate of our insured. No one can question the right of the stockholders to derive from their investment a proper and legitimate reward, but it requires no argument to prove that in this respect the stockholders of the Prudential have no just cause for complaint. It should not be a difficult task to do justice both to stockholders and policyholders, and the great success of the company itself is evidence that good care has been taken of both interests. Our position of justice and equity in all our dealings with our policyholders is neither new nor novel, but traditional with the Prudential, and this will ever be our policy so long as my voice prevails and so long as I am sustained by the judgment, good will, and good faith of those who, throughout these many years, in unison and without a dissenting voice, have administered with rare skill the affairs of the Prudential, in due appreciation of the great trust committed to their care."

But how long would John Dryden's voice prevail?

He was an old man now, and tired. Many of his old associates had succumbed to age or disease, and he was beginning to feel alone. On July 10, 1910—just a few weeks after the frustrating compromise decision in the Blanchard law suit—Dryden suffered a heavy blow: his earliest and most loyal backer, Dr. Leslie D. Ward, died in London. Announcing the death to the Prudential staff, Dryden wrote, "Personally, I have lost in Dr. Ward a friend and companion through a long association not often paralleled in the relations existing between men in business affairs. I can bear testimony to his valuable services in the building up of this great company, to his integrity, to his fidelity to principle, to his lovable and charitable disposition, to his optimistic and enthusiastic temperament. . . ."

The months passed. The newspapers made a fuss about Teddy Roosevelt's married daughter smoking cigarettes. Woodrow Wilson was elected Governor of New Jersey. Leo Tolstoy died. Amundsen reached the South Pole. The Supreme Court ordered the dissolution of the Oil Trust. The streets were beginning to fill up with automobiles; the next President would ride to his inauguration in a car. Although few sensed it at the time, the first World War was fast approaching, and it would change the world in unimaginable ways.

On Saturday, November 18, 1911, John Dryden was operated on in his home at 1020 Broad Street in Newark, so that gallstones could be removed. He was said the next day to be "doing well," but within another day or two the doctors were expressing "little hope." Pneumonia had set in. Late on the afternoon of Friday, November 24, death came to the man whom *The New York Times* described the next morning as the "Father of Industrial Insurance."

As preparations were made for the funeral, the press was filled with the praise usual on such occasions. But the most telling comment had been made two years earlier, by a Newark publication called the *Expositor:*

> John F. Dryden . . . is a remarkable illustration of greatness arising out of a long and arduous, but always determined, struggle for success in a new and venturesome field of human endeavor. He succeeded because he possessed traits and characteristics which have always been a prerequisite to greatness; above all, remarkable energy and conscientious application to the details of his daily life, and absolute intellectual honesty. . . .
>
> To have had faith in a new idea is not rare, for the world is full of day dreamers who hopelessly struggle against overwhelming odds. But to have had an abiding faith in an almost hopeless aim and effort, and to have carried the idea through the years, against all odds, to a successful termination, is given to few men, and of these few John F. Dryden ranks foremost as a truly great man of his time.

He was, indeed, a man of his time. By modern standards, many of his views and his acts can be judged harshly. But a man or woman should be judged against the values of their times. By that yardstick John F. Dryden was a truly great man.

He was tough. He had to be, in a time when the financial world was like a wild, lawless frontier.

Dryden was fiercely independent. At a time when many other life insurance companies fell under the domination of one Wall Street giant or another, he kept the Prudential a thing apart, as the investigations of the time showed. He would make alliances—when it benefited the Pru—with various interests, but in the end the Pru always stood alone, representing no interests but its policyholders'.

There can be little doubt that Dryden truly cared deeply about the welfare of his policyholders and his employees. Nobody ever accused him of attempting to drain profits out of the Pru. Indeed, he fought bitter battles with important stockholders in order to defend the company's surplus against demands for higher dividends. As a result, the Prudential's assets, at the time of his death, amounted to $259,186,137 —more than a quarter of a billion dollars—all of it built up from his dream and a few thousand dollars invested by businessmen whom he and Dr. Ward had converted to the cause.

It is true that Dryden, after so many failures and frustrations in the first half of his life, achieved great wealth, but it could not be said that he got his money dishonorably. He had seen how to satisfy a social need, he had struggled against long odds to bring his dream to realization, and he had reaped the rewards. After his death *The New York Times* estimated his fortune at $50,000,000—not much less than the $68,000,000 left by J. P. Morgan on his death two years later. Morgan led the honorary pallbearers at Dryden's funeral, and a most distinguished group it was. The rites ended at Mount Pleasant Cemetery in Newark, within sight of the upper floors of the Prudential headquarters building today.

In the introduction to his collected papers and addresses, published in 1909, Dryden had left a statement of philosophy which could sustain the Prudential through the challenges that would face it in the decades after his passing:

"Social institutions, like political institutions, can endure only . . . if they prove their social utility by successful adaptation and re-adaptation to the ever-changing conditions and circumstances of political and social life."

9/ The Customers Take Over the Business

It had always been understood in the company that Forrest Fairchild Dryden would one day succeed his father as the head of the Prudential. In fact, his grooming as the heir apparent had cost the Pru one of its best men in 1897, when John B. Lunger, actuary and manager of the Ordinary Branch, resigned. Lunger left because John Dryden reneged on a promise that he would be the next man elevated to a vice presidency; Dryden had decided that his son had to be the next vice president as part of his progression to the top. Lunger became a vice president of the Travelers and later vice president of the Equitable.

As a boy, Forrest had worked part time in the office. After attending Newark Academy and the Phillips Academy at Andover, Massachusetts—he later married the daughter of his mathematics teacher there—he started to work full time for the Pru as a clerk in 1882. By 1890 he not only bore the title of secretary, but he was also a member of the board of directors. In 1903 he was elected third vice president, in 1906 second vice president, and in 1911 vice president. On January 8, 1912, he was elected president, filling the vacancy created by his father's passing.

Anyone would have found it difficult to follow John F. Dryden. Despite his reserve and formality, the elder Dryden had been regarded with respect that almost amounted to awe. Now some Prudential people complained privately that the younger Dryden was too much a stickler for rigid rules, that his insistence on the proprieties was sometimes stretched so far that it reached pomposity, that he lacked the feeling for people which had softened his father's aloofness. These or other criticisms probably would have been leveled at anyone who succeeded John Dryden, but they were more readily believed about Forrest Dryden because of the preferment he had enjoyed.

Fortunately for all concerned, Forrest was willing to be guided by his father's wise adviser, general counsel Richard V. Lindabury. It was fortunate because Forrest had a crisis on his hands even before his election, when he was just acting president.

The problem involved the close interrelationship of the Prudential and the Fidelity Trust. At the December 1911 meeting of the Fidelity's board, the bank's president, Uzal McCarter, named the proxy committee which would vote the Fidelity's shares of Prudential stock at the Pru's annual meeting in January 1912. McCarter said the committee would consist of himself; his brother, Thomas N. McCarter, the president of the Public Service Corporation; Frederick W. Egner, vice president of the Fidelity; Forrest Dryden; and Dryden's brother-in-law, Anthony Kuser. In other words, the Fidelity interests would have a three-to-two edge over the Prudential group, thus, in effect, giving the Fidelity control of the Pru.

Forrest Dryden protested immediately, saying that he'd understood the fifth member was to be Wilbur S. Johnson, vice president and comptroller of the Pru. (That was the way it had always been handled when John Dryden was alive—the Fidelity's proxy committee had a majority of Prudential men, and the Pru's proxy committee gave the edge to the Fidelity people, thus assuring that neither could wrest control away from the other.) Uzal McCarter conceded that he had discussed such an arrangement before his death with John Dryden, but he said he didn't feel bound now to hold to that plan. The ensuing "discussion was prolonged and acrimonious," according to Edward D. Duffield, then the Pru's general solicitor, who wrote a long, confidential account of the whole affair.

Duffield said, "It developed that it was the purpose of Mr. [Uzal] McCarter and his brother and others who, by reason of Senator Dryden's death, controlled a majority of the board of the Fidelity at that time, to take control of the Prudential, dictate the composition of its board of directors, and control the conduct of its affairs."

But matters were not as clear-cut as McCarter thought. In the course of the discussion, it emerged that six members of the Fidelity's board thought that the Fidelity should control the Prudential, six thought the insurance company should control the bank, and three of the directors were wavering but essentially felt that it would be better if the two institutions "were completely divorced." In the end, a committee was appointed to consider some way of separating the two companies.

In the meantime, there remained the problem of Fidelity's proxy committee and the Pru's annual meeting, which was always held on the second Monday in January. The Fidelity's annual meeting was scheduled for the second Tuesday in January. In 1912 New Year's Day fell on Monday; thus, the second Monday that January preceded the second Tuesday, so the Pru's meeting would come before the Fidelity's annual meeting—and there would be nothing to prevent the Fidelity group from electing a Prudential board which it dominated.

At that point, Duffield's account falls silent, but it appears that somebody in the Pru faction—probably Lindabury—realized that the advantage did not lie with the other side, as everyone had supposed. For the Fidelity's annual meeting was fixed by state law, and could not be changed except by the legislature—but the Prudential's annual meeting was established in the by-laws of the company, which could be amended at any meeting by action of the board. Thus the Prudential board could, if it wished, change its annual meeting to the third Monday in January. The Prudential board would then be in a position to vote its shares in the Fidelity for a board in which it had absolute control, and the McCarter faction could be rendered powerless—even ousted, if need be.

It was like a game of chess, and the Fidelity men were in check. Faced with such a complete turnabout in advantage, they withdrew their takeover threat. The special committee which had been appointed recommended that the Fidelity shares be voted at the Prudential's annual meeting for the existing board, with the vacancy caused by John Dryden's death to be filled by a person to be chosen by the Pru's management. In return, the insurance company's management would bind itself to vote for the bank's existing management. Finally, both sides agreed that Prudential should be mutualized—that is, converted into a mutual life insurance company, which has no stockholders, being owned and controlled by its policyholders. The policies issued by a mutual life company are called "participating" because they provide for the policyholder to share in any earnings which may be realized over and above the needs of the business. The policyholders' portion of those surplus earnings is paid out to the policyholders as "dividends." Obviously, a company owned by stockholders can only be turned into a mutual by purchasing their shares from them, using for this purpose money which comes from the company's surplus funds. In the Prudential controversy, both sides said they would work together to devise a method for mutualizing Pru which would be fair to the Fidelity and to the other stockholders, as well as to the policyholders.

The crisis had been averted.

But the problem still remained—how to turn the Prudential into a mutual company, owned by its policyholders?

The Pru couldn't simply buy its shares back, because that would throw control into the hands of the minority stockholders if they chose not to sell their stock. And it was that minority which had been trying for many years to take more money out of the Pru.

If Duffield's recollection was correct, it was Dr. Leslie D. Ward's brother, Edgar, the retired general counsel of the company, who suggested a solution: arrange for a trustee to vote the re-purchased shares until the entire outstanding stock had been acquired.

While this strategy was being worked out, a ruling was handed down on April 26, 1912, by the Court of Errors and Appeals in the law suit by the Blanchard heirs in which they had demanded a greater share of the profits and an end to concessions to the policyholders. Lindabury had been right in his prediction: the high court decided the case in favor of the Prudential.

During the fall of 1912 Lindabury asked Thomas N. McCarter whether the Fidelity would be willing to transfer its shares to a trustee who would hold them for Prudential policyholders. McCarter said his group would be agreeable to that, provided the Pru paid at least $300 for each of its shares.

At the same time, McCarter said he wanted to buy the Fidelity shares held by the Prudential. It later developed that he felt he had an understanding with Lindabury that those shares would sell to McCarter at a price of $600 per share. However, when it became known the following year that the Prudential was going to be mutualized, the market price of Fidelity shares rose above the $600 figure. When Lindabury said rather heatedly that it had not been his understanding that he had made a commitment for the Pru to sell at the $600 price, McCarter, who tended to be hot-tempered, complained angrily that the Pru men were trying to back down on the deal. Again feelings rose on both sides.

It was on the unlikeliest of occasions that the matter came to a head. On September 24, 1913, a bronze statue of John Dryden by the sculptor Karl Bitter was dedicated in the rotunda of the company's main building, ''where the tide of our employees ebbed and flowed past it for more than 40 years,'' as a later president of the company, Robert A. Beck, said when Dryden was inducted posthumously into the Insurance Hall of Fame. (The statue served a useful, if irreverent, purpose over the years, according to Henry Schlegel, who worked in the Actuarial Department in Newark before going out to the Western Home Office years later. Schlegel said the rotunda lobby "confused newcomers with its maze of doors," but "we soon learned that the true street exit was directly in line with the nose on John Dryden's statue.") At the dedication luncheon, Uzal McCarter asked for a meeting of the mutualization committee.

When the ceremonies were concluded, the meeting was held that afternoon in Forrest Dryden's office. At the meeting, the McCarter brothers said they'd go along with the mutualization plan only on condition that they could obtain the Prudential's shares of Fidelity stock at the $600 price. If that condition were not met, "they would proceed with their original plan of placing the Fidelity in control of the Prudential," in the words of Duffield's memoir.

Another committee meeting was held on October 6, at which Duffield reported tentative agreement on the basis of the deal the McCarters had sought. The state's Commissioner of Banking and Insurance also approved the arrangement.

Lindabury and Duffield drafted a bill permitting the mutualization of the Prudential and providing for the naming of a trustee for policyholders. When the bill came up for a hearing, the minority stockholders, who opposed it, were represented by Samuel Untermyer—a fact which would later have great significance to the fortunes of Forrest Dryden. Despite the opposition, the bill passed, and was signed by the Governor on March 24, 1913.

In accordance with the law, the Chancellor—who was then head of the state's Court of Chancery—appointed three men not connected with any of the interested parties to serve as a committee of appraisal. After a series of hearings, the appraisers fixed the value of Prudential's stock at $455 per share, or 910 per cent of par. The majority stockholders sold their holdings back to the Pru at that price in 1915, but nearly 30 years passed before the remaining shares could be acquired. In the meantime, the majority shares remained in the keeping of the trustee for policyholders, State Senator Austen Colgate of Essex County serving as the first trustee.

The outstanding shares earned their owners an annual dividend of 10 per cent over the intervening years. Those stockholders also received each year the earnings on the capital determined by the appraisers to be the property of the shareholders.

From a practical point of view, however, the Prudential operated as a mutual company after 1915. Mutualization was the principal achievement of Forrest Dryden's administration, and a great accomplishment it was.

During the years that followed, the Prudential wrote its first Group insurance policy, besides broadening and liberalizing its individual life insurance policies.

With U.S. entry into the first World War in 1917, the company organized the "Prudential Home Guard," a military unit whose purpose was never quite clear. But the faint-hearted could take cheer in the thought that if the Kaiser managed to bring his troops up the Passaic River or into Port Newark, Prudential's latter-day Minutemen were prepared to repel the invader.

However, the war was a deadly serious business for 1,729 other Prudential employees—those who served in the armed forces. Fifty of them lost their lives in the war.

Some Prudential civilians had to deal with death and maiming on a mass scale, too, after a munitions ship bound for Europe collided with another vessel in the harbor at Halifax, Nova Scotia, caught fire, and exploded with a noise heard 61 miles away. Two square miles of the city were totally destroyed, more than 1,600 men, women, and children were killed, and upwards of 4,000 persons were injured. There were so many Prudential policyholders among the victims that John H. Glover, the company's local manager, couldn't handle the job alone, so he appealed to the Home Office for help. The assignment was given to Albert C. Joyce—the same Joyce who had sold John Dryden a policy eight years before—and he sped from Boston to the Canadian city. For the rest of his life he was haunted by the scenes of horror—the endless piles of debris, the bodies still buried under the rubble, the shocking wounds suffered by so many, the lack of shelter for the survivors and the rescue workers in the midst of a Canadian snowstorm, the threat of typhoid.

A year later the terrible influenza epidemic was sweeping North America, having ravaged Europe. Some idea of the impact of the epidemic can be gained from these facts: in 1917, there were 51 flu deaths in Boston; by October 1, 1918, there were 202 deaths *a day* in that city, and for many days the flu death rate was 175 a day. One out of four persons in the U.S. and Canada fell ill; of every 1,000 stricken, 19 died. The total number of deaths was estimated officially at between

400,000 and 500,000. As someone pointed out, the death lists were three or four times the length of those for the London Plague of 1665, the dread Black Death.

For the people of Prudential, it was the most demanding time they had ever known as a group. Although Newark was not hit as badly as most cities—the death rate went up only 250 per cent there—the Home Office, where claims had to be processed, was undermanned because of the number of clerks who were sick. And in the agency offices across the continent men and women worked valiantly to serve their policyholders in a time of heightened need.

From September 26 to October 19, 1918, the Pru paid $1,000,000 in influenza death claims. In one day it paid $506,000 in all kinds of death claims, a record up to that time.

One of the hardest hit cities was Philadelphia, where the death rate shot up 700 per cent. Harry I. Leonard, who had been "walking a debit"—as Prudential people put it—for many years in south Philadelphia, found the epidemic "unbelievable." One day he'd be talking to one of his clients, and the next day he'd hear that the man or woman was dead. Undertakers could not handle so many funerals. The district ran out of coffins. At the office he worked out of, Philadelphia No. 9, everybody pitched in to help adjust and pay claims as fast as possible, but even so long lines formed at the cashier's window as though seeking tickets for a Broadway hit.

One day Leonard's boss, R. J. Pedrick, realized that the agent had been working for weeks in houses visited by the deadly flu.

"What do *you* do for medication, Harry?" he asked.

"My prescription calls for a quart a day," Leonard replied, "but I believe I'm a little ahead of the prescription."

By the end of the war people all over the continent were complaining that there weren't enough apartments and houses. Housing shortages invariably follow wars because so much labor and so many materials are diverted to war production during the conflict that very little new building takes place. And yet the number of persons marrying and the percentage of families having babies tends to increase in wartime, resulting in an increased, pent-up demand for housing after the fighting is over.

When new construction fell to 58 per cent of normal in 1919 and to 37 per cent in 1920, the New York state legislature decided that it had a responsibility to look into the matter. State Senator Charles Lockwood was named chairman of an investigating committee, and he appointed a distinguished member of the bar, Samuel Untermyer, as committee counsel. Untermyer, who was famous for his legal erudition, his urbanity, and his intellectual agility, was a Wall Street lawyer turned crusader against what he saw as the "money power" of that financial center. During the Armstrong investigation Untermyer had represented the Equitable. Later he had represented the Prudential's minority stockholders in testifying against the Prudential mutualization bill in the New Jersey legislature.

Despite his legislative appearance against the Pru, the company's officials had no reason to feel alarm when his appointment as the Lockwood Committee's counsel was announced, because the declared target of the investigation was the building industry. During 1920 the committee explored that industry at length, uncovering all manner of deplorable practices and earning admiring editorials in the press.

One of the reasons for the housing shortage, the committee found in that first phase of its work, was a lack of mortgage money. Untermyer used that as his justification for turning the investigation into an inquisition into the life insurance industry, on the ground that insurance companies ought to be encouraged to invest more of their funds in mortgages.

This time the Prudential, which had fared well in the Armstrong investigation, took the kind of beating which had been handed out to the other companies then. Untermyer subjected Forrest Dryden to hours of merciless questioning, seeking to show that Dryden was involved in financial deals that adversely affected policyholders. For example, evidence was produced showing that two thirds of the Pru's funds were deposited in New York and New Jersey banks in which Dryden owned stock.

To make matters worse, Dryden was an incredibly poor witness. Although he had spent his entire life in the insurance business, most of his answers were to the effect that he didn't know, that he didn't keep up with developments of this or that sort, or that he didn't understand. Several times he was threatened with a contempt action, but it is hard to read the testimony without believing that he really didn't know what to answer.

When he did make a forthright answer, it was disastrous in its effect on public opinion. Asked if he saw anything improper in depositing funds of which he was a sort of trustee in banks from whose operations he profited, Dryden replied firmly, "I do not."

Despite his reputation as a first rate investigator, Untermyer obviously had not familiarized himself with many of the basic facts about the Pru. In the beginning, he proceeded on the assumption that John F. Dryden had owned all of the original stock of the company, a suggestion that the elder Dryden's ghost must have heard with a rueful chuckle. He also thought that Forrest Dryden had bought the Blanchard stock—and *that* must have startled the Blanchards!

Untermyer kept insinuating that the Prudential's mutualization was a fake. To that Lindabury had a ready response: he asked the New Jersey Commissioner of Banking and Insurance to conduct an investigation of his own into that question, using examiners from other states as well, so that there could be no suggestion that the Pru had used political influence to get a rigged verdict. The investigation was carried out by a team of insurance experts from the state staffs of Massachusetts, Indiana, Missouri, and New Jersey, as well as New York. It cleared the Prudential of all of Untermyer's charges about the mutualization.

"If there ever was a mutualization of a life insurance company in which its policyholders were protected," said the New York Superintendent of Insurance, "it was the mutualization of the Prudential, from beginning to end. If the public will examine the records it will find out the facts. But some people are not so anxious to find facts as they are to distort them. I am perfectly satisfied that the affairs of the Prudential, so far as mutualization goes, are satisfactory."

Besides Forrest Dryden's ownership of bank stocks, Untermyer did come up with one fact that proved highly embarrassing to the Prudential: it still owned 20 per cent of the stock of the Fidelity Union Trust Company, as the Newark bank was now called.

As soon as he decently could, Forrest Dryden took a leave of absence while the other directors and officers tried to repair the damage done to the company by the Lockwood investigation. It was said that Dryden was in poor health. He went to Bermuda to recover.

During his absence the board of directors voted to sell the Prudential's shares of Fidelity Union stock. He wasn't told about the action until his return to New Jersey, at which time he resigned from the Fidelity Union Bank's board of directors. But Dryden didn't return to his office; he continued on his leave of absence, this time at a resort in New England.

With the sale of its Fidelity Union stock, the Pru made the divorce of the two institutions final. In the years that have passed since then—more than half a century—banks and insurance companies have been investigated at every level of government, but no one has ever suggested the slightest impropriety in such dealings as the Pru might have with the Fidelity Union, for they were the sort of transactions that the Prudential had with hundreds of banks throughout the U.S. and Canada.

On August 14, 1922, Forrest Dryden, two weeks before the end of his six-month leave of absence, tendered his resignation, which the board accepted with suitable expressions of regret and appreciation. For Dryden, it had been a personal tragedy.

For the Prudential, it had been a cleansing and strengthening ordeal, from which it had emerged healthier and more vigorous than before. The X-rays had found the suspicious growths within the sturdy body, and they had been cut out.

Rightly or wrongly, many Prudential people at every level thought that nepotism had been the root cause of the Pru's difficulties, and a consensus developed that it had to be ended. The company enacted anti-nepotism rules that are today surely at least as restrictive as those in any American or Canadian company.

The total absence of nepotism seems somehow to underline the truth that the Prudential is a company that belongs to its customers.

10/'Paddlefoot' and the Colonel

During the long administration of Edward D. Duffield, who succeeded Forrest Dryden as president of the Prudential in 1922, the world was wracked by painful transformations in every area of life, but within the company, life went on in almost cloistered tranquillity. Less than two weeks after Dryden went on leave of absence, the U.S. Supreme Court unanimously upheld the constitutionality of the 19th Amendment, which gave women the right to vote. At that time, the Teapot Dome scandal was still in the future, and so were Herbert Hoover's "chicken in every pot" and Franklin D. Roosevelt's New Deal. Mussolini did not yet rule Italy; Hitler had not written *Mein Kampf;* and in the Soviet Union, Lenin was alive, Trotsky was a power to be reckoned with, and Stalin was a colorless secretary of the Communist Party. In China, Sun Yat-Sen was still trying to establish an independent republic on a sound footing. On Wall Street, the height of the bull market was far in the future, and even further off were the Crash of 1929 and the Depression of the 1930's.

Of course, there was no television. There were not even very many radio stations. Multi-lane highways were undreamt-of—indeed, most roads were unpaved. Most travelers could not go by air; there was only one, undependable airline. At the University of Toronto, Banting and Best had just discovered insulin, but antibiotics were still in the future, and so was commercial production of vitamins.

George Gershwin had yet to do his best work, and the same was true of Aaron Copland, Eugene O'Neill, Ernest Hemingway, Sinclair Lewis, Theodore Dreiser, and F. Scott Fitzgerald. The *New Yorker* magazine had not yet been founded, nor *Time*.

During Duffield's administration, much of the earth would be explored. Motion pictures would be produced with sound, and even in color. The roads would be crowded with cars which would give people the mobility and privacy to complete the destruction of Victorian manners and morals. Millions of Americans would learn to drink in speak-easies before Prohibition was repealed.

At almost precisely the halfway point in Duffield's 16 years as president of the Pru, the world was shaken by the worst economic crisis in history. People wondered if democratic governments could survive; political extremists thrived on the right and the left. Millions were without work and many without food or shelter.

All of those developments had their impact on the Prudential and on the people who worked for it, but the effect was always muted and subdued. It was as though Duffield, a sound, no-nonsense, paternalistic sort of fellow, simply wouldn't stand for too many of the jolts and strains of the outside world penetrating the cathedral-like walls of the Prudential. It is likely that the 1929 stock market crash did not have the lasting influence on the Pru that the benevolent personality of Duffield did.

It was while Duffield led it that the company came to be known for "the three P's": Princeton, Presbyterianism, Prudential. (Some added a fourth: Prissiness.)

Until the end of World War II a cachet of the Prudential employee who was likely to rise in the organization was a degree from Princeton. Duffield himself was a direct descendant of the first president of Princeton, Jonathan Dickinson (the middle initial in Duffield's name stood for Dickinson). Since the beginning, Duffield's family had been associated with Princeton. His father taught mathematics and the classics there for 56 years, from 1845 to 1901, and Duffield's brother Henry worked for the university for 40 years, the last 30 as its treasurer. Born on the campus, Duffield was elected a trustee in 1920 and in 1932–1933 he doubled as president of both Princeton and Prudential, while the university conducted a search for a permanent president.

At meetings of the Princeton trustees, Duffield was particularly impressed by the contributions of another trustee, Franklin D'Olier—so impressed that in 1925 he asked D'Olier to come to work at the Prudential. After due consideration, D'Olier accepted the proposition and became Pru's vice president in charge of administration.

The son of a Philadelphia cotton broker, D'Olier, after graduation from Princeton, had worked as a millhand at Talladega, Louisiana, in order to get an understanding of the business at the workingman's level. At the outbreak of the first World War he was head of the family textile business, but he nevertheless volunteered for service. On Armistice

Day he was a colonel in the Quartermaster Corps in France; for the rest of his life everybody called him "Colonel D'Olier." He was one of the 20 American officers who met in Paris on February 15, 1919, to organize what became the American Legion, and later D'Olier was elected its first national commander.

Duffield had particular need of D'Olier because the Pru had just lost the services of one of its most able advisers, Richard V. Lindabury. Still strong at 74, Lindabury had been in the custom of riding every morning at his 600-acre farm near Bernardsville. On July 15 his horse apparently threw him, and the fall killed Lindabury.

Despite the loss of Lindabury, the Prudential prospered throughout the Roaring Twenties, operating in a very conservative fashion and changing its customs and practices only when the forces for change could no longer be resisted. Nevertheless, with Duffield—who was called "Paddlefoot" behind his back because of his painfully flat feet—as president and D'Olier as his right-hand man, the obsolete was gradually eliminated and the innovative introduced.

Thus, in 1922 the three-cent Weekly Premium Industrial policies were discontinued, although the company still wrote the five-cent policies. The following year the company opened its first mortgage loan branch office, in Toronto. The year after that a Group insurance plan covering Home Office personnel was inaugurated.

On May 7, 1928, the first policies on an Intermediate Monthly Premium plan, a contract combining some characteristics of an Industrial policy and some of an Ordinary policy, were issued. Later that year the company introduced the Modified 3 policy, a whole life policy with a change of rate at the end of three years; it began with a low rate which was increased after three years, by which time the dividends offset the higher premiums. Before the year was out, the Accidental Death Benefit was added to Weekly Premium policies retroactively—an action by which Prudential beneficiaries received an extra $3 million in the next 12 months alone.

During the 1920's another building was erected as part of the Home Office complex in Newark: the Gibraltar Building, which still occupies the block bounded by Bank, Academy, Halsey, and Washington Streets. The "Gib" Building, as it has always been called, was connected at the sixth floor by a bridge over Halsey Street with the North

Building, which in turn was connected by a third floor bridge with the Main Building across Bank Street.

Within the Pru buildings, life and work went on pretty much the way it always had. Skirts were shorter, supervisors had given up wearing morning coats, and elevators and cafeterias were no longer segregated by sex, but otherwise very little had changed. The atmosphere was still very formal and authoritarian. The restrooms were checked regularly to make sure that nobody was smoking in them. Young women had to leave the company when they married; some, who felt they needed the money, hid their marital condition. Inevitably, some also hid pregnancies, and at least one baby was born unexpectedly in a restroom.

The Depression which began in 1929 had relatively little direct effect on the company. In 1932, like most other companies, the Prudential cut salaries, the deepest cuts being made in the pay of senior officers, but by that time the cost of living had dropped so sharply that less money went further than before.

Actually, after the worst of the Depression was over, the Pru found that in the six years from 1930 through 1935, the face value of its life insurance policies in force had *risen* by more than $1.5 billion and it had paid out more than $471 million to its policyholders in dividends. It had also made policy loans totaling upwards of $396 million. All of this, of course, was on top of the usual payments for death benefits and other claims.

In fact, so busy was the Prudential that it acquired more property, at High and Warren Streets in Newark, to house some of its operations.

During the terrible days of massive unemployment throughout the country, nobody lost a job at the Prudential—unless he or she was incompetent, insubordinate, unreliable, or otherwise unsatisfactory. In order to relieve the general distress in the community, the company established a temporary rule that no more than one person would be hired from any household.

In a 1929 report, statistician Frederick L. Hoffman said that the murder rate in the U.S. had doubled since 1900. Despite Chicago's reputation in the Roaring Twenties, he also found that the murder rate there was far below that of 10 major cities in the South. Anticipating a public debate of the 1970's, Hoffman opposed capital punishment, asserting that his statistical studies convinced him that it was not a deterrent to homicide; instead, he favored restrictions on the purchase and possession of firearms.

The following year—after the stock market crash—Hoffman disclosed that the 1929 suicide rate had set a record. "When the suicide rates for a period of years are correlated to business failures," he said, "there is a fair consistency in the correlation . . . though sometimes the highest suicide rate follows the year after the highest rate of business failures."

Many of the most famous murder cases of the 1920's and 1930's affected the Prudential. Late in the Twenties, for example, Ruth Snyder and her lover, a corset salesman named Judd Gray, killed her husband, Albert Snyder, an art editor, with a sashweight. Presumably they wanted to get rid of an obstacle to their romance, but they were practical about their project; Mrs. Snyder took out $95,000 in insurance on her spouse's life before she ended it. The unfortunate Mr. Snyder never knew how heavily he was insured, because Mrs. Snyder persuaded her Prudential agent to copy her husband's signature onto the application. As soon as the agent's act became known, the Pru fired him for violating company rules, and then it fought successfully against paying the policy on the ground of fraud.

A classic claims case of the Thirties involved a well-nigh-indestructible gentleman by the name of Michael Malloy, an Irishman of uncertain years who liked liquor as much as he disliked work. One day in 1932 Tony Marino, the owner of a New York speak-easy which was one of Malloy's favorite haunts, got together with the neighborhood undertaker, Frank Pasqua, and suggested that they join in a project to insure Malloy and then bring about his demise. However, they could not be accused of thinking in grandiose terms: they only insured the unsuspecting Malloy for $1,200—again with the help of an agent who violated company rules by not talking with the insured personally and not getting his signature on the application. With the help of the bartender, Red Murphy, Marino and Pasqua saw to it that Malloy drank five shots of antifreeze on top of his usual heavy dose of alcohol. But Malloy didn't die; he just slept it off.

During the following week Malloy, whose taste buds probably couldn't tip him off to what he was drinking, consumed vast quantities of wood alcohol, which did nothing but make him drowsy. So the conspirators decided to have him die of ptomaine poisoning by eating sardines out of a can which had been standing open for days without refrigeration. Just to make sure, Marino had the can ground into little slivers of metal, which he mixed with the rotten fish. Malloy ate the metal-and-rotten-fish sandwich and washed it down with antifreeze, and felt none the worse for it.

In desperation, the plotters waited one night until Malloy passed out from antifreeze and then carried him into the park, where they left him after taking his jacket and opening his clothes to expose him to the elements. It was the first week of January and a heavy sleet storm was beating at the city. To help nature along, Marino poured five gallons of water over the head of the unconscious Malloy. But the only result of that night's work was that Pasqua caught a cold. Malloy felt fine after he woke up in the park.

Another attempt on Malloy's life—by running him down with a car—had to be called off because people in the neighborhood almost witnessed the aborted murder. Later that night, however, they managed to shove the unconscious man in front of a taxicab, which hit him hard.

But nothing about Malloy's death appeared in the newspapers for a couple of weeks, and a check of the local hospitals by telephone did not uncover a corpse named Malloy. Lacking even the intended victim, the persistent plotters then picked another man, named McCarthy, stuffed his pockets with papers identifying him as Malloy, slipped him a mickey, and then ran over him with a car. McCarthy didn't die immediately, and while Marino and Pasqua were waiting in the speakeasy for word of his death, an unexpected patron strolled into the saloon—Mike Malloy.

He had been in the hospital since his "accident," he told the conspirators, who soon were in need of him again: McCarthy was out of danger, according to the doctors. This time Malloy was finally killed, by having a rubber hose attached to a gas jet held in his mouth after he passed out from drinking.

Prudential paid off, but even in those days $1,200 wouldn't go far, and Marino and Pasqua, in the course of their efforts, had felt compelled to bring in, one at a time, four other men. In the subsequent quarreling over division of the modest loot, one of the plotters was killed. The others talked so much, complaining about one another, that the gossip finally reached the ears of the police. In the end, Marino, Pasqua, and two others died in the electric chair at Sing Sing; the fifth man got off with a stretch in prison.

Another claims story from the Thirties concerned a fraud ring in Philadelphia that caused the death of at least 50 persons. It started with a South Philadelphia faith healer named Dr. Morris Bolber, who arranged for a friend of his named Paul Petrillo to seduce housewives whose husbands had grown indifferent. After insurance had been bought on the husbands' lives, Bolber provided a poison that made the wife a widow.

Since it wouldn't do to keep using poison, the two murderers recruited one of Paul's cousins, Herman Petrillo, who proceeded to push people off roofs, dump non-swimmers into rivers, and otherwise contribute substantially to the city's death rate. Herman Petrillo also acted as a stand-in, when needed, for insurance medical examinations of intended victims. A physician acting for Prudential examined him twice in one year—Petrillo using different names each time, of course—and thought, the second time, that he'd seen the man somewhere, but he couldn't place him.

In time, Bolber and his accomplices joined forces with a North Philadelphia woman named Carino Favato, who was also a faith healer and "adviser" to troubled wives. Thus they were able to extend their operations to another populous part of the city.

For five years, from 1932 to 1937, the ring worked its deadly business, until the day when Herman Petrillo told a man just out of prison that if he located somebody who could be insured and then killed, the ex-convict would get part of the proceeds. The ex-convict may have been a crook, but he wasn't a murderer. He went to the police with his story, and before the books were closed on the case, the Petrillos had been executed, and Bolber and Carino Favato each got life sentences.

More important than the unusual claims of the period, however, was the staggering problem posed for the Prudential by its farm and home mortgages. As the national economy ground almost to a halt, companies went bankrupt, people were thrown out of work, and millions could not meet their financial obligations. The Home Office and offices in the field were swamped with delinquencies. The flood of correspondence was so great that specialists had to be sent into various areas to work out problems on the spot. Out of some of those emergency headquarters emerged the Pru's later regional real estate investment offices.

Whenever possible, the Pru tried to avoid foreclosure. The terms of mortgages were revised, or mortgages were extended, if there seemed to be any possibility of keeping the property in the hands of the mortgagors. Often this process was resorted to several times, in order to prevent foreclosure, before the mortgagee finally found himself in the clear, able to pick up the payments again without ruining himself.

In one—by no means rare—case, a Columbus, Ohio, home was purchased in 1927, and Prudential made a home loan on it. Time after time the mortgage terms were eased or payments suspended to enable the couple who owned the house to get on their feet. It was not until 1937 that the family was able to resume regular payments.

All over the country this sort of thing was going on with Prudential mortgages during the Depression. In Lakeland, Florida, a railroad engineer was laid off, and for four years the Pru not only did not demand payments, but also even paid the taxes on the house. When the man was able to go back to work and resume payments, he wrote to the Pru, "My family and I are certainly grateful to you for helping us keep a roof over our heads."

When farm mortgages were involved, the Prudential went to even greater lengths to help farmers keep their land. All representatives of the company were notified that it was the Pru's intention not to foreclose on any farm whose owner was making "every effort in his power to meet his obligations." If there was any possibility that the farmer could ultimately get on his feet, the Pru would abstain from foreclosure.

But farmers had been battered economically during the 1920's and for many the Depression was the final, crushing blow. Vice President Kenneth J. Jackson, in a 1974 study, gave a terse recapitulation of that period: "The mortgage loan account grew to a total of $1,150,000,000 in 1931 before acquisitions forced a decline to a low point of $787 million in 1935. Foreclosed properties reached a peak of $258 million in 1936—about 20 per cent of the total loan and property account. Recovery was evident in the late Thirties."

Whether the mortgaged property was a farm or a home, if the Pru did have to foreclose, the company always gave the original owner preference—that is, the original owner could buy the property back for the amount of the mortgage or the market price, whichever was lower.

With farms, an arrangement frequently made was for the Pru to foreclose on the property, which it would then proceed to improve.

Equipment would be purchased, buildings repaired and painted, fences restored. The Pru paid the taxes and bought seed, which the original owner, now living as a tenant on the farm, could plant. The crop would be divided between the company and the farmer, until the farmer had stabilized his financial condition and farm prices had risen to the point where he could again accept the burden of mortgage payments. Because of this approach, in many rural areas any farm in good repair, with fresh paint, was assumed to have a Prudential mortgage on it.

Many unsolicited letters came into Newark from farmers who emerged from the Depression with land which they had held on to, or re-purchased, with the help of the Prudential. A typical letter was signed by John Koistenen, of Hamlin County, South Dakota:

"During the drought and Depression I had a $4,000 loan and I wasn't able to pay the interest or taxes and the interest was $600 already and they renewed the loan and that gave me a chance to get on my feet and since then I have paid that loan and paid the loan on another quarter [that is, 160 acres] and have bought two tracts of land since. I have also improved the place for about $10,000 worth. So the Prudential Insurance Company has treated me right and will recommend them to anyone who needs money."

Forty years later Prudential men and women still spoke with pride of their company's actions during the Depression. Undoubtedly there were some cases of distress that were handled clumsily or callously; in the torrent of delinquency it was inevitable. But the overwhelming majority of property owners were treated with the dignity, compassion, and understanding to which they were entitled.

"The only excuse for the existence of an organization like this," Duffield once said, "is the fact that it is an organization that serves somebody. We are not here merely for the purpose of gratifying ourselves. This organization has developed and it has grown because, although it may be imperfect, nevertheless, from its inception to the present day, it has been a service to the people of America."

As the U.S. and Canada began to climb up out of the Depression, Duffield could take comfort in the knowledge that during a time of trial the Prudential had indeed been of service.

Late in the summer of 1938 Duffield relaxed at his summer place in Rhode Island. On Monday, September 12, he returned to his office, attended to some urgent business, and then took a train to Toronto, where a meeting of field men was being held. On Tuesday, Wednesday, and Thursday he talked to the group—and Duffield was regarded as a magnificent public speaker. His last talk, on Thursday, emphasized that the qualities by which one is judged are unselfish service, the willingness to do a kindly deed, and a consideration for the rights and needs of others.

On the afternoon of September 15 he boarded a train for Newark, where he arrived the following morning. About noon, in his office, he suffered a cerebral hemorrhage. The following evening he died, and Prudential mourned a kind and decent man. In the halls and offices in Newark, many would miss the tall, stooped man with the gentle eyes, the eloquent voice, and the ludicrous gait—the man they called ''Paddlefoot.''

11/A Scottish Black Sheep

If the internal world of the Prudential was tranquil during Duffield's 16-year administration, it was the quiet of fertility—like a snow-covered Dakota field, sown with wheat in the autumn, dormant through the winter, but ready to germinate and yield a rich crop when it is warmed by the thawing sun of spring. So the Pru during the 1920's and the 1930's gathered into itself—or sheltered for a later, more creative, time—a number of men and women who would make important contributions in the course of time.

They included four men who would be presidents in later decades: Carrol M. Shanks, Louis R. Menagh, Orville E. Beal, and Kenneth C. Foster. But there were many others who would play key roles in the Pru's postwar leap into the future—agents, actuaries, underwriters, accountants, marketing specialists, management experts—the whole wide range of skills that are used within a huge and complex life insurance enterprise. Their backgrounds were varied. Some came from Newark blue-collar precincts, and others from Princeton. A number were Canadians. A few had been recruited from other insurance companies. It was a mixed bag that included a good many provocative, strong-willed, dynamic individuals.

But the most colorful of the lot was a gifted but fey Scotsman named Edmund Boyd Whittaker. By the time the Pru's centennial occurred, Whittaker had been dead for 17 years, but he was still being spoken of at informal sessions during company conferences as though he had just retired from his job.

Those who believe that there is something inherently drab and dull about the insurance business should have known Whittaker, who put the lie to that myth every day of his exuberant but ill-starred life.

Whittaker was a non-conformist, an iconoclast, an innovator, a dreamer, a lover of facts, an aesthete, an amateur musician, a collector of crude scatological humor, a subtle wit, an admirer of excellence, an original and daring thinker, a born leader, a natural salesman, and, in the opinion of many who knew him, one of the most brilliant men ever to grace the Pru's premises.

Starting with almost nothing, Whittaker built the company's Group business to the point where the Pru often wrote more Group business in a year than any of its competitors, most of whom had a long head start on the Pru. Among his major achievements were Major Medical protection, low-cost Group Credit insurance, the first Group insurance coverage in a multiple-employer collective bargaining context, and the development of an astonishing aggregation of actuaries. His accomplishments were of such a lasting character that his admirers nominated him for the Insurance Hall of Fame many years after his death.

Yet this man of genius drank himself to death.

To his legion of drinking companions, in the Blue Diamond and various other bars in and out of Newark, Whittaker used to describe himself as "the black sheep of the family."

Apparently his father at one time so regarded him. His father was Sir Edmund Taylor Whittaker, mathematician, astronomer, and philosopher, a figure of world renown. In 1902, when the future "black sheep" was born, Sir Edmund was at Cambridge University, where he was a fellow of Trinity College. In 1906 Sir Edmund packed up his family and moved to Dublin, where he had been appointed Royal Astronomer of Ireland and astronomy professor at the University of Dublin, but six months later he went to Scotland, where he spent the rest of his life. He was professor of mathematics at the University of Edinburgh.

According to the *Dictionary of National Biography,* "three of Whittaker's scientific books have had a great influence," and many analytical concepts and entities still bear names he gave them. The recipient of many honors, he died in 1956. His passing, said the *D.N.B.,* "marked the end of an epoch, for he was almost the last polymath who took all mathematical knowledge for his province."

Sir Edmund's second son, John, was professor of pure mathematics at the University of Liverpool from 1933 to 1952, and vice chancellor of the University of Sheffield from 1952 to 1965. A daughter, Beatrice, married a professor of mathematics at the University of Dundee. "Note three professors of mathematics [in the family]," the Prudential's Whittaker, the eldest of Sir Edmund's three sons, once scribbled on the company's personal data sheet. "I should be very academic, but I'm not."

Therein lay the problem.

Sir Edmund's firstborn son (there were two sisters) was told by his father, at the age of 19, "You'll never make university, so go out and get a job."

It wasn't that the younger Whittaker couldn't easily handle university work. It was simply that he rebelled against the rigid structure of university studies. In his latter years he told J. J. Bates, one of his associates at the Pru, that he wished his own children, instead of going to college, would use the money for travel.

If young Whittaker had to get a job, there was, apparently, scarcely a moment's hesitation about what line of work he would enter. Among the many frequent visitors to the home of his father, who was a gregarious man, were a number of actuaries, Edinburgh being an important insurance center. Through the good offices of one of the actuaries, young Whittaker went to work as an apprentice actuary for the Scottish Widows Fund in Edinburgh.

Actuarial work was an ideal compromise for him, combining as it did the taste for mathematics that he had absorbed from his father with the involvement in the broader life outside the campus, which young Whittaker craved. An actuary applies mathematics—especially the laws of probability—to various aspects of the insurance business, including the calculation of premiums, policy reserves, and other values. Because of their unique training and experience, many companies put the talents of actuaries to work in other sectors of the business, like sales or administration. The Pru's sixth president, Louis R. Menagh, was an actuary. Whittaker used to call actuaries "the engineers of the insurance industry."

After five years with the Scottish Widows Fund, Whittaker came to the U.S. at the invitation of a New York Life Insurance Company actuary who was a friend of the elder Whittaker. (Sir Edmund, incidentally, did not limit his own theoretical work to pure mathematics. An important contribution to actuarial science is the "Whittaker-Henderson Graduation Formula" for predicting mortality rates, which is based on a paper he first made public in 1919; it was refined as a practical tool for actuaries by Robert Henderson in 1924.)

During the three years that he worked for New York Life, Whittaker married Nancy Livingstone, to whom he had been engaged when he left Scotland. Their marriage produced two daughters and a son.

Whittaker's move to the Prudential was recalled by him in an article he wrote for a trade journal, *The Eastern Underwriter,* some years later.

"Back around 1928," he wrote, "the Prudential almost ran out of actuaries, and our then executive vice president, Colonel [Franklin] D'Olier, decided something drastic should be done about it. In order to take care of immediate needs he hired Val [Valentine] Howell from the Guardian, Bruce Gerhard from the State Insurance Department, Harry Blagden from the Sun Life, Pearce Shepherd from the North American Reinsurance Company, and me from the New York Life. This represented a fairly considerable capital expenditure, and the Colonel vowed that from then on we would produce our own actuaries."

For some reason lost in the mists of time, Whittaker was given the title of "mathematician" when he joined the Pru in November 1929, although he was doing actuarial work. In 1935 he was named assistant actuary, in 1941 associate actuary, two years later a second vice president, and three years after that—in 1946—a vice president.

In the light of the authoritarian prissiness that characterized the Prudential at the time Whittaker went to work there, it is rather astonishing that he got along so well, for he was the most unorthodox, unpredictable, and uninhibited of its thousands of employees. Probably the explanation lies in the fact that from the first the other actuaries, including Howell, who became chief actuary in 1938, recognized Whittaker's extraordinary attributes—which might have been described in the same words that were applied to his father after the latter's death; Sir Edmund's "amazing intellectual powers," said one of his colleagues, included "his rapidity of thought, his infallible memory, and his remarkably lucid style of exposition."

Of course, Whittaker's influence within the Prudential was helped immeasurably by his engaging personality. He was the sort of fellow who is admired by men and adored by women. A "big, handsome man," as Dr. Ronald Buchan recalled, he had tremendous strength physically as well as mentally. To James R. (Jamie) Deans, a fellow Scot at the Pru who worked with Whittaker and was one of his closest friends, it seemed that "he had arms like legs." He was "not a fashion plate," as his longtime secretary, Eleanor Jensen, put it charitably. Indeed, Virginia Vogt, who was married to one of Whittaker's Group men, Martin D. Vogt, used to threaten to remove Whittaker's disreputable but beloved raincoat by force and take it to the dry cleaners.

Unawed by his superiors, he was generous and helpful to his subordinates. People who worked for him knew that they would get full credit for their work; nothing pleased him more than to see men he had chosen and trained get ahead. And get ahead they did—in the 1960's and 1970's the senior ranks of management were heavily seasoned with men whose hearts still belonged to Whittaker.

Throughout the business world, official reports are always picked up reluctantly by those whose duty it is to read them, for the prose is almost invariably stilted, the thought behind the words pedestrian, and the general air of the paper pompous. But Whittaker's reports were approached with eagerness, and with good reason. Once, for example, he was asked to set down on paper an account of the development of Group insurance at the Pru, as he recalled it. This small excerpt suggests the flavor of his style:

"When I became Group underwriter in 1934, the sales head was one Theodore Tortemittschlager.* He was a statistician par excellence, who lined in the second decimal point. I understand that his previous assignment had been going around graveyards reading inscriptions on tombstones to see how many people lived beyond the limiting age of the American Experience Mortality Table, namely, 96. This was considered ideal training to head up the Group sales organization.

"He spent most of his day signing his name, which he did with a great flourish. Any time any agent wrote a Group or Wholesale case he would sign his name on letters to the agent, the assistant manager, and the manager. When he was not signing his name he was compiling inconsequential statistics with which he used to regale us at the sales conferences. I have often thought how lucky we were that his name was Theodore Tortemittschlager and not H. E. Dow [a close associate and friend of Whittaker's], or he would have had time to compile at least five times as many irrelevant statistics and we would have had to listen to them for a week."

Discussing the actuarial student program which he set up and conducted with great success—spotting college students in their sophomore

---

* For the purposes of this book, the present author has substituted a fictitious name for the one cited by Whittaker.

year or even earlier, hiring the best prospects for summer jobs at the Pru, and then employing them upon graduation, while encouraging them to work toward passing their actuarial examinations—Whittaker said:

"The most important thing is to send out the right man, because it is well known that people attract their own likes. If you send out an old fuddy-duddy to do your actuarial student hiring, because his time is more expendable than that of the rest of the actuarial officers, he will hire a bunch of young fuddy-duddies and you will be stuck with them for all time."

Until the start of World War II, Whittaker did all the recruiting himself. After the war he formed a committee of five persons, each assigned a small number of colleges. But Whittaker still went out, taking the newest member of the committee with him.

"We don't hire these boys because we need their labor," he said. "We hire them as an investment in young men. We want them to absorb the office atmosphere and the spirit of friendship which prevails throughout our company. . . . The whole spirit of the program is to convince the students of the fundamental decency of the company."

Whittaker himself set the tone for the company's "fundamental decency" by his stand on the employment of Jews. Over the years various Jewish organizations and equal-rights groups have criticized large segments of the insurance industry for what they see as a pattern of discrimination against Jews in executive positions. But that criticism has never been raised against the Pru—at least, not since the early 1930's, when Whittaker appeared on the scene.

To him, it simply didn't matter what a man's religious or national background might be; he only cared about the man's mind and how well he could use it. One of Whittaker's earliest recruits through the actuarial student program was William Chodorcoff, whom Whittaker found at the University of Manitoba. After joining the Pru in 1930, Chodorcoff rose through the ranks until, at the time of his death, he was executive vice president. As the Pru approached its centennial, its executive ranks included at least three senior vice presidents who were Jewish, and many others of that faith at various levels of management, including vice presidents.

Whittaker wouldn't hire anybody *because* of that person's background. On the other hand, if the prospective employee appeared otherwise desirable, Whittaker would not be *deterred* from hiring him because of his creed or nationality. (To be sure, Whittaker was not sufficiently sensitive to social justice to take the "affirmative action"—as it came to be called 40 years later—that would have brought blacks into the Pru's executive ranks, but it would have been difficult to find many white Americans who saw that problem clearly in Whittaker's day.)

In one egalitarian way, Whittaker did discriminate—if it could be called that—in hiring: he sometimes said he would not hire anyone with whom he wouldn't want to spend an evening in conversation.

In 1948, when some life insurance agents felt that Group insurance—then just beginning its fantastic growth—ought to be hobbled by restrictions because they incorrectly saw it as a threat to their own self-interests, Whittaker, addressing a conference of agents, spoke like a Dutch uncle:

"Most life insurance agents, just like our own agents, are very glad to participate in any and all forms of welfare programs that are offered to them. It does seem to me that you, as career men, owe one obligation to your profession. You ought to take pride in making available, wherever possible, to all employees in the United States through these welfare programs the same degree of social and economic security that you enjoy yourselves."

Oddly enough, that speech, entitled "The Social Responsibility of the Group Insurance Industry," was so well received and widely reprinted that Whittaker later told one of his men, George Walker, that the speech "was the making" of him.

Two years later, in 1950, addressing an insurance conference of the American Management Association, Whittaker was equally astringent:

"We who are trying to compete with the ideas of nationalized programs are required to be social engineers. So far we have been good salesmen and good managers. We have not measured up too well as social engineers. If we don't do better, our system of private enterprise will pass by default to social planning. So far, our competitive position is not all it might be. What I have to say about current trends will indicate areas for improvement.

"All of us concerned with social insurance problems need [to practice] skepticism today. We're not as objective sometimes as we might be. Loyally, we tout the progress we have made in voluntary plans. We whitewash the ideas to which we have been adhering. But respect for reality should cause us to drive around the block to look at the other side of the house. Our blind acceptance of the obvious, otherwise, may defeat our aims.''

Long before such speeches gave him a broader reputation in the business community of North America, Whittaker's work as an actuary had made him an important figure in that profession. Moreover, his progress in his chosen field had smoothed his relationship with his father. Every other year he and his wife would go over to the United Kingdom for a visit. According to Jamie Deans, Whittaker was never so happy as when he was staying in the ''Western Isles''—the Hebrides, off the northwest coast of Scotland—the wild and wind-swept islands which have given the world, among other things, Harris tweeds and a famous liqueur made of Scotch whisky and heather honey.

Among Whittaker's recreational activities was his own odd form of golf—odd not because of the rules, which were the same as everyone else's, but because of his clubs. He only used three: a driver, a niblick (now usually called a nine iron), and a putter. There was also, during most games, a couple of bottles of liquid sustenance tucked away in his golf bag.

On one visit to Scotland Sir Edmund suggested that his son go to the golf professional at St. Andrews for some tips on improving his game.

''Let's see ye swing,'' said the Scottish golf pro.

Whittaker wound up and swung at the ball in his own, free-form style.

''Mon,'' said the pro, ''ye're nae a golfer—ye're a killer!''

Everything he did was done with vigor, enthusiasm, and some special touch that was Whittaker's own. Contract bridge, for example, was one of his many passions; at one time he was president of the Commercial Bridge League of Northern New Jersey. He was a brilliant player, even in the days when alcohol was taking its toll. Pru veterans remember with awe how Whittaker could play winning bridge when it was difficult for him to sit at the table because of his drinking.

Another passion was limericks. On one company questionnaire he wrote, in answer to a query about special interests: ''Believed to have the best collection of limericks in the Pru or out of it.'' Of course, most were unprintable.

Generally, Whittaker's family and friends rejoiced in his eccentricities. The reaction to his traits by people who were not so close to him was sometimes one of acerbity. When Eleanor Jensen, Whittaker's

secretary, told Pru president Carrol Shanks that she was going to a night
school course in Abnormal Psychology, Shanks replied with a question:
"Are you taking the course—or teaching it?"

But Shanks and Whittaker shared at least one taste—an interest in the
piano. Whittaker loved to sit at the piano, playing, especially with his
friend Jamie Deans singing along with him. Deans, who had been a
concert baritone in Britain before the second World War, was clearly the
more talented of the two in that sphere. "No convention was complete
unless I sang 'The Road to Mandalay' with Eddie accompanying me,"
Deans said recently. "I grew to hate it."

At one Prudential gathering Whittaker asked a young woman what
she'd like him to play. When she named an operatic aria, Whittaker, to
the surprise of many in the room, was able to play it.

At least one of Whittaker's attributes was the cause of undisguised but
not unfriendly envy on the part of other Pru executives. That was his
ability to get six or eight of his key people together, discuss with them
what ought to be in the department's annual report, and then dictate
rapidly the entire report, running to perhaps a dozen pages, so flawlessly
that it needed no rewriting or editing.

When he was switched from actuarial work to the top post in Group
insurance, he found the change "very pleasant, much to my astonishment," he noted some time later. The men who worked with him
regarded him as the perfect salesman—self-confident, knowledgeable,
persuasive, congenial. But in the end his sales work may have contributed to his untimely end, although it certainly didn't cause it. Salesmen
are more likely to have occasions to drink than most people, and
Whittaker drank more than enough without an excuse, for he was a clear
and, ultimately, tragic victim of the disease of alcoholism.

By the early 1950's, his drinking had become a matter of concern to
his friends and associates. Carrol Shanks, who was then president,
summoned Whittaker one day.

"You've got to stop drinking," Shanks said. "It's getting serious."

"I can't," Whittaker said simply.

About that time, his friend Jamie Deans noticed a change in him, a
kind of pervasive fatalism, as though Whittaker had seen his fate and
accepted it as inevitable. "If the Pru had had, years ago, the kind of
program for alcoholics that it does today," said Deans, now retired and

heading the Monmouth County (New Jersey) Council on Alcoholism, "Eddie wouldn't have died when he did."

By the time Shanks talked with Whittaker about his problem, Deans believed, "Eddie had reached the point of addiction. I think that what he said to Shanks was quite literally true at that point—he no longer was able to make the decision to stop. He was just trying to stay alive long enough for Nancy to get her widow's pension."

About three or four years before his death, the first signs of his decline were noticed by his friends. He wasn't quite as sharp and fast in his thinking. His lunch hours were noticeably longer. He began leaving the office early. His moods indicated that he was very troubled. But he never talked about his drinking. He just did it.

Despite the obvious physical deterioration, it still came as a surprise to everyone when Whittaker entered a hospital early in 1958. He never left the hospital alive.

A week or two before his death, Eleanor Jensen, who had been his secretary for so many years, visited him in the hospital. His condition finally made her realize that he might be dying. But her reaction was similar to that of his many other friends: "Even then, I couldn't conceive of it—the man had so much vitality!"

Toward the end, Whittaker lapsed into a hepatic coma. He died the night of March 10, 1958. He was just 55 years old. His untimely death was a terrible waste of an enormous talent and a great heart.

12/The Last Days of the Old Pru

Franklin D'Olier used to tell his family privately that he wouldn't advise young people to go into the Prudential. Advancement within the company was governed largely by seniority—as indeed it was generally throughout the insurance industry—and young men, he felt, "would have a very long haul" before they got anywhere. More likely, they'd be buried most of their lives in some unchanging job.

"He used to say that the dead wood at the top was absolutely frightening," recalled one of his daughters, Mrs. Mahlon Pitney. But while D'Olier's friend and sponsor, Edward Duffield, headed the company, D'Olier's opportunities to bring more flexibility and life in the organization were limited. And when the death of Duffield, in 1938, propelled D'Olier into the presidency, the timing was all wrong.

D'Olier was 61 years old, and men of that age do not usually engage in efforts to overthrow the established order of things, no matter how clearly they see the need nor how vigorous they may still be—and he was extraordinarily active. For 13 years D'Olier had pushed as far as he could in the improvement of administrative practices, despite the inertia of the complacent and anachronistic bureaucracy. After all his exertion, the changes had not basically affected the true nature of the company, and D'Olier, one senses, had almost given up hope of moving it along much further.

But the biggest barrier to any drastic changes by D'Olier after he became head of the Pru lay in the events outside the involuted world of the company. War was in the air. Earlier that year Hitler had sent his tanks rumbling into Austria as he absorbed it into his Third Reich, and in the very month that Duffield died the Munich conference, intended to bring "peace in our time," began the dismemberment of Czecho-slovakia. The Spanish Civil War, which was being viewed increasingly as a proving ground for a general European conflict, raged on. Japan, having invaded China a year earlier, was attempting to strengthen her

100

hold on that huge and hostile land. On the very day that D'Olier was elected president—November 14—the U.S. Ambassador to Germany was recalled to Washington "for consultation," to demonstrate American shock and horror at the anti-Jewish pogroms which had just erupted across Germany. To a war horse like D'Olier, whose American Legion leadership activities had kept him in close contact with military chiefs in the nation's capital, the need for him to lend his support to the mounting campaign to strengthen the armed forces overshadowed the far less pressing problems of the Prudential.

Not that he neglected the company. Far from it. When the federal government set up the Temporary National Economic Committee, which would investigate the life insurance industry as part of its study of the concentration of economic power, D'Olier personally supervised the preparation of the Prudential's presentations. Ironically, although the TNEC had been established in part on the premise that bigness is more or less equivalent to badness, the committee—whose special counsel, Gerhard A. Gesell, was one of the two major judges in the Watergate case in the 1970's—found that the three biggest life insurance companies, including the Prudential, were generally free of the abuses that were uncovered in some of the smaller companies.

In the end, few of the evil effects of concentrated economic power were found to be present in the life insurance industry. The TNEC found no decline in competition, but actually an increase. There was no evidence presented to indicate that any of the companies was acting in restraint of trade. There was no suggestion that life insurance companies were engaging in the cartels which the TNEC found in some other industries, which with foreign competitors had carved the world into spheres of influences. Despite their great investments, the TNEC did not accuse the life insurance companies of controlling, or even attempting to control, the companies in which they invested.

There were criticisms, of course. The cost of Industrial insurance—a continuing problem—was singled out, although the Prudential was able to demonstrate that it had been working to reduce costs. In the area of investments, the TNEC said the life insurance companies should do more to help finance small business, and the Securities and Exchange Commission, in a study requested by the TNEC, urged that legal restrictions on common stock investments by life insurance companies, which the SEC called "by far our most dynamic savings institutions," be relaxed. "The continued flow of funds to life insurance companies which are prevented from purchasing common stocks is certain to have serious effects on the economy," said the SEC. "Common stocks of substantial corporations with an established record of earnings are clearly as 'safe' as many bonds."

When the bulk of the evidence was in, 151 companies submitted a long, somewhat irate statement to the TNEC disputing some of the evidence. Later a second statement, supplementing the first, was sent to the TNEC. Among the points which it attacked were those dealing with investments in small business enterprises and in common stocks. Businesses in need of venture capital, the statement said, "have not proved their worth" and so were not safe enough. As for common stocks, "what the policyholders want is safety for their insurance estates and not the risks inherent" in equity investment.

In its analysis for the TNEC of the statements of the life insurance companies, the SEC said in part, "It should be pointed out that the Statement on Life Insurance is not signed by many leading companies whose representatives appeared at the hearings. Among such companies not signing the Statement are the following: Acacia Mutual Life Insurance Company, The Prudential Insurance Company of America, The New York Life Insurance Company, The Mutual Life of New York, The Northwestern Mutual Life Insurance Company, The National Life Insurance Company of Vermont, and the Western and Southern Life Insurance Company."

The SEC had spotted a disagreement in philosophy within the life insurance industry. Within 15 years the Prudential would be investing in common stocks and in small businesses that looked promising.

As though a major government investigation were not enough, D'Olier had his hands full of an old problem—mutualization. When the company was mutualized in 1915, the owners of 2,700 shares refused to sell them at the appraisal price of $455 per share. Gradually, over the years, most of those shares were surrendered, but in 1937 there were still 584.76 shares outstanding. That was the year that heirs of Noah Blanchard filed two suits, demanding five to six million dollars in deferred dividends and challenging many of the company's acts over more than a quarter of a century.

The litigation dragged on, as law suits of that kind always do, until 1940, when general counsel Charles B. Bradley brought Frederick H.

Groel into the company. Groel had been the youngest member of the state legislature in 1925, and since then he had been Newark's Assistant Corporation Counsel and later Assistant Secretary of the New Jersey Senate. A man who knew his way around Republican politics, he had been the Pru's legislative representative at Trenton since 1936.

Groel began working on the mutualization problem with Bradley's most trusted aide, Carrol M. Shanks, whose title was general solicitor. As a result of their work, including conferences with lawyers representing the Blanchard heirs, a bill was introduced into the state legislature permitting the Prudential to go over the previously fixed price of $455 for its shares. When negotiations for purchase of the stock began in January 1941, D'Olier himself sat in on them, but as time went on he left it to his executives to try to get a tentative agreement. By February 1942 the Pru's special counsel, Josiah Stryker, was almost ready to give up—and then, suddenly, an informal chat with opposing counsel led to a compromise agreement. Under the terms of the arrangement, the Prudential would pay $1,500 per share for all the outstanding stock.

After approval by the board, the company formally agreed to the deal on February 17, 1942. Under the law, the chancellor of the state was required to pass on the proposal. He held a hearing at which D'Olier defended the agreement as the best that could be reached in the interest of the policyholders. On July 29, 1942, the chancellor approved the arrangement, and on September 1 all of the outstanding shares were turned over to the company. Legally, however, the company had to obtain legislative action before mutualization would be accomplished. Three acts were passed—one providing for the election of directors, another amending the charter, and the last amending the mutualization act so as to define the legal position of the company after the process was completed. With the passage of those measures, the Prudential became, in fact and in law, a wholly mutual life insurance company on March 30, 1943, when the board of directors surrendered their shares to the trustee for policyholders.

Of course, not all of the time of "the Colonel," as everyone called D'Olier, was taken up with such weighty matters. He seemed always to be conferring with one or another of his executives. That was his forte; as he used to tell his family, "there are half a dozen fellows at the Pru who are smarter than I am, but I can get them working together and keep them working together."

He had an aristocratic air about him, but an unfeigned, plebeian interest in people. Restlessly roaming the complex of buildings, he poked his nose into every corner of the operations until he knew hundreds of lower level employees by name. When he died, in 1953, long after he had left the presidency of the Pru, one of the mourners at his funeral turned out to be a boiler room worker who had always looked forward to the Colonel's frequent visits for a chat.

It was D'Olier's custom to pop into the offices of his subordinates, instead of asking them to go to his office. He used to say that there were two advantages to this practice: first, it gave him a chance to see how his men operated in their own departments; and second, it enabled him to terminate a conversation whenever he wished, without the nuisance of trying to nudge a long-winded caller out of his office.

A terrible public speaker but a great storyteller, D'Olier most often recounted incidents in which the humor was directed at himself. At the annual Field Day held for Pru employees, featuring athletic competitions as well as games and picnicking, D'Olier used to give out the prizes, wearing his battered felt hat. One year he told of the girl who had accepted a prize from him and then told her friends he was a nice man.

"That's your president," somebody standing nearby said.

"President! With a hat like that?" she exclaimed.

Many Pru officers had heard how D'Olier had once been called "Also Ran" as a youth because the local newspaper, in reporting sports events, often mentioned that "Franklin D'Olier also ran" in the competition. (Although he stood six foot one, he weighed only 98 pounds in his youth, and his weight never exceeded 134 pounds.)

Even D'Olier's avid interest in military matters, dating back to his service in the first World War, was a safe subject for good-natured humor. When D'Olier asked Fred Groel what time it was, Groel, mocking D'Olier's precise military manner, replied, "Ten minutes and 37 seconds after two o'clock."

D'Olier got the joke, and he was kind enough not to point out that Groel should have said, "1410 hours and 37 seconds," if he wanted to mimic military style.

Always on the periphery of national politics—as one might expect of a former national commander of the American Legion—D'Olier was caught up in the tensions of a world on the eve of war. In September 1939, when Nazi planes flew across the borders of Poland to bomb

Warsaw, the Prudential's Canadian employees and policyholders found themselves at war. But still the U.S. remained apart from the conflict, although it began sending an endless stream of supplies of all kinds to the democratic forces in Europe.

After the Nazi war machine overran most of Europe in 1940, however, one uneasy sign of the times appeared at Pru's headquarters in Newark. Acting on instructions, Rudy Domonkos ordered an 18-month supply of all reprints. "I also deleted our old cut of Gibraltar with the slogan, 'The Prudential Has the Strength of Gibraltar,' " he later recalled. "Apparently it was felt [German Lieutenant General Erwin] Rommel might capture it" after seizing North Africa.

As the European countries fell to the Nazis and Great Britain struggled valiantly to prevent an invasion, mimeographed war bulletins were published for executives twice a day by Frank J. Price, Jr., the company's publicity manager. In the 1970's when news of almost equal importance, including the impeachment of a President, was absorbing the attention of most Americans, the Pru's Public Relations and Advertising Department would publish a similar, but more professional, news summary called "News at Noon."

As the U.S. moved closer to war, an increasing number of young men were drafted from their jobs at the Pru to enter the armed forces. After Pearl Harbor hurled the U.S. into the midst of the fighting, so many men left that women were recruited for all sorts of jobs, including some never filled by women before. Moreover, the longstanding rule that Pru would not permit married women to work there was also suspended for the duration of the war.

Altogether, 6,412 men and women from Prudential served in uniform in World War II, and 111 of them gave their lives.

In 1942 the company completed its newest building, the Washington Street Building—just in time to have it commandeered by the Army, which used it as headquarters for its Office of Dependency Benefits.

On every side there was activity associated with the war, but D'Olier was not a part of it. He couldn't stand not playing a role in this struggle. When the Republican leadership in the state urged him to run for Governor, he brushed the idea aside impatiently. He wanted *action*.

Somehow, he managed to get into the midst of things, despite his age. When he was almost 64, in 1941, he was one of three Americans permitted to fly to England to study civilian defense methods in use there. D'Olier and his associates were received by King George VI at Buckingham Palace.

Five months later Mayor Fiorello LaGuardia of New York, who was national director of Civilian Defense, appointed D'Olier head of defense measures for the civilian population in New York, New Jersey, and Delaware. At the same time, D'Olier headed the state's USO appeal. Later that year he was chairman of the war bond drive in the state. (During the war, the Pru invested more than $3 billion in war bonds. Its employees bought some $19 million in bonds on the payroll deduction plan and millions more during the bond drives.)

Although D'Olier took part in many other war-related activities—the National War Fund, for example—they were not enough to satisfy his need to participate in the war effort. Pru employees were donating blood, working at servicemen's canteens, helping out at military hospitals, enforcing the East Coast "brown-out" so that enemy submarine crews could not see Allied ships silhouetted at night against city lights ashore; and, best of all, many of the Pru people were serving in uniform—not only men, but also girls who had gone from being clerks to marching in the WACs (originally the WAACs), the Waves, the Spars, or the Women Marines.

Even the Prudential's printing plant had gone to war. It was turning out waterproof survival maps in nine colors for Allied pilots who might find themselves forced down at sea or in enemy-held lands.

One significant service which the Pru performed in 1944 was to make it possible for men in the armed forces from New Jersey to vote in the presidential election that year. After Governor Walter E. Edge told D'Olier that the state simply couldn't handle the job of furnishing the state's 21 county clerks with the names, home addresses, and military addresses of 400,000 men and women of voting age who were serving their country, the Colonel took two Prudential officers, Albert F. Jaques and Harry J. Volk, with him to Trenton to see if the Pru could help. A system was worked out which incorporated a number of elements: D'Olier's Civilian Defense volunteers made house-to-house canvasses to get the vital information, which was put on cards and cross-indexed at the Prudential. In the end, the county clerks received both lists of the men and women in uniform and gummed labels for mailing ballots to those who were eligible to vote.

But even that wasn't enough for D'Olier. He really wanted to get into the theaters of war. To some men, like D'Olier, war is a narcotic; its "high" makes all civilian life lackluster by comparison.

Later in 1944 D'Olier got his chance. Henry L. Stimson, the Secretary of War (a title no longer in use), and General Henry H. (Hap) Arnold, commander of the Air Force, summoned him to Washington. There they asked him to organize and direct a survey which would indicate whether the Allied bombing efforts had been as effective as hoped in their impact on the enemies' economies and war efforts. When he accepted, President Franklin D. Roosevelt formally appointed him Chairman of the Strategic Bombing Survey Commission—an assignment that would find a permanent place in U.S. military histories.

Although the survey entailed a good deal of on-the-spot examination in Europe and Asia, many of the commission's conclusions were drawn from analysis of statistics on file in Washington. Unfortunately, the statistics were buried in literally millions of reports on bombing raids —reports that contained such data as the kind of aircraft, the time of takeoff, the primary target, the weather, the kind and amount of bomb load, the altitude from which the bombs were dropped, the amount of antiaircraft fire, the severity of fighter interception, the time over target, and the losses incurred.

Before the statistics could be analyzed, they had to be extracted from the mountains of reports. Again, D'Olier turned to Harry Volk. Then 38, Volk, after graduating from Rutgers University in 1927, had gone to work for the Prudential because the company gave employees time off to further their education; that's how he got his law degree in 1930. Early in his career at the Pru he had come to the attention of D'Olier, who tagged him as "a very able man." Although he had worked in several departments, Volk was considered outstanding as a systems man, as the term is now used. In 1944 he was head of the biggest punch card operation outside the U.S. government, and punch cards were the means that enabled him to develop the data needed for the bombing survey. However, even for Volk the survey required many months of work in Europe.

Inevitably, the responsibility for the analysis of the data and the interpretations fell to Volk, who feverishly assembled 12 teams of writers and statisticians in Europe, despite the chaos of wartime. He snatched a printing plant in England from the Office of War Information, and soon the first volumes of what would, in the end, be a 208-volume report were emerging from the bindery.

The gist of the report was that the bombing of factories had been relatively ineffective in crippling war production, that transportation was the preferable target. "Evidence from all sources clearly indicates," said the report, "that the continuous aerial attacks on transportation facilities prevented the enemy from effectively concentrating his men or material at critical times and places. Transport proved to be the weakest link in the logistic chain. Its failure was the immediate cause of the breakdown of the supply system and, consequently, was a decisive factor in the collapse of the German army."

The findings of the Strategic Bombing Survey were a critical factor in the decision of the White House and the Congress that the postwar military organization must be restructured. All of the armed services were unified under a Cabinet-level Secretary of Defense, under whom were the Army, the Navy, and the now separate Air Force.

At the time he accepted the bombing survey assignment, D'Olier designated Carrol Shanks, by then executive vice president, to be acting president in his absence. In fact, the Colonel was rarely in evidence at the Pru after 1944. As the conclusion of the bombing survey approached, toward the close of 1945, D'Olier decided to make his retirement official. On January 1, 1946, D'Olier, then 65 years old, became chairman of the board and Shanks took his place as president and chief executive officer.

Despite his retirement, D'Olier had one last public service to perform. When President Harry S Truman asked former President Herbert C. Hoover, in 1947, to head a commission which would study the federal government structure and recommend changes to improve efficiency and economize on operations, Hoover in turn called upon D'Olier to be chairman of one of the commission's four task forces.

When D'Olier died, on December 10, 1953, his family and the Prudential were overwhelmed with expressions of sadness from the famous and the obscure. The Newark *Star-Ledger* voiced the feelings of many when it said he was "a man who lived a full life to the advantage of himself and his fellow man."

13/An Unlikely Revolutionary

For most persons, an "acting" appointment is a kind of limbo, an impossible position of maximum responsibility with minimum authority. Because there is usually no assurance that the appointment will be made permanent, one has an inclination to tread lightly, stepping on as few toes as possible, lest failure to obtain permanent tenure open the way to reprisals.

But that was not true of Carrol Meteer Shanks, the seventh president of the Prudential. From the moment he became acting president of the company, at the beginning of 1945, he was as firm, decisive, tough, sure, courageous, and, when necessary, ruthless as he was 16 years later, in the last year of his administration.

"Shanks was a hard-driving, hard-bargaining, take-charge man with complete disdain for insurance industry traditions," *Business Week* said in a cover story about the company in 1967, six years after Shanks left it. "Men with Pru at the time remember him as cold and calculating, but exciting and inspirational, too. Competitors thought he had more guts than brains, and took far too many chances. Says one executive [of another company] today: 'In retrospect, of course, Shanks's bold moves worked OK, and no one was hurt. Maybe the Pru has just been damned lucky.' "

Maybe. But it would be hard to persuade most of the men and women who worked at Prudential in the Shanks years that chance was a major element in his achievements. During those years he reorganized and modernized the company, encouraged the development of an astonishing corps of talented young men, set in motion a tidal wave of creativity, reshaped the company's investment policies into an aggressive force for the policyholders' benefit, and carried out a program of regionalizing the Pru's operations that was—and, to a large extent, still is—so extraordinary and unique that its implications are still not truly understood by most people outside the company. Shanks's revolutionary

109

actions at the Pru not only turned the entire insurance industry upside down, but also had an impact on all business enterprises, directly or indirectly.

To many Prudential people it seemed as though fate had intended Shanks to head the company during that critical postwar period. However, he had not been D'Olier's first choice as a successor. According to the Colonel's daughter, Mrs. E. Esty Stowell, the heir apparent had been Caleb (Pete) Stone, who was vice president in charge of the Pru's Bond Department. Stone and D'Olier were close personal friends, a relationship that may have been related to Stone's background as an Army brat, his father having been a colonel in the regular Army, which always fascinated D'Olier. But Stone suffered a heart attack, and D'Olier decided that the burdens of Prudential's presidency might be too much for him. As it turned out, Stone, an able businessman, lived an active life for another 23 years.

If D'Olier's initial intention to put up Stone may have reflected the Colonel's boyish impulse to play soldier, his later choice of Shanks demonstrated that D'Olier, despite his own conventional background, was not a prisoner to tradition, for Shanks was in every way a sharp break with the past.

He was not a Princetonian. He was not an Easterner. Unlike Forrest Dryden, Edward Duffield, Franklin D'Olier, and most of the Pru's officers for half a century, he had not grown up in comfortable circumstances. Indeed, in many ways Carrol Shanks was a throwback to the company's founder, John Dryden.

His father was the postmaster and school board president of Fairmont, Minnesota, a small town near the Iowa border, where Carrol Shanks was born on October 14, 1898. In 1912 a political upset cost the elder Shanks his mail job, so the family packed up and moved to Payette, on the Snake River in Idaho, northwest of Boise. There they tried to operate a 20-acre fruit farm—"very definitely a mistake," according to a family chronicle, "as none of us had any farm experience whatsoever." To help out the family finances, Carrol and his older brother Mick worked summers at a brickyard.

Always a keen student, Carrol followed Mick to the University of Washington, where he worked so hard as a shoe salesman—five hours every weekday and all day Saturday—to earn money for his schooling that he was only able to see one football game. But he made straight A's, Phi Beta Kappa, and the presidency of his fraternity, Beta Theta Pi, graduating with honors in 1921, when he married another member of that year's class, Martha S. Taylor.

Shanks's college work had been interrupted by World War I, when he entered the Army. At war's end he was at officer candidates school at Waco, Texas. He got on a train for New York, where his brother, who had been in the Navy, met him. Until September 1919 the two young men worked for a Wall Street house selling municipal bonds. Their money was only sufficient to get them to Minneapolis, where the Milwaukee Railroad hired them as part of a track gang assembled for work at Avery, Idaho. After working two weeks in Idaho, the brothers took their pay and left, riding a freight train. The empty boxcar into which they had climbed turned out to be occupied by three tramps. As the train rolled west, the tramps threatened to kill the Shankses for their meager hoard of money, but Carrol, brandishing a piece of lead pipe, discouraged the would-be robbers so much that they decided to jump off the train. They were not the last to find out how tough Shanks could be when he was challenged.

After graduation and marriage, Shanks headed east to go to the Columbia University law school, inspired by a grandfather who had been a judge. During his first summer in New York he applied for a job with one of the top three banks there. The bank lost interest in him when its executives found he'd gone to the University of Washington. Instead, they chose for the job another applicant who had gone to an Ivy League school, the University of Pennsylvania. The experience did nothing to build Shanks's confidence in the judgment of the established authorities—although 20 years later, when Shanks, then a member of that bank's board of directors, went to the trouble of checking the record of the man who had beaten him out for the job, Shanks "found he was a top man."

Supported by his wife, who worked as a teacher, Shanks attended Columbia's law school in a class that included men ranging from Thomas E. Dewey, a conservative who would one day be a Republican candidate for President, to William O. Douglas, a liberal who later enjoyed an extraordinarily long term of service as an Associate Justice of the U.S. Supreme Court. Like Douglas—who remained a lifelong friend—Shanks taught at the law school for a couple of years after his graduation in 1925, while at the same time working for a leading Wall Street law firm.

In 1928 Douglas rebelled against the conservative leadership of

Columbia Law and went off to teach at the Yale University law school. "We induced [Carrol Shanks] to join the faculty and work with me in the field of corporate finance," Douglas wrote in his recent autobiography, *Go East, Young Man.* "He spent a year at Yale, only to find practice more to his liking, but during that year we started a project that ended with several Douglas and Shanks casebooks."

The casebooks on various aspects of law were published in the early 1930's and were widely used by law students in the years that followed. "I've had people say those were the books that put them through school," Shanks said many years later.

Shanks returned to the firm of Root, Clark, Buckner & Ballantine, where he was working in 1932 when John W. Stedman, vice president of the Prudential in charge of its Bond Department, realized that he was badly in need of top-flight legal counsel because so many railroads whose bonds were held by the Pru had been plunged into bankruptcy by the Depression. Stedman turned for help to Root, Clark, two of whose partners were friends of his.

"I approached them, requested that they give me the names of some of the younger, promising men in their office, and asked permission to invite them to consider the job I had in mind," Stedman later told a Prudential historian. "Among those names was that of Carrol M. Shanks."

One of the others whose names were given to Stedman was Francis T. P. Plimpton, whose distinguished later career would include service as U.S. Ambassador to the United Nations and the presidency of the Association of the Bar of the City of New York. Plimpton turned down Stedman's job offer but recommended Shanks, with whom he had become friendly.

Shanks's first contact with the Pru was embarrassing. So was his second.

The first occurred when Shanks received a telephone call from a woman who said she was calling for a Mr. Stedman of the Prudential Insurance Company. Shanks told her crisply that he had all the life insurance he wanted at that time and he wasn't interested in discussing with Mr. Stedman the possibility of taking out more.

A few minutes later she called back to say that Shanks's firm had given Stedman his name, that Stedman wanted to talk with him about a matter of business. This time Shanks remained on the line and spoke with Stedman, who outlined the job that was open. After some discussion, Shanks said he'd like a little time to think it over. Stedman suggested that he phone in a few days.

Two or three days later, Shanks had his secretary put through a call to Stedman. He told the Prudential executive that he was interested in the post. At Stedman's suggestion, Shanks agreed to go to the Pru the next day for lunch with Stedman and some of his associates. So the next day, about a quarter to twelve, Shanks checked the telephone book to find out where, in the Wall Street district, the Pru had its Home Office. It was then that he discovered, to his dismay, that the company's headquarters were located in Newark, which he could not hope to reach by noon. A hurried, apologetic telephone call to Stedman smoothed over the mix-up.

It was agreed that Shanks would begin his employment by the Pru on Tuesday, July 5, 1932, at an annual salary of $12,000. At noon on his first day, a notice was sent around to all officers of the company: salaries of executives were being cut because of the Depression; Shanks would now get $10,000 a year.

Despite the pay cut, Shanks liked the work at the Pru. Life was livelier there, in those Depression days, than it had been at Root, Clark. "Law is bookish," Shanks said. "I like the action, the battle, the campaigns."

With responsibility for salvaging what he could of the millions that the Pru had invested in the bonds of now-bankrupt railroads, Shanks saw plenty of action. He was named chairman of the Bond Committee and reorganization manager of two railroads, the Norfolk Southern and the Eastern Illinois.

The Pru gave him complete authority, and he ran with it. He pulled off all manner of unorthodox deals. For example, he once swapped $200,000 in virtually worthless railroads bonds for 200 miles of railroad track, and then sold the steel rails for $60,000 in cash. The buyers were Japanese. Neither Shanks nor probably any other Americans realized at the time that the Japanese were turning the scrap metal into the armaments for the coming world war.

Such free-wheeling approaches to business problems seemed incongruous for Shanks, whose appearance belied his spirit. He looked austere, aloof, somewhat forbidding—"glacial" was an adjective often applied to him, although he could, when he wanted to, display real warmth. To most of the world, he was the epitome of a 19th-century,

Calvinistic banker; but inside, he harbored the fiery passions of an adventurer, a revolutionary.

Little more than a year after he joined the Pru, Shanks was promoted to associate general solicitor. Five years later he was elected general solicitor, then the No. 2 post in the Law Department. A year after that he was also made a vice president. Less than five more years passed before he became an executive vice president. Sixteen months later he was president—at 47, the youngest president of a major life insurance company in the U.S. or Canada.

His first moves as president—indeed, as acting president—were characteristic of the man: he attacked the problem that underlay all the other problems, he went at it in a wholly untraditional way, and he displayed the same impersonal willingness to inflict necessary pain that one might expect of a surgeon.

That central problem was the "dead wood at the top" which D'Olier had lamented. Many of the men at the head of various operations had reached their positions as the result of an absurdly rigid seniority system which prescribed, for example, where each man sat in the executive dining room. Under that system, if the president, the executive vice president, and all the vice presidents were out of town at the same time, the executive in charge of the Home Office for the moment would be the second vice president who had first attained that rank. It was a system to encourage caution, not innovation—all the more so since the Prudential, like other life insurance companies at that time, almost never fired anyone except for dishonesty or similarly serious violations of company rules.

Until Shanks.

His solution to the dilemma of executive inadequacy was to force the resignation or early retirement of men he regarded as incompetent. Within months of his becoming acting president, the company had a new general counsel and a new head of the District Agencies Department, and not long after that there was new leadership in the Ordinary Agencies Department. The same sort of process was carried out in many other areas of the company, and it reached down beyond the top level of authority to the ranks of middle management. Some called the weeding-out "brutal" but there were few who survived the massive surgery who did not feel that it had been necessary.

Obviously, such a widespread catharsis caused overwhelming apprehension among many who feared that they might be sent packing, but the more alert, ambitious, and creative—especially among the younger men (for women still would not begin to move into positions of responsibility for another two decades or more)—saw the breaking up of the old order as the beginning of a new era of hope for the company.

"The change was electric," said Orville E. Beal. "Prudential had great possibilities, great potential, which was yet unrealized. Up to then, Prudential had been willing to follow the lead of other big companies; if they tried something and it looked pretty good, we might try it out. We didn't blaze many new trails in the insurance industry before Shanks took over. Many folks felt Prudential was a sleeping giant at the time Shanks moved in, and he woke it up.

"He didn't hesitate to spend money to modernize the company and its facilities. He made momentous decisions, sometimes against the advice of his top officers, and those acts paid big dividends. He prodded people to spend money on research—to find new methods of doing things.

"Sometimes he was too impatient. Sometimes he was a little too rough on people. But he shook up the organization. He shook it up and woke it up and got us going again."

To Jack T. Kvernland—then in his twenties, he would one day be senior vice president and chief actuary—Shanks's first speech to the organization was an occasion of curiosity, anticipation, and hope.

"He was absolutely the world's worst speaker," Kvernland remembered. "But as time went on, he got so much better. And what he said was more important than how he said it."

The reaction of Kvernland and his young friends was, he said, "Gosh, Shanks has shaken us up. That's good."

In the eyes of the young men like Kvernland, "The people who reacted with fear to Shanks were some of the old school crowd who would have been afraid of any kind of change, no matter who was doing it, or how."

When the shakeout was over, Shanks was surrounded by a group of strong, tough-minded, and sometimes contentious men.

His closest aide was Harold M. Stewart. Shanks promoted him to vice president in charge of the District Agencies Department in 1944 (it was not until the 1960's that the rank of senior vice president was established). Less than three years later Stewart was named executive vice president.

The son of a Prudential agency manager, Stewart was a tall, big-boned man whose frugality was legendary. He wore cheap clothing and went to considerable lengths to avoid incurring any personal expenses. A bachelor who finally married not long before his retirement, he would let his paychecks accumulate in his desk until the accountants pleaded with him to deposit them so the books could be cleared.

Shanks found Stewart to be "stiff," a good deal of a "stand-patter"—just the opposite of Shanks himself—but nobody, it was generally agreed, knew the District Agencies business the way Stewart did, and the District Agencies (as the old Industrial Insurance Department, with agents acting as premium collectors as well as salesmen, was now called) was by far the biggest part of the company.

"My God, there wasn't anything he didn't know about the District Agencies system," said Charles B. Laing, later a senior vice president, who was one of the legion of Pru men who had grave reservations about Stewart.

It was said that Stewart liked to browbeat many of his subordinates. "He wanted to get acquainted with the people around him just well enough to find their weaknesses," said one man who worked for him. "Then he had them."

Stories were told of how he had humiliated men by criticizing them savagely and at length in the presence of others, including their own subordinates. Some said it was done to help men he respected, so they could learn and improve—surely an odd way of going about a worthy goal, if that was his intention. To at least one man Stewart said he only criticized him on small things which he could do better, not on the basic thrust of a man's work or ideas, but he almost got that same man fired. And if he was hard on men he considered able, he was "unmerciful," as one of his few defenders put it, "on people he considered not worth teaching."

The chief actuary was Valentine Howell, "brilliant and charming," in the words of a peer. Vice president and treasurer was Robert M. Green, a popular executive who had the appearance and the air of a British military officer; he would make one of the most important contributions in the company's history. F. Bruce Gerhard, who was in charge of general office administration, was an actuary—part of a Prudential tradition of using actuaries and other specialists in other areas to which they could bring a fresh viewpoint. G. E. Potter had responsibility for Home Office buildings and plant, and also, curiously, for public relations and advertising. The Bond Department was headed by Caleb Stone. Ed Whittaker was in charge of Group insurance; Sayre (Pat) MacLeod, Ordinary Agencies; and Orville Beal, District Agencies. Real estate investments were the responsibility of Charles Fleetwood, who would, in time, put his stamp on the Southwestern Home Office. Sylvester C. Smith, Jr., general counsel, would later be the first full-time head of a corporate law department to be elected president of the American Bar Association. Frederick H. Groel, as vice president and secretary, worked closely with the board of directors.

And then there was Louis R. Menagh, Jr., another complex figure—and one of great and growing importance—in that crowd of dynamic, highly charged men. He had started with the Pru in 1914, when he was 22 and fresh out of Rutgers; when Shanks was elected president, Menagh was 54 and had 32 years of company service behind him. It had been a long, hard pull, with many disappointments and frustrations, all of which had taken their toll.

During the 1920's James F. Little, then the chief actuary, encouraged Menagh to take the actuarial examinations.

"I had never taken any mathematics in college," Menagh recalled, shortly before his death in 1973. "When he asked me, I thought he might as well have asked me to go to the moon. I had to study that stuff and I didn't like to study."

But study he did, and he passed the examinations, which are extraordinarily difficult. Despite his new status as a fellow of the Society of Actuaries, Menagh felt that he was never wholly accepted by the Actuarial Department as a fellow professional, and there is some basis for believing that his feelings were more than mere oversensitivity.

In November 1939 Menagh was made comptroller of the company. Until then, the Comptroller's Department had been weak and ineffective—a dangerous state of affairs, especially for a financial company. Under Menagh's direction, the department became one of the strongest in the entire corporation; indeed, some felt that it was too strong, especially after an expense control program instituted in the early 1940's began providing Menagh with more information about the activities of many executives than they thought he needed.

"Before he was elected vice president [in 1947]," said one man, "Menagh had a certain sweetness about him, but afterward . . ."

Afterward, men began to worry about the information that was flowing to Menagh, and about his increasing influence with Shanks.

Menagh earned the confidence that Shanks placed in him. Even in the late 1930's, Menagh told Shanks about problems in areas which Shanks had been assigned by Duffield, and later by D'Olier, to deal with. The information helped the company, and it helped Shanks.

After Shanks reached the presidency, he asked Menagh what the comptroller saw as the company's most immediate obstacle to growth.

"He told me that the New York companies only paid one-third the taxes that the Prudential did," Shanks said. "That put us at a competitive disadvantage."

Characteristically, Shanks confronted the city and the state with demands for tax adjustments. He said, in effect, that the Pru was willing to bear its fair share of the tax burden, but as a mutual company it had an obligation to its policyholders to keep costs as low as possible, and that included keeping its tax costs about the same level of those of its competitors in other states.

During the ensuing political furor, Menagh and Groel, who had the best political contacts, worked out with the leaders of both parties a system of taxation that could be accepted as fair by the state, the city, and the company. Before the end of Shanks's first year as president, the tax dispute had been resolved. A major obstacle to the company's growth had been removed.

14 / 'Break the Whole Thing Up'

World War II ended with VJ Day—Victory over Japan—on September 2, 1945, 19 days after Japan announced that she would surrender. In Europe, peace had come that spring, on May 7. By the end of the year, most of the U.S. and Canadian troops had been demobilized and returned home, although other young men in much smaller numbers were still being drafted to take their places in the armies of occupation overseas. Some of the men who came back into civilian life at that time would one day be major figures in the Prudential.

Donald S. MacNaughton had no reason to think that he was destined to be chairman of the board and chief executive officer of the Pru in the days when he went back to his high school teaching job in upstate New York after serving in the Pacific as a flight controller in the Air Force. When the school board in Pulaski, a small town in Oswego County, at the eastern end of Lake Ontario, refused to raise his pay to compensate for his after-hours work coaching the basketball team (he had also augmented his meager income by playing for a professional basketball team in Syracuse), MacNaughton quit his teaching job and entered the Syracuse University law school under the GI Bill of Rights, while his wife, Winifred, supplemented the government's $90-a-month payments by going back to work as an elementary school teacher.

A future president of the company, Kenneth C. Foster—witty, tough-minded, often irascible, and generally regarded in later years as one of the most brilliant men ever employed by Prudential—was immersed in a small controversy as soon as he got back to Newark. After joining Pru in 1938, he had earned a doctorate in law from Rutgers in 1940 and his Chartered Life Underwriter (CLU) degree in 1941.

Then he was drafted as part of the mobilization during that last year before the U.S. entered the war. Released from service in the fall of 1941, he was told that his superiors were so impressed by his work as assistant manager of the Newark Ordinary Agency that they were trans-

119

ferring him to the Home Office in the Ordinary Agencies Department. Foster, who had been returned to civilian life because he was over 28 years old, had been working in the Prudential Home Office less than a month when Pearl Harbor was attacked; the following month he was back in uniform.

When Foster was finally discharged from the service after the war, having risen from private to captain, earning the Commendation Medal along the way, he went back to Pru. Sayre (Pat) MacLeod, the head of Ordinary Agencies, suggested that he go back into the field. Foster pointed out that the law protected the right of veterans to get their old jobs back, and his old job was the one he held at the Home Office for three or four weeks before Pearl Harbor. Foster got the job, and MacLeod did not hold his stand against him. In four years, after a series of rapid promotions, Foster became a second vice president (equivalent to the later rank of vice president).

Many others returned to civilian life and to Prudential, where they were destined to play prominent roles in the company. One such was Robert A. Beck, who would become president of Pru one day. Beck, who had been a paratrooper during the war, started to work for Pru as a part-time agent while attending Syracuse, from which he would graduate *summa cum laude* in 1950.

Then there was handsome Robert W. Harvey, who had been a navigator in the Air Force; he returned to the Actuarial Department. So did former Navy Lieutenant Fredrick E. Rathgeber. Thomas Allsopp, who had, like Foster, gone into the Army a private and emerged a captain, having earned the Bronze Star, went back to the Organization and Methods Department, which would be at the heart of Prudential's revolution. Among the others returning to that department were Floyd H. Bragg, late a major in the Air Transport Command, and a former Navy lieutenant, Raymond W. Cobb.

Some wartime links carried over into civilian life. Charles W. Campbell, a colonel in the Adjutant General's Department in the Army, came back to become manager of the company's Newark agency; in 1954 he would marry Helen Crabtree, whom he had met when she was a major in the service. And a Navy man, Warrant Officer Joseph M. Savage, after returning to the Pru, persuaded E. Carroll Gerathy, who had become his friend in wartime, to join the company, too.

Some of the returning veterans—like John J. Marcus, an actuary who had served as an Air Force meteorologist—had completed their higher education before the war, but many more completed their college work during the immediate postwar years before going to work for Pru. For example, an Air Force lieutenant colonel, Frank J. Hoenemeyer, back in civvies, earned an M.B.A. from the Wharton School of the University of Pennsylvania before entering the company's Bond Department. And Duncan Macfarlan, who had been an aviation cadet in the Navy, became a Prudential special agent (that is, an agent in the Ordinary branch). An infantryman named Donald R. Knab took his bachelor of arts degree and his law doctorate, passed his bar examinations, and joined the Pru's real estate investment office at Cincinnati. After getting out of the Air Force, Raymond A. Charles, who had been a prewar graduate student at the Massachusetts Institute of Technology, took an M.B.A. at the University of Chicago before accepting a post with the company in Newark.

Not all who had been engaged in war work needed to switch from uniforms to civilian clothes. Not Harry J. Volk, for example—back from the Strategic Bombing Survey. Nor John D. Buchanan, who had served in the War Assets Administration and was now a Prudential agent in Omaha.

None of that mass of men and women who came out of the war to work for the Prudential could have been called typical. They were a generation who had felt the heady breezes of the Roaring Twenties, the icy gales of the Depression Thirties, the scorching blasts of the wartime Forties. They were full of ideas, ready to change the world.

And change it they would. As cultural anthropologist Margaret Mead was to write two decades later, "The gulf separating 1965 from 1943 is as deep as the gulf that separated the men who became builders of cities from Stone Age men."

In that process of national—and world-wide—change, the postwar generation of Prudential men and women would play their part. To use one example: if anything epitomized the enormous advances in technology, it was the computer—and probably the first developmental contract for a computer for commercial use was one signed by the Pru in the late 1940's.

Many of the changes that were made in the late 1940's appeared less than monumental, but often they were more significant than they appeared to be at first. For example, the employment of women. When the men began to come back from the war, women were taken out of "men's jobs" and on October 1, 1947, the company reinstated the prewar rule that women had to resign when they married.

The rule didn't last long—just six months, in fact. F. Bruce Gerhard reported, "It became apparent . . . that the policy was unpopular with the public and our employees and was difficult to justify. Furthermore, studies of the cost of employing and training replacements for girls who left revealed that the policy was costing more than the value of any intangible benefits it might have. Accordingly, on April 7, 1948, a change was made so that now female employees who marry may continue in our employ on the same basis as single women."

For one young couple in the Group Department, the change occurred just in time. Virginia Baumann didn't want to leave the Pru after she married Martin D. Vogt on May 22, so the announcement of the new policy was greeted by her with cheers. For a few more years Virginia and Martin—whose mother had worked for the company during World War I—were able to go on working together.

The rule change regarding married women undoubtedly reflected, in part, the findings of two surveys of employee attitudes—studies which would have been unthinkable in the old Pru. One of the surveys, by a firm of management consultants engaged for the purpose by the Prudential, "indicated that the majority of Prudential employees did not think that age, length of service, or sex should be important factors in a salary policy."

The other inquiry was conducted by the Survey Research Center of the University of Michigan, sponsored and financed by the U.S. Office of Naval Research. Its purpose was "to determine the relation between employee production and employee attitudes to specific aspects of work." The results were published as *Satisfactions in the White-Collar Job*, by Nancy C. Morse, although the Prudential was not named as the organization under scrutiny.

The study found a substantial majority of the employees expressing "financial and job status satisfaction"—except among the older men and women, trained in the old regimentation, who found the new, less formal ways sometimes more than they could cope with. Majorities of employees, often running to more than 70 per cent, were satisfied with their pay and their work, and this was true at every salary level and every level of responsibility. However, the women were more contented than the men, and married employees than single. By and large, the study concluded, the company was viewed by its employees as enjoying "high prestige in the community" and providing "favorable working conditions."

One finding with future significance to the company was this: "The need for skilled, varied work is quite widespread in the white-collar population and those who are doing highly routine work will tend to be less satisfied with their jobs than those doing skilled, varied work." A quarter century later, the acknowledgement of that need would underlie the Prudential's "job enrichment" program, intended to diminish the number of routine jobs and to enable every employee to feel a greater sense of accomplishment.

By the end of 1948 there were 11,526 employees, nearly 65 per cent of them women, working in a rabbit warren of seven buildings in the heart of Newark, the most important of the structures being linked by a tunnel which was completed in 1947. The older buildings were modernized—and the Washington Street Building, lately vacated by the Army's Office of Dependency Benefits, was renovated—during 1946 and 1947.

Throughout the buildings concealed loudspeakers broadcast recorded music. Candy vending machines appeared in 32 locations. Smoking was authorized in the offices "during recess and lunch periods and before and after closing hours"; before long, all restrictions would quietly be abandoned. In the cafeterias, where free lunches had been provided for employees since the early 1920's, there was a new air of relaxation.

The employees' association resumed its program of dances, moonlight sails, snow trips, roller-skating parties, basketball games, fashion shows, and bowling and bridge tournaments. In July 1946 almost all the employees and their families—including thousands of children—climbed aboard 10 special trains for a holiday at Asbury Park, an outing they had enjoyed every summer before the war.

The general feeling of renewal pervaded everything. In 1946 the Prudential re-entered Texas, from which it and all the other major life insurance companies had withdrawn in 1907, after enactment of an extremely restrictive law there. "The selection of capable managers and suitable office quarters was very greatly aided by Rear Admiral Gerald A. Eubank, U.S.N.R., manager of our Downtown Ordinary Agency in

New York City and a native Texan,'' said Ordinary boss Sayre MacLeod—struggling, one suspects, to suppress an unseemly grin as he dictated the straight-faced statement to his secretary.

For Admiral Eubank was one of those colorful figures who brighten the Pru's history in every period. As an Admiral, he was not quite in the class of a Nelson; although he was always addressed by that title after his return to civilian life, his naval skills were displayed mostly in the marketing of war bonds, reminding irreverent Pru people more of Gilbert and Sullivan than of Oliver Hazard Perry. But as a shrewd salesman, a clever self-promoter, and an intelligent manipulator, it was hard to find his equal.

In 1920, for example, he moved to Detroit and started to work as a life insurance agent. The word soon spread that he was rather shiftless —spent all his time at the horse races. But his critics were stilled the following year when he sold over a million dollars' worth of life insurance to people he had met at the track.

"He was extremely able," said Carrol Shanks.

A native of Navasota, Texas, Eubank served as a Navy supply officer in World War I. At the beginning of the second World War, he was assigned the same duties at the Philadelphia Navy Yard, but somehow—using his remarkable ability to influence people—he suddenly burst into the limelight as organizer of a world-wide war savings bond program for the Navy, the Marine Corps, and the Coast Guard.

One Prudential man remembers Eubank, who retired in 1960 and died in 1969, as having bright blue eyes. He was short, "but people didn't think of him as being short because he dominated any room he was in."

His big belly was a source of humor for the Admiral. Ruefully patting his paunch, he used to sigh that he had lost 2,000 pounds in his lifetime.

The stories about him were legion. It was said that once, when every hotel in the country seemed to be crammed full of people, he was refused a room by the desk clerk. He went down to the street to a pay telephone, dialed the hotel, asked for the assistant manager, and snapped in his crispest, most naval fashion, "This is Admiral Eubank. I want a room. High up. Quiet. A corner room would be best." When he showed up an hour later, he got the room.

He seemed to know people everywhere, and everybody who knew him liked him, and many were impressed with him. "He was the kind of person who would push himself in," Shanks said.

Soon after the war, as a result of one of Robert Green's ideas, Eubank had ample opportunity to "push himself in" all over the country.

It was an idea Green had carried about within himself for some time, waiting until the time was right to propose it to Shanks. One day he was summoned to Shanks's office. He found the company president "boiling mad" over some dispute with the city authorities. Earlier that day Shanks had told Fred Groel, the board secretary, that he didn't like the situation the Pru found itself in. "All our eggs are in one basket," he'd said.

To Green, Shanks raised the possibility of moving enough of the company's operations to the suburbs so that it would not be wholly at the mercy of the city politicians.

"I told him we were sure [in the Methods Department] that the operation would not suffer too much and that communications could be handled with trucks, telephone, etc.," Green remembered in later years. "However, I told him that I did not think that was the answer to his problem."

(In fact, Green did not even think that the Pru's big problem was the issue they were discussing. But the solution to the real problem—which was, as Green saw it, coping with bigness, especially with respect to the uncovering and development of talented personnel—also was the answer to the matter vexing Shanks that day.)

"Well," asked Shanks, "what should I want to do?"

"You ought to break the whole thing up in pieces and spread it over the United States and Canada," Green replied.

Green said he "was convinced that we had the most efficient home office of anybody, but still were a long way from the quality of performance that I had hoped for."

"I told him that we were suffering from bigness and the inevitable bureaucracy that comes with bigness in any human operation," according to Green's later recollection. "By breaking into small parts, *each with the greatest possible authority and responsibility*"—the key to the success of the whole concept—"we could lick the disease we were suffering from. I told him that we could enjoy the advantages of the smaller companies. . . . I told him to wait for two weeks and I would give him a memorandum outlining the whole thing."

"Fine," Shanks said. "But this thing is dynamite, so please keep it quiet."

With two other men, Paul W. (Pete) Stewart and E. C. Brigden,

Green left the next day for Toronto to talk with his old friend, Edwin C. McDonald, who was head of Metropolitan's operations in Canada. Several decades earlier, the Met had established a satellite "home office" of sorts at San Francisco and another at Toronto. Although both had been maintained ever since, neither was regarded in the industry as having had a significant impact on the Met's fortunes. Green hoped that his visit to Toronto would provide him with an explanation for that lack of effect.

"Up there I found out why the Metropolitan had not fully succeeded in its effort at decentralization," Green said. "The responsibility had been delegated to the local executive, but very little authority. Every single part of the Canadian head office had to report back to the equivalent part of Madison Avenue [the Met's headquarters site in New York City]. They even had to pattern their organization exactly after the Madison Avenue organization. In many cases, this didn't fit well at all.

"Fortunately, my friend was quite outspoken. In fact, I would say he was typical of the Regional Home Office vice presidents later developed by the Prudential."

Back in Newark, Green and his assistants amassed a three-inch-thick collection of data and other information bearing on his proposal, including the amount of insurance of various kinds written in each state, the total investments of the Pru by geographical area, population and projections, and many other details. Green made extensive studies of how the country might be carved into regions by the Pru for its purposes. He drew up an organization chart to indicate what functions a regional home office might carry out and how it would do it. Finally, he sat down and dictated a six-page, single-spaced memorandum. After his secretary transcribed her notes and typed the memo, Green found he didn't need to change a word.

Green took the memo and the pile of supporting research material to Shanks, who sat and read it without saying a word, his face, as usual, expressionless. There was not a flicker of an eyebrow to indicate to Green how Shanks was reacting to the proposal.

"I have never worked with any man whose mind worked faster than Carrol Shanks's," Green often said, so the suspense was not drawn out. When Shanks got to the end of the memo, he said, "This looks good."

Shanks thought for a moment, then asked Green, "How many people know about this?"

"Just Pete and Ed and the stenographer to whom I dictated the memo."

"Well, please keep it quiet," Shanks instructed him. "I want to take my time before announcing it."

It was clear that Shanks did not intend to identify Green with the idea—at least, not at first. And he was right to conceal Green's part. He was not attempting to steal the credit for an idea, as Green fully understood and always acknowledged in later years. No, the reason for Shanks's desire to keep Green out of the picture was that he knew the plan would meet widespread disapproval from most of his senior officers, and the commonplace jealousies and frictions that exist in any large organization might only harden the opposition to the proposal.

Because Green's connection was not publicized, the people of Prudential sometimes disputed among themselves in later years who deserved the credit of the company's decentralization program, one of the most sweeping and powerful reorganizations ever carried out by any large corporation. In fact, Green and Shanks both were due the honors. The concept, an incredibly daring one for any organization, let alone one just emerging from its long torpor, was Green's, and the depth of his vision is indicated by the fact that a quarter of a century later all of the strengths that regionalization would give to the company were being realized. For example, many younger men, assuming incorrectly that administrative convenience had been the underlying reason for decentralization, said in the 1970's that one of the best *incidental* features of the system was that it developed such strong pools of skilled, experienced manpower—but that was one of the *primary* advantages foreseen by Green.

But Green's idea would have been just that—an abstract thought, unrealized and unrecognized—if Carrol Shanks had not had the similarly profound vision to see the virtues in the audacious scheme, the courage to commit millions of dollars (hundreds of millions, as it turned out) and years of man-hours to an untried concept, and the strength to see the program through to a successful conclusion over the initial opposition of his most powerful and determined officers. Even some members of the board of directors expressed vigorous disagreement with the plan, but Shanks remained unswayed, fortunately for the Pru.

Green's memo, dated July 27, 1945, set forth three principal objectives: "to make the company a truly national institution, to give the company stronger local significance in various sections, [and] to develop executive personnel."

Decentralization was desirable as a cure for five faults that Green found "inherent . . . in the high degree of concentration of the present organization." The faults, as he enumerated them, were these: "Too much specialization, almost from top to bottom. Too few men with broad responsibilities. Too many levels of authority between the president and the lower levels—the clerks and agents. Too much tendency toward bureaucratic organization involving intricate rules and red tape. Too much of an attitude of caution and timidity down the line."

Before going into the merits of decentralization, and how to achieve it, Green paused to mention two possible disadvantages:

> 1. Cost of operation. It is reasonable to expect that smaller units will be more costly than the mass production operation possible in the Home Office. Home Office cost, however, is such a small part of the total cost of operation that if sufficient gain in other directions is obtainable by a change in plan of operation, we can stand the probable additional cost of operating the office. It is conceivable that certain costs may be reduced. I shall discuss the question of cost and size later.
>
> 2. Lack of control. The company has always operated on a system of very strong centralized control. This has undoubtedly been necessary and desirable. If the branch Home Offices suggested in this proposal are going to function properly, centralized control will have to be relaxed to some extent, as the executives in the branch offices will not develop as we wish them to if they are under too severe restraint from the Home Office. They must be allowed plenty of leeway. This adjustment in thinking may be one of the most difficult things to accomplish in connection with the suggested plan. It seems to me that it will have to be made if the plan is going to be a success. I believe that any anticipated weakening in control of accounts and expenses can be overcome by proper organization.

The tentative plan of organization for the company under Green's program was set forth:

"A central executive Home Office in Newark . . . would confine itself to centralized company administration and be separated from any local branch office, even that which will cover the Newark territory.

This office must have an equal interest in each branch. In this office, as I visualize it, there will be the senior officers of the company, practically all of the actuarial evaluation work, and staff departments of officers necessary for the supervision and control of the functions of which they have charge throughout all the branch offices. A great deal of study will have to be given to the whole question of that portion of the company's operation which must be handled at the central executive Home Office. The objective, as I see it, should be to decentralize as much as possible. . . .

"At the top [of each branch Home Office] should be a senior vice president of the company who has complete responsibility for the operation of the branch. He should occupy, in effect, the same position as the president of a smaller company, being capable of passing judgment on sales problems, investment problems, and general administration problems. He should have good public relations sense and devote his interests and energy to promoting the Prudential throughout his area in all branches of the business. Below him should be a group of preferably not more than four men with a rank equivalent to that of second vice president, these four, together with the senior vice president, to form the executive committee of the branch. Each of these men would have a definite part of the business for which he is responsible, but should, through committee discussion, maintain a current familiarity with other parts of the business in the territory covered by the branch.

"The responsibilities of these four men would be: sales, investments, general management of the branch, [and] charge of all insurance policy matters from issue to claim. Under these four men would be a series of junior executives with approximately the following responsibilities: general accounting, bank accounts, cash; underwriting; claims; Ordinary policy work, issue to claims; Industrial policy work, issue to claims; Group insurance administration; Ordinary agencies; Industrial agencies; Group insurance and Group Annuity [*i.e.,* pension] sales; personnel and methods; mortgages and securities; and medical work."

This meant, as Green pointed out, that the Regional Home Offices, or Branch Home Offices, as he called them, would carry out these functions: "supervise sales organization; supervise mortgage offices; take some active part in securing investments for the Bond Department; do the underwriting, both lay and medical [that is, determine whether an applicant was insurable, and if so, under what rates and conditions];

issue policies; make policy loans; pay surrenders and claims.'' Green said he was ''inclined to feel that actuarial evaluation must be done at the centralized executive Home Office, but possibly this can be decentralized.''

In his discussion of the type of organization to be established in the Branch Home Offices, Green said, ''We must be careful to view the problem objectively and not be too much influenced by the existing Home Office organization. The Home Office organization is the result of certain traditions, often influenced by personalities. In my opinion, in many respects it is not strictly logical and would not be as it is today if worked out on a blueprint basis with a complete disregard for the particular abilities of certain officers. We have an opportunity to start fresh in branch offices and set up our organization upon sound and logical lines [although] there is room, no doubt, for wide variation of opinion on the blueprint that should be established.''

In his summary of the memo, Green said that ''the most important objective'' of decentralization was the ''developing [of] executive personnel.''

One day that fall, in October or November 1945—picking a day when he knew Green would be meeting with the War Manpower Commissioner to argue for more Home Office help—Shanks assembled his senior officers and had Valentine Howell, the chief actuary, read the memo, from which Green's name had been deleted. Apparently Shanks chose Howell because he expected the most vehement disagreement to come from him. It was his intention to give Howell the overall responsibility for carrying out the plan, knowing that no man can bring himself to oppose a program that is his baby.

A decade later Howell, who had learned that Green was the author of the program—indeed, Shanks used to make a point of crediting Green with it whenever he was speaking to Canadian employees during Green's later tenure as head of the Canadian Head Office—saw to it that Green was properly honored. By that time decentralization had turned out to be more than a successful idea: it was the key to the company's astonishing leap forward over the next quarter-century.

15/Afloat on the Tar Pits

One day late in 1945 or early in 1946 Gerald Eubank, the Prudential's exuberant Admiral, was flying from Washington, D.C., to Los Angeles aboard a Navy transport airplane. When he found that the passenger beside him was Norman Chandler, publisher of the powerful Los Angeles *Times*, he couldn't resist telling Chandler that the Pru was considering seriously the possibility of establishing a separate Western Home Office—not a branch field office, but an autonomous Home Office—in Los Angeles. As Eubank expected, Chandler was excited by the prospect that such a step held out for the economic development of southern California, and impressed by the inside knowledge and connections of the Admiral. Chandler asked to be informed when a firm decision was reached, and he promised to do everything he could to help the project.

The conversation would have been of interest to Valentine Howell, Robert M. Green, Harold M. Stewart, Sylvester C. Smith, Jr. (he was then the Pru's general solicitor), and Harry J. Volk. Those five men in Newark had been named by president Carrol Shanks to be members of a committee, with Howell as chairman, charged with the responsibility of looking into the question of "whether it would be desirable to establish one or more Branch Home Offices in the U.S. and Canada." Apparently the committee was simply a device used by Shanks to defuse some of the opposition that he foresaw. Although there were rumbles of discontent, the committee, after delaying as long as the chief resisters dared, came up with the recommendation that its members had known Shanks wanted in the beginning: start with one Regional Home Office, probably in California, and see how it affected the company's operations before setting up a second.

That recommendation was handed up toward the end of 1946, many months after Eubank's conversation with Chandler. In February 1947 a firm decision was made to go ahead with the plan. Shanks summoned

Howell; Volk; George Potter, who was in charge of Home Office buildings; and Charles Fleetwood, who would later that year be named head of the Mortgage Loan and Real Estate Investment Department, succeeding the retiring Paul Bestor. Shanks told them to go out to Los Angeles at once and select a site for the new regional headquarters. Volk, he said, would run the West Coast operation.

They went by train. Because of the number of cars, there were two sections to the train. Howell, Volk, and Potter were in the first section. Fleetwood was in the second section. The first section got to Chicago more or less on time, and the three Pru men aboard it changed there to another train which would carry them the rest of the way.

But Fleetwood, in the second section, was stranded in a snowstorm. By the time he got to Chicago, the others had left. So he took an airliner to Los Angeles and arrived a day ahead of the others. In those days, most of the people of the Pru still traveled by train, but Fleetwood's speedy flight convinced a good many of the company's executives that it was time to switch their patronage from the rails to the air.

In Los Angeles, the four men looked at a number of sites, under the guidance of Bill Schroll, who was head of the company's mortgage loan office there. They had a cover story—they were looking at sites for a client of the Prudential—because it was thought that property owners might hold out for more money if they knew that a company with the Pru's huge assets was buying land for its own use. They didn't know that Eubank had tipped their hand long before.

The first site they examined was a ten-acre piece of land on Wilshire Boulevard, between Curson and Masselin, a block away from the La Brea tar pits. That is, from the tar pits open to the public; in fact, the tar pits extended under the land that the Pru men were considering buying. Nevertheless, an engineer assured the group that a building could be erected on the site, provided that it did not go above ten stories—but that was no handicap, because a city ordinance at that time prohibited the construction of buildings higher than ten stories or 150 feet. The engineer said that because of the underlying tar, the building would have to float on a concrete slab, without a foundation or pilings.

That was the site favored by Volk and Fleetwood. Howell and Potter preferred another piece of land. On the train, heading back East, they played cards and argued. It was not until they were approaching Newark that Howell finally said to Volk, "Harry, you'll have to run the operation. As far as I'm concerned, it's your choice."

So the group recommended purchase of half the site, which was all they thought the company would need. Shanks shook his head.

"Buy the whole thing," he said.

In later years, some of the doubts of Howell and Potter bore fruit in a minor way. The underlying tar made it necessary to keep repairing the parking lot. (In 1963 the tar pit under the Pru's property disgorged the bones of a sloth and of prehistoric birds, all more than 14,000 years old.) On the other hand, there was a useful aspect to construction over the tar pits: the tar absorbed most of the shock during earthquakes. In two major tremors—July 21, 1952, and February 9, 1971, neither of which occurred during normal working hours—there was no significant damage to the building. Despite the mess caused by broken glass, overturned files and desks, and spilled water from coolers, the only real damage was to the lights, and after the second temblor, the company installed a new kind of light which could sway, like a lamp in a ship, during a quake.

The public announcement of the establishment of a Western Home Office, as it came to be called (like the later Regional Home Offices, it usually was referred to simply by its initials, WHO), was made simultaneously on both coasts. In the East, Carrol Shanks told the news to the company's leading agents and managers at the Pru's annual business conference, held on March 16, 1947, at the Hotel Commodore in New York City. At the same time, Harry Volk disclosed the Pru's plans in a talk to a large assembly of business, civic, and political leaders who had been invited by Norman Chandler to a luncheon at the California Club in Los Angeles.

Within the company, most people were puzzled. The company had field offices all over the continent already—was this to be a sort of super-field office? Was the dramatic announcement just a promotional gimmick or was there real significance to this development?

The reaction in Los Angeles was altogether different. The Los Angeles *Herald,* an evening newspaper, gave the story a streamer headline across the top of the front page. The next morning Chandler's Los Angeles *Times* ran the news in the top spot on the front page of its local section, under a five-column headline that said: "Prudential Will Erect $7,000,000 Western States Headquarters Here." Both newspapers emphasized how much the Prudential's action would mean to the economic development of southern California and the rest of the West.

Moving quickly to establish the Prudential as an integral part of the community, Volk asked Chandler to serve as chairman of a committee to advise the new WHO. The advisory committee consisted of Justin Dart, president of United-Rexall Drug Company; LeRoy M. Edwards, vice president and general manager of the Pacific Lighting Company; James E. Shelton, president of Security-First National Bank; and P. G. Winnett, president of Bullock's, Inc.

The enthusiasm of Angelenos was understandable. Pru's proposed WHO building would be the first major office building erected in the Los Angeles metropolitan area since 1934, as Harry Bennett, who had been engaged as the company's public relations consultant there, remembered. It was also the first fully air-conditioned building in Los Angeles. Because the site of the new building at 5757 Wilshire Boulevard was well to the west of the downtown district, WHO also helped to influence the westward flow of new construction. "Prudential not only started off the construction boom in Los Angeles but it also started the construction of major office buildings along Wilshire Boulevard," Bennett said. In time, the boulevard—far beyond Pru's WHO, into Beverly Hills and Westwood and West Los Angeles —became, as Bennett put it, "a corridor of tall structures," the height limitation existing in 1947 having been later removed.

On May 5 of that year Shanks and Mayor Fletcher Bowron took part in a ground-breaking ceremony at the site. In the meantime, back in Newark, Volk had already begun to set up his new organization. By the end of the year he was able to report:

"Top supervisory personnel was first selected, and the WHO head of each division was charged with the responsibility of organizing the functions under his direction. In June the organization of the Debit Policy Division of the Machine Records Division was begun and has now been practically completed. Other divisions were organized, one by one, from June through the balance of the year, and on December 31st more than 625 persons were engaged in WHO operations. These persons were doing work that eventually will be transferred to California. This work did not represent a duplication, but an actual segregation of the functions from the parent departments in Newark. The amount of work presently being done by the WHO [in Newark] represents approximately 70 per cent of the total task. . . .

"To illustrate the size of the record separation problem, it is interesting to note that more than 2,000,000 punched cards, representing policies in force on our debits, had to be reproduced, sorted in various classifications, and listed. From these listings 2,000,000 policy applications have been picked from the files. . . . Over 400,000 cards were punched from our in-force Ordinary renewal cards. These cards were used as a picking means for segregating Ordinary applications, register records, loan records, dividend records, and other necessary forms."

The creativity released by decentralization was foreshadowed at that early date by the development of new methods of carrying out almost every kind of function while the WHO unit was still working in Newark.

In October 40,000 square feet of office space was rented in the Horton-Converse Building at 431 South Fairfax Avenue, a few blocks from the WHO site, for use until the new building was completed. Later additional space was taken, temporarily, in the Citizens Bank Building at 5780 Wilshire Boulevard. Soon those offices began to fill up with Prudential employees, some transferred out from Newark, others hired locally.

The first person to be transferred to Los Angeles was James Hunter. Because he would be manager of the new building, he was needed at the site during construction, so he arrived in Los Angeles toward the end of 1947. In the meantime, two Angelenos familiar with employment practices and conditions in the West, Mildred Radanovich and Victor Alberti, had been hired and sent back to Newark for training in the Pru's methods and philosophy.

During the first two weeks of 1948, Alberti and Miss Radanovich were part of the first group to be sent out from Newark. The others were Manuel (Doc) Allen, Personnel manager; Leroy Decker, Payroll; Dr. Albert H. Domm, the medical director; Clifford Hermey, Purchasing; Eleanor Schmidt, Personnel (her father, Louis H. Schmidt, was a second vice president—equivalent to the present rank of vice president—in Newark); Isaac Wood, Payroll; and Louis Yuhas. Eleven years later Miss Schmidt married Hunter, whom she met on her first day in Los Angeles. Although they had both worked for the Pru in Newark, they had not known each other there.

Soon the people being sent from Newark were moving out with increasing frequency, and the groups were getting larger. The responsibility for organizing and transporting the groups fell to Jan Bout, who ultimately became head of the corporate Conference and Travel Division.

Dutch by birth, Bout had spent seven or eight years in California as a boy and returned to the U.S. again after his schooling. Before he was drafted into military service in World War II, he had been working for the Santa Fe Railroad, so he ended up in the Army as an officer in the Transportation Corps. After the war he returned to the railroad, and he was on duty in Los Angeles as a passenger travel agent in May 1947 when he noticed two angry men in the railroad station. They were Harry Volk and Admiral Eubank, and they had been treated rudely by a railroad ticket agent. Bout not only solved their ticket problem, but even got them a table at Earl Carroll's nightclub after they had been told, by telephone, that none was available. The next day Eubank asked Bout for a resumé of his background, and a few weeks later Bout was working for the Pru.

The first group that Bout took from Newark to Los Angeles consisted of 29 persons, including eight or nine children, all in one sleeping car. Although he had retired from the presidency of the company two years before, Colonel D'Olier went along, too, riding in a private car at the rear of the train. As a director of the Pennsylvania Railroad, D'Olier could travel by private car whenever he wished.

The next movement filled three sleeping cars. After that, people began moving out in such numbers that the Pru's sleeping cars would be run as second sections to the trains of which they were technically a part. During 1948, 522 employees and 644 dependents moved from Newark to Los Angeles—and, thanks to Bout, not a single passenger ever got lost, nor one piece of baggage misplaced. The Pru also moved 150 van loads and 12 full freight-car loads of household effects. Sixty freight cars brought 240 automobiles across the continent, although some, like Dr. Domm, preferred to drive out from Newark. One man, Daniel J. De Norch, turned the journey into a honeymoon. His last working day in Newark was April 1, 1948—a date some might consider inauspicious. But not De Norch: on April 3 he married Vincey Jaso of East Orange, and they headed for California by car.

For those who went by train, it was an exciting trip. The departure was a ceremonial event. Friends, relatives, neighbors, and office colleagues would gather at the Pennsylvania Station in Newark for prolonged, tearful, laughing farewells. Top officers of the company would put in an appearance to wish the departing troops Godspeed. Dr.

Domm, who had gone back to Newark in order to escort one trainload of "Pioneers," as they came to be called, said, "We left Newark on a steaming day in August. I can still remember, 26 years later, how Shanks stood there on the platform, ramrod straight, melting in a starched collar."

William W. Meelheim was aboard one of the trains, consisting of four sleeping cars and a club car. After the usual frenzied farewells, the train pulled out of Newark at 5 P.M. Thursday.

"Soon after we left," he said, "somebody discovered that Winnie Hale, the nurse who was traveling with us, was celebrating her birthday, so we all joined in a big, unplanned birthday party for her. It was great fun. At one point we were all joined in a big conga line snaking through the train. In those days there weren't transistor radios, of course, but we made our own music."

On every train there was a party atmosphere, with sing-alongs, games, and jokes to while away the time. Some people drank, some played cards, some entertained the kids. A number of romances got their start on those trips, for about a third of the people were unmarried. Some marriages eventually resulted.

Usually the train would arrive in Los Angeles about noon on Sunday. The last couple of hours everyone spent at the windows, staring at the sun-drenched land. The orange groves held a special fascination for these transplanted Easterners. "I still remember the fragrance of the orange blossoms," Meelheim said.

A few traveled by plane. One was Bob Larkin, who climbed aboard a Constellation operated by Trans World Airlines. With him Larkin had not only his wife, but also his five children. Flying was still a novelty for most people, and there was a good deal of fear associated with it, so TWA was mightily impressed by Larkin's simple demonstration of faith in the safety of flying. Airline officials were so impressed that they interviewed Larkin and his family at LaGuardia Airport before the flight and used the recorded interview as part of a commercial on radio. But the commercial was only broadcast in the New York area, so the Larkins, to their disappointment, never heard it.

The company accommodated all of them in hotels at first. Later, some, especially married couples, moved into apartments in one of several buildings which had been taken over by the Pru. After a few months, everybody found an apartment or a house of his own. Most of the houses were in the San Fernando Valley, which was then sparsely populated and inexpensive.

Eleanor Hunter, who at that time was Eleanor Schmidt, stayed at the Park Wilshire, but most of the other unmarried women had rooms at the Alexandria. So did many of the unmarried men.

"There was a sorority house atmosphere at the Alexandria," Mrs. Hunter said. "There were always parties, moving from room to room. It took a while for everyone to realize we weren't on vacation."

In the apartment courts, life was more sedate but still somewhat communal. Dr. Domm recalled, "Charlie Ives brought with him a television set with a five-inch screen that he'd assembled from a kit. [The last official figures, for the end of 1947, had shown that there were only 250,000 television receivers in the country, and only 20 stations were telecasting, so TV was still a strange new phenomenon.] The Iveses would invite all of us over to watch TV at least once a week. Wrestling matches were big in those days—remember Gorgeous George?—and we'd sit or stand, a room crammed full of people, watching that little, flickering picture, joking, talking. They were BYOB—Bring Your Own Booze—parties, and good fun."

Many had volunteered, and none had been compelled to make the move. So it was natural that they should have a unique *esprit de corps*. Rightly or wrongly, they felt that the company had skimmed the cream from Newark to staff this new operation. They felt, as one put it, that "only the most venturesome wanted to come out to a new, untried experiment in a part of the country unfamiliar to us." Many had been led to California by ambition; they hoped that in a new organization they would have a better chance to show what they could do. Some simply wanted to get away from the cold and snow and humidity and the old cities of the Northeast to the sun and warmth and dryness and the newness of southern California.

Mrs. Hunter, for example, had been working for the Pru for 12 years in Newark, in Personnel. In December 1947, on her way to work, she slipped on the ice and fell into the snow.

"That does it," she told herself. "I'll put my name in."

She did—and three weeks later she was on her way to California. But obviously weather was not the only factor in her decision.

The cadre from Newark, besides doing its own work, also had to train men and women who had been hired locally. The veterans found themselves working long hours. Meelheim recalls that he would do his own work in Debit Loan Approving at night and spend his days training new employees. The need for trained people was apparent; Meelheim, who had originally been asked to go out to WHO for a month, spent seven months there, and then returned only because of a death in the family. But the new people caught on quickly, and eased the burden of work. By the end of 1948, WHO's people consisted of 377 who had been transferred to Los Angeles, 46 who were only temporarily assigned from Newark, and 908 who had been hired in Los Angeles.

Among the "Pioneers" in WHO were a number of persons destined for high office in the company, including Fredrick E. Rathgeber, who became executive vice president; and William Ingram, James B. Jacobson, Kenneth C. Nichols, and Alan M. Thaler, all of whom became senior vice presidents.

Many of the inconveniences of those days, working long hours in temporary quarters, were mitigated by the presence of Harry Volk. He was a natural leader, capable of inspiring real loyalty and affection, and he reciprocated by showing pride, faith, and understanding toward the people who worked for him. Everyone, it seemed, knew him, if only by sight, because he was liable to pop up anywhere. There was a general feeling that Volk was sharing the difficulties with his people.

On June 1, 1948, the cornerstone of the new building, which was to be called Prudential Square, was laid. The cornerstone had been shaped from a two-ton piece of the Rock of Gibraltar which had been presented to the Pru by the British government. (By the time the last Regional Home Office had been built, so many massive pieces of the Rock had been bestowed on the company by the Crown that one might have been justified in wondering whether the Rock might not resemble a Swiss cheese. But it was sure-fire publicity for the Pru.) Inside the cornerstone were microfilms of most of the leading Western newspapers and a letter from Shanks to a future head of the company. In his letter Shanks said, at one point:

"The growth and maturity of the nation, together with the advantages of regional handling of affairs and the disadvantages of continued piling up of work and control in one locality, have made the time ripe for this first step toward regional control of our large business. The future will tell whether additional steps toward decentralization will be taken."

In September Carrol Shanks and Harry Volk undertook what Harry Bennett called the Pru's "road show." They visited Salt Lake City, Spokane, Seattle, Portland, San Francisco, and Denver before returning to Los Angeles. In each of those cities, including Los Angeles, Shanks addressed Chambers of Commerce, service clubs, civic groups, informal meetings of leading citizens, and the press.

"In each city the pattern was very much the same," Bennett recalled. "We would arrive in the evening and the next morning around 10 o'clock we would have a press conference featuring Shanks. He would have a great deal to say about the local area, and he'd relate Prudential to the area. He would especially emphasize that it was not Prudential's goal to come in and collect insurance premiums to be sent East, draining the Western economy and pouring funds into the East. Instead, Western money would be accumulated in the West and would create a greater fund of resources that could be quickly invested in the West to aid the Western economy.

"At noon there would be a luncheon for 100 to 200—or more—of the leading business executives, civic officials, and others who could be called opinion makers. At this Shanks and Volk would tell very much the same story as they had at the press conference. They would constantly emphasize the important part that Prudential had been playing in the local economy, how much had been invested in that area by Prudential, and how the new WHO would now make it possible for Prudential to speed up this function of aiding the local economy. They continually underlined the fact that decisions affecting the economy now would be made by people living in the West and understanding the West and its peculiar problems."

Later in the day there would be tours of local Pru offices, a reception at which Pru employees in the area could meet Shanks and Volk, and, finally, a dinner to which perhaps a dozen of the leading local citizens might be invited. It was a schedule that made for very full days.

The movement out of temporary quarters and into the new building began even before the structure was finished. On April 26, 1948, the fifth floor was occupied—although the windows had not yet been installed. "People had to put rocks on the papers on their desk so the breeze wouldn't blow them away," according to Fred Heimall, of Building Maintenance. "We'd watch the fog roll in one window and out the other.'' But the windows finally were in place throughout the building. More space became available in August and September.

With the dedication and official opening set for November 15, the company invited the public to an ''open house.'' More than 10,000 visitors took advantage of the invitation. On the 16th, 400 leading citizens attended a luncheon at the Biltmore at which Chandler presided and Shanks spoke.

The die was now cast. The question remained: would the gamble be successful?

Shanks had done everything with Volk to help launch the new Regional Home Office. Now Volk had to follow up.

One of Volk's first moves was to announce, as an incentive to agents, that a District agents' conference, ''with new high standards for qualification,'' would be held at Sun Valley.

The Pru had never held such a conference at a luxury resort before. Some in the District Agencies Department in Newark were scandalized. But Volk knew what he was doing. He wanted his agents to see the kind of higher standard of living they could aspire to, if they applied themselves to their work and increased their income. And he also wanted them to become familiar with places like Sun Valley, so that they could talk about them with ease when meeting with sales prospects.

It was only one of many changes that would be wrought in the Pru by the Western Home Office, and by the other Regional Home Offices, too. Even before the dedication, the Pru's Eastern formality was crumbling before the more casual folkways of the West. Employees were calling bosses by their first names, a thing unheard of in Newark. Even though one young woman had been fired that summer for coming to work in a halter top one hot day, the style of dress in the offices was clearly more casual than in Newark.

Although Harry Volk himself would never stop looking like an Easterner, pinstripe proper, it was generally understood that he approved of the Westerners' attitude toward life—and that feeling, too, contributed to the high morale of WHO.

Nevertheless, it is the bottom line, in all business, that determines success or failure. For WHO, 1949 was the first full year of operations. At the end of the year, Volk reported, with pride, that sales in his region had increased by 20.1 per cent over 1948, and by 12 per cent over 1946, which had been the best prior year. The improvement in production—as the insurance business calls sales—occurred in all departments.

"Results show that the Prudential in the West is doing better, as compared to previous years, than is the Prudential in the balance of the country," Volk wrote. "The Prudential has improved its position substantially with respect to the total [insurance] industry in the West."

This financial improvement, he pointed out, had been achieved while the Pru, through WHO, was improving its service to policyholders in the West, producing new ideas for more effective operations, and developing new levels of experienced and confident manpower.

In his letter in the cornerstone, Shanks had left it to the future to tell whether the company should continue down the road of decentraliza- tion. Now, it seemed, the future had spoken.

16 / 'We of Canada'

Even before the end of 1949, WHO's first full year of operations, Carrol Shanks made his next move. On December 9 he announced that the Prudential would establish a Canadian Head Office* in Toronto.

"For 40 years we have been one of you," he said in an address at the York Club on December 12, "but now we are to become even more closely knit through further decentralization of management. . . . It seems to me very logical that Prudential of America should set up a separate Canadian [Head] Office. Authority and responsibility belong in Canada, and our people who run this new office will be urged to use freely their own initiative and imagination in providing insurance protection to Canadians. They will be expected to invest Prudential dollars in Canada in such a way that it will strengthen your economy. Working independently and with your banking and business groups, they will pay particular attention to the money needs of small businesses, to the financing of farms and homes. They will use our nationwide status in Canada to invest the funds of areas where money is plentiful in areas where it is scarcer but where there are national assets to be developed."

Pointing out that Prime Minister Louis St. Laurent, two months earlier, had called for leadership from businessmen in a drive to satisfy the aspirations of the Canadian people, Shanks said, "The step we are taking will develop *more* drive, initiative, and resourcefulness in my company. Enterprise is strengthened by a move such as ours that creates new centers of initiative. We believe moving general management into the region for which it is responsible releases the creative faculties—the drive and imagination—of our managers."

The head of the CHO—as the Canadian Head Office was usually called—was Robert M. Green, the man whose memorandum on decen-

---

* Conforming to Canadian usage, Prudential used the term "Head Office," rather than the U.S. form, "Home Office," for its Toronto operations.

tralization four years earlier had set off the sweeping changes now under
way. Although a U.S. national—he was born and raised in
Cincinnati—Green had Canadian roots. One of his great-grandfathers
was a Baptist minister who had emigrated from Yorkshire, in England,
to Sherbrooke, in the province of Québec. Green's grandfather, a
graduate of McGill University, was superintendent of schools at Brock-
ville, Ontario, up the St. Lawrence River from Montreal, for many
years before moving to Ohio. Green himself was a Princeton man who
had served as an artillery officer in the U.S. Army in Europe in the first
World War and, after the war, was named a Chevalier of the Star of
Romania for his work in that country as a representative of Herbert
Hoover's American Relief Administration, seeing to it that emergency
rations of food and other supplies got to the people who needed them. A
man who stood tall and straight, Green had an air of self-possession that
was impressive. "He is one on whom the cloak of authority sits
naturally," said one Canadian periodical.

"There is a certain type of U.S. citizen whose breadth of vision and
experience are such that one tends to think of him as North American
rather than as an exclusive representative of one nation," said the
Monetary Times of Toronto. "To Canadians, such men typify everything that is expansive and dynamic in American tradition. A notable
example is Robert M. Green. . . . This grandson of an Ontario
educator brings to Canada the detachment and affection of an old
neighbor—free of regional prejudices, ready to promote the interests of
the whole [continent]. He had flown the length and breadth of the
Dominion [of Canada] more than once, and knows the temper of the
people in the various provinces. For many years, he had holidayed with
his family at Pointe au Baril on Georgian Bay, so his knowledge of the
land is based on decades of association."

The emphasis on Green's ancestral and personal connections with
Canada was significant, for the ambivalence of Canadians toward their
more populous neighbor to the South has rarely been understood by
Americans. (The very fact that U.S. citizens have pre-empted to themselves that designation, "American," which should be applicable to all
the people of the hemisphere, rankles many Canadians.) But Green was
always able to empathize with the Canadians.

"Canada is a proud and independent nation," Green once told a
Newark newspaper, "and Americans are apt to take Canadians for

granted. . . . Eighty per cent of the industries on the Niagara peninsula are foreign-owned. . . . What do you suppose happens to the feeling of nationalism under those conditions?''

From the first, Green, with his sensitivity to Canadian attitudes, made it clear that the Prudential had not set up its Canadian Head Office to exploit the people of the North, but to be of more service to them. Other Pru officers joined in the effort to reassure Canadians. For example, Shanks, in a speech at the Château Laurier at Ottawa in 1950, made the point that capital accumulation is one of the most urgent needs in a country struggling to realize its full potential for development. The funds of life insurance companies, he said, are a key factor in capital accumulation.

"A healthy portion of [Canada's] growth rightfully can be attributed to the work done by these life insurance dollars," he said. "They have given support in the form of loans to the industrial production which is becoming increasingly dominant in Canada. They have contributed to the development of the forests of British Columbia, the fisheries of Nova Scotia, the oil production of Alberta, the wheat farms of Saskatchewan, the electric power, the factories, and the offices of Ontario and Québec—and to homes of Canadians everywhere.

"Canada's mineral wealth, her farms and factories, fisheries and forest industries, wherever located in this rich land, as well as the homes of her people, have benefited from the investment of the life insurance savings of thrifty Canadians. Individual enterprises, large and small, have found insurance assets a highly available and satisfactory source of capital."

Instead of erecting its own CHO building at once, the Pru rented seven floors in the Bank of Nova Scotia Building, which was then under construction in Toronto. There was one other change from the methods used in setting up the Western Home Office: instead of shipping great numbers of people from Newark, Green hired most of his staff in Canada and sent them to Newark for training. Of the original permanent staff of 546, only 14 per cent had been transferred from Newark, and some of them were Canadians by birth. (Six years later, only seven per cent of CHO's employees were U.S. nationals, and a majority of the management jobs were held by Canadians.)

Those new Canadian employees who were to be trained in Newark traveled South on two special trains on successive Saturdays in June.

The women under 21 years of age were housed at Drew University in Madison, New Jersey, not far from Newark; they had to observe the regular university rules, which at that time included a curfew and weekend passes. Women 21 and older, and men, were put up in student quarters at Upsala College in East Orange, closer to Newark. To keep the young Canadians entertained, weekend trips to points of interest in the area were organized, and there was a program of extracurricular activities. Toward the end of the training period, which lasted all summer, the young women at Drew wrote and staged a review entitled "Dear Mom."

Over the Labor Day weekend the trainees, along with experienced employees being transferred on a permanent or temporary basis, were all transported to Toronto. On the morning of September 5 the Canadian Head Office opened for business. But the formal opening did not take place until three months later.

At a breakfast meeting of Canadian agents December 1, Shanks reported that in October, the latest month for which figures were available, the field force had doubled its previous record for sales in Canada. "That did not happen accidentally," he said. "What occurred here is the same as took place in the Western Home Office. First you fellows in the field raised your sights, then you helped the people you serve to raise theirs. As a result you are thinking bigger."

After the brief dedication ceremony later that morning, company officers, public officials, and others who attended went to a luncheon with leaders of the business community. There H. L. Enman, president of the Bank of Nova Scotia, described the move from Newark to Toronto as "staggering to the imagination," and added, "Whatever it is that Prudential has, it is most amazing to us the way they get things done."

Over the years that followed, the Prudential came to be viewed as a natural part of the Canadian economic environment. The Canadian operations were conducted almost as though they were a separate company. That could not be avoided, for the Pru in Canada did business in a nation shaped by different historical, economic, social, and cultural forces than those that determined the form and substance of the U.S. Contrary to the belief of many U.S. nationals, Canada is not "just like the U.S.," and Canadians are, in many ways, unlike their cousins across the border.

The historic association with Great Britain, for example, posed for Pru the dilemma of establishing a strong corporate identity in a country where it had been competing for years with another insurance company named Prudential. That company was the Prudential Assurance Company, the English pioneer in Industrial insurance which had served as a model to John Dryden nearly three quarters of a century before. The presence of the two Prudentials occasionally caused a certain amount of confusion, especially for the postal service, which sometimes sent mail to one company which had been intended for the other. Nevertheless, the U.S. company was able to assert its identity in the minds of most Canadians.

There was never a problem for the Prudential of America when it came to the economic nationalism of Canadians, for the company's investment policies did not offend Canadian sensibilities on that score. As the Toronto *Star* said in a headline in the early 1970's, "Prudential Plows Profits Back into Our Economy." All of the money collected from Canadian policyholders by the Pru was invested in Canada, as was a great deal of money paid in by U.S. policyholders. To be precise, at the end of 1974 the Pru had invested over $2 billion in Canada, of which $1.3 billion came from Canadians insured by the company, and $860 million from U.S. nationals. Moreover, the Pru's investments did not represent shares in the ownership of Canadian enterprises, generally speaking. The overwhelming bulk of the investments was in corporate and government bonds and in residential and farm mortgages. Only a few millions of dollars were invested in common stocks and in real estate.

From the first, the Pru had to cope, as everyone in Canada must, with the issue of bilingualism and biculturalism, for the nation, of course, has a dual heritage, British and French. One out of four Canadians speaks French as a mother tongue, and one out of five speaks no other language. But language is not the only difference between the Francophones—those who speak French—and the Anglophones. The whole fabric of law, customs, and outlook is a thing apart.

For example, in Québec, under a statute dating back to 1774, disputes involving civil matters and property are judged by the old French civil law, and not by the English common law which underlies civil litigation in English-speaking Canada.

Unlike most Western societies, Québec has retained a traditional society which was only beginning to change in the 1960's and 1970's. People tended to remain in the community where they grew up. This made for stability, but it caused problems for the Pru when the company wanted to promote and transfer people. One man in the city of Québec refused to transfer to Lévis, across the river, just five miles from his home, because he would be leaving the community in which he had not only lived but worked—refused even though he could have commuted from his home to Lévis easily. In October 1973 there were 30 such refusals of transfer on the desk of Jean Paul Labonté, Prudential's regional vice president for Québec.

Long before opposition to the use of English was felt strongly in Québec, the Pru acknowledged Francophone sentiments on that issue. In 1956 the company's letterheads, advertising, and other materials began featuring the French translation of its name: La Prudentielle d'Amérique, Compagnie d'Assurance. Policyholders were given the choice of conducting their business with the Pru in either French or English. By the 1970's, every Pru employee in Québec was a Francophone. This made communications within the company easier, too, because, of 485 agents in the Québec region, 410 spoke only French.

In 1968 some of the difficulties posed by Canada's dual heritage were vividly portrayed in an article in a company periodical, *Prudential People:*

>   If you speak English well and French poorly or vice versa, you hope, if you telephone a field or regional office [in Canada], that the person who answers your call knows both languages well.
>
>   "Perhaps I can avoid the issue," you might think. "If I call the Valleyfield office, surely everyone there speaks English well. After all, the name of the town is English. But the Verdun District? They must speak French most of the time."
>
>   So you call Valleyfield and ask to speak to Jean-Claude Cécyre. ("He's obviously French," you think, "but if he works in Valleyfield, he must speak English well.")
>
>   Jean-Claude does speak English, but he has some difficulty with normal (that is, rapid) conversation. He has little need to speak English, although he reads and writes it quite well, because 99 per cent of the people in his agency speak only French.
>
>   Jean-Claude's brother, Yvon, a District agent in the French-

named town of Verdun, speaks English with more ease. About half the people in the Verdun area speak only English, and Yvon, who learned conversational French in school, had plenty of opportunity to practice speaking it on the job. Quite naturally, he now speaks both languages like a native—a native of bilingual Canada.

Because there is so much material that must be translated between the two languages, the Canadian Head Office found it necessary to develop a Translation Service with a staff of 17 persons, who included not only persons born in Canada, but also natives of France, Finland, Egypt, Morocco, China, and Mauritius.

Those who know only standard French—that is, the French of literature and of Paris—find they must learn the peculiarities of the *Québecois* patois, for the language has developed differently, in some instances, in the New World. For example, the word *malle* means a "trunk" or a "large suitcase" in France; in Québec, it may mean "mail." To a Parisian, *un char* signifies "an armored tank"; to a Montréal resident, it's "an automobile." A used car is *une auto d'occasion* in France, but may be *un char usagé* in Québec (in that example, even the gender is different). A speech is *un discours* in standard French, but *une adresse* (again, a gender change) in the vernacular of Québec. Some of the departures of Canadian French from the standard tongue represent importations from English: a summer cottage may be *une maison de campagne* in the dictionaries, but it's more likely to be *un camp* in the Laurentian highlands.

If all this proves confusing to those with some knowledge of standard French, it does not compare with the difficulties faced by the Pru when much of the correspondence was turned over to computers, according to Mrs. Cecile Brooks, the head of the Translation Service, and Mrs. Marcelle Eisen, one of her translators. The trouble with the computers was that their programming, which was done by English-speaking people, made no allowances for accent marks—and in French, an accent mark can change the whole meaning of a word or a phrase. Here is an example:

Biscuits salés (note the accent over the *e*) means "salted crackers."
Biscuits sales (no accent) means "dirty crackers."

Bilingualism and biculturalism are important to the Pru because Québec is a major element in the company's Canadian operations. In 1973, more than 39 per cent of the new insurance sold, by face value, was credited to the Québec region. According to regional vice president Labonté, the Pru has sold more Group insurance in Québec than in all the rest of Canada.

One of the first agents recruited by the Prudential when it began doing business in Canada in 1909 was French-speaking Edmond Bourassa. In his first week with the company he earned about $25, which was considered a handsome income in those days.

"When I figured out what my business . . . was to bring me in commissions," he said after his retirement, "I became dizzy. My wife and parents insisted that I be very watchful and careful because, said they, 'It must be a company of thieves to pay so much money. Maybe they won't pay the death claims and you'll be responsible for them.' "

Life in Canada has changed a great deal since Bourassa's day, and so have the methods of its agents. Years ago, when the late Fred Smith was one of the leading Canadian agents, he used to travel on snowshoes as he made his calls at remote lumber and mining camps in northern Ontario. Today a number of agents ride snowmobiles on their rounds in winter.

In 1973 Viateur Carufel was a typical agent in Montréal. He was employed as a streetcar man when a friend who worked for Prudential suggested that he become an agent. That was in 1946. His debit, or territory, was an area ten blocks long and three blocks across in Rosemont, a working-class section at the east end of the island on which the city is situated. Carufel was close to his people; he lived in the territory covered by his debit. To his policyholders—400 of them, of whom he saw about 100 a month—Carufel was confidant, financial adviser, father confessor, comforter. He heard about deaths, of course, but also about births, school graduations, engagements, weddings—and he kept a record of it all. After all, the young couple getting engaged today would need to review their life insurance when they got married, n'est-ce pas?

On one occasion, when a policyholder was dying, Carufel accompanied the man's wife and his two daughters to a cemetery and helped them make arrangements for a lot. The two daughters were so impressed by his helpfulness that they bought more insurance from him.

Whenever possible, Carufel made sure that the people on his debit heard about actual incidents illustrating the benefits of life insurance, like the 32-year-old man who had paid in only $132 in premiums when he died of heat stroke in a Turkish bath, leaving his widow with a two-year-old baby—and $19,000 from the Pru. Carufel's favorite account concerned a fireman who took out a $29,000 insurance policy when he got married at the age of 24. Eighteen months later, after he had paid in $270 in premiums, he died of cancer. The fireman came from a family of 15, many of whom later bought insurance protection from Carufel.

"It is only service that counts," Carufel said. "If you don't give good service, you can't expect success in our business."

If that were true, the Prudential must have provided good service, for it enjoyed marked success in Canada as an increasingly autonomous operation. Over the years there were changes of both practices and personnel, of course. In 1953 Green reported to Shanks his regret at losing the services of Thomas Allsopp, who "had been among the first to join the Canadian Head Office organization and . . . played a most important part in building the organization and setting policies of organization from the very beginning." Allsopp had just been transferred to a new South Central Home Office at Jacksonville, Florida.

By 1957 the Prudential had moved into third place in life insurance sales in Canada and it was time to consider a permanent home for the Canadian Head Office. Green consulted with Shanks, there was some discreet examination of possible sites, and in June 1958 Green announced that the Pru would erect a new CHO building at King and Yonge Streets, in the heart of the financial district.

Before the construction was completed, Green retired. He would be missed. He had been accepted wholeheartedly as an adoptive son of the North, and with reason: soon after he moved to Toronto, he had begun using in his speeches the phrase "We of Canada," and there was no question that it fairly represented how he felt.

Green was succeeded by Howard A. Austin, who had been transferred to Canada in 1958. It was during Austin's administration at CHO, on February 2, 1961, that the new building, a 20-story structure, was dedicated by Louis R. Menagh, who had been president of the Pru for little more than a month.

A year and a half later Austin resigned because of ill health. His place

was taken by William Ingram, whose remarkable career had already
included service at four of Pru's Regional Home Offices, as well as the
Corporate Home Office in Newark—and after his tour of duty in
Toronto he would go on to still another Regional Home Office, giving
him experience in six of the nine.

During the 1960's Prudential was confronted with an unusual problem. The newspapers carried a report that an organization called the
Prudential Finance Company, in the first block of King Street East, had
been declared bankrupt. Many readers understandably confused the
foundering firm with the Prudential Insurance Company, which was in
the first block of King Street West. A few days later the public's
bewilderment was compounded when the courts turned the bankrupt
company over to the Metropolitan Trust Company and a newspaper
came out with the headline: "Metropolitan Takes Over Prudential." As
quickly as possible, Pru published advertisements straightening everything out for its policyholders and sales prospects.

Ingram made a significant contribution as head of the Canadian
Head Office by his persistence in persuading the Corporate Home
Office in Newark to change its accounting procedures so as to segregate
Canadian investments. Thus the Canadian operation was able to claim
the usually higher yield of its Canadian investments, rather than using
the lower yield on the overall company portfolio. As a result of this
change, the Canadian Head Office, working with senior management in
Newark, was able to find solutions to the many legal and actuarial
problems, so that Canadian policyholders would have their insurance
rates and dividends based on Canadian experience only—and that was
true of investment return, mortality, and expense rates.

In 1967 Floyd H. Bragg, who was then in the District Agencies
Department in Newark, made a telephone call to his wife.

"You'll never guess where we're going," he said.

"Canada," she shot back, with wifely omniscience.

Bragg was going to Toronto as successor to Ingram, who was being
moved to Chicago to head the Mid-America Home Office, where he
had been stationed a decade earlier. Soon after he settled into his new job
in Canada, Bragg, as a result of his initial observations, decided that the
time had come to carry "Canadianization" to its logical conclusion.
The current of nationalism was clearly running more strongly, and there
seemed little probability that it would slacken in the foreseeable future.

So a new policy was quietly formulated: no more transfers of U.S. nationals to Canada unless the transfer was essential to the welfare of the company. In addition, Bragg told those U.S. nationals who had been working in CHO that he would help any of them who might want to be repatriated. Raymond W. Cobb, who was setting up a new Central Atlantic Home Office at the time, took a number of persons who wanted to go back to the U.S. Soon there were only a few on the CHO staff who were not Canadians.

The process moved forward a short time after that when Donald S. MacNaughton, the Prudential's chief executive officer, accepted Bragg's proposal that CHO titles be upgraded. CHO's head now became "president, Canadian Operations." Some of the persons reporting to him were designated senior vice presidents, and there were several vice presidencies. CHO became "Head Office, Canadian Operations," with the intra-company code, "CDNO."

At the same time Bragg won the consent of senior management in Newark to his proposal to engage an outsider, a Canadian, to be the No. 2 man in the Canadian Head Office. Bragg knew whom he wanted for the spot: W. James D. Lewis, who had been with the Confederation Life Insurance Company, a Canadian organization, since 1949 and was then its vice president in charge of individual insurance. A World War II artillery captain in the Royal Canadian Army, Lewis had taken his bachelor's and master's degrees at the University of Toronto and was an actuary.

To observe the proprieties, Bragg asked the head of Confederation Life if he would object to Bragg's talking with Lewis about a move to the Pru. Lewis's boss said Bragg was welcome to discuss the proposal with Lewis, but he added that he had already chosen Lewis to be his successor. The man said that he would do his best to dissuade Lewis from the proposal.

In the end, Bragg's powers of persuasion proved superior, and Lewis joined the Prudential on September 1, 1971—the date on which CHO's titles were upgraded.

A year later, Bragg was transferred to Minneapolis and Lewis was promoted to president, Canadian Operations—the first Canadian to head the Pru's organization in that country. He was also head of the Prudential Growth Fund Limited, a mutual fund designed to be sold by Pru agents who were able to qualify under provincial licensing regulations. (Unlike a Prudential equity product marketed in the U.S., the Canadian effort was a pure mutual fund, without insurance features.)

During Bragg's tenure in Toronto, the Pru had begun publicizing "Great Moments in Canadian Sports," including paintings, broadcasts, community health-through-sports programs, and other activities. (One "Great Moment" starred Violetta Nesukaitis, a coding clerk in CDNO's Underwriting Division, who was an internationally recognized table tennis champion.) Pru's identification with Canadian national pride through the sports program further strengthened its bonds to the Canadian people.

As the Prudential's first hundred years approached their close, the company took a major step to express its faith in the Northern nation by investing $125 million of U.S. policyowners' funds in the bonds being used to finance the billion-dollar Churchill Falls hydroelectric project in Labrador. The power project was designed to produce 5.4 million kilowatts. "The Churchill Falls project is an excellent example of the role U.S. capital can play in Canada," said the Pru's board chairman, MacNaughton, in 1971. "It would not have been possible without outside help."

On another trip to Canada two years later, MacNaughton told an interviewer for the CBC—the Canadian Broadcasting Corporation —his philosophy of business. The first obligation of business, he said, is to "produce business services of quality that are wanted by the public at a reasonable cost." But that is not enough. Each company must go about its business in a "responsible way." In addition, it must "do all of the other things that any good citizen of a community has to do."

The CBC interviewer called it "the new philosophy of business—a far cry from the old 'profits come first' attitude."

To Canadians, who had been able to observe the Prudential since 1909—and especially since the Canadian Head Office was opened in 1950—the Pru had indeed established its credentials as "a good citizen" of the community. It was not born in Canada, to be sure, but it had, over the years, become a naturalized citizen of that great country of the North.

17 / A Ferment of Men

Leroy A. Lincoln, who became president of the Metropolitan in 1936, was widely, and justifiably, regarded as a wise and able executive. But he could be annoyingly tactless at times—at least in his relations with officers of the Prudential.

One day in the 1930's Alfred Hurrell, then general counsel of the Pru, was playing golf with his assistant, Carrol Shanks, at a country club in Montclair, New Jersey, when they encountered Lincoln, who was in a group playing another hole. Lincoln, who had first met Hurrell when they both worked for the New York State Insurance Department, called out to him, "I see you're playing golf with someone that even you can beat."

"That guy insults both of us in one sentence," the usually unflappable Hurrell muttered to Shanks.

About 1950, when both the Western and the Canadian regional offices were in operation, Shanks found himself seated next to Lincoln at a luncheon meeting of the presidents of life insurance companies. Bringing up the Pru's decentralization program, Lincoln said, "You know that we did that years ago."

Shanks acknowledged that the Met had, indeed, established regional offices on the West Coast and in Canada.

"We put an end to our regional office trend," Lincoln went on.

Shanks simply nodded his head and went on eating, but Lincoln persisted.

"I understand that you give your regional offices considerable responsibility—pretty much a free hand," Lincoln said.

Shanks said briefly, "Yes, we do."

"Carrol," said Lincoln, "I hate to say this, but if you don't change your approach to this, you people aren't going to get ahead at all. You've got to handle this sort of thing the way we do. Our people have to follow the book. That's the stand you're going to have to take."

155

By this time Shanks had had enough.

"Roy," he replied, "You're right about one thing—our men do have the authority to go ahead on their own. We trust them to make decisions for themselves.

"And let me tell you this, Roy: If you don't come around to our way of doing business, you won't be able to compete with us."

In effect, Shanks had thrown the gage of battle at Lincoln's feet. The latter's condescending advice had only strengthened Shanks's determination to press forward with his policy of decentralization. To be second—as the Pru then was—had been sufficiently galling to a man of Shanks's pride, but to be patronized, too—that was more than he could bear. So the announcements of additional Regional Home Offices (RHOs, as they have always been dubbed within the company) at regular intervals during that decade were like barrages fired at Lincoln and the Met: the Southwestern Home Office (SWHO), at Houston, in 1950; the Mid-America Home Office (MAHO), at Chicago, 1951; the South Central Home Office (SCHO), at Jacksonville, Florida, 1952; the North Central Home Office (NCHO), at Minneapolis, 1952; the Northeastern Home Office (NEHO), at Boston, 1957.

The opening of so many regional offices provided scores of Prudential people with the chance to show how they could handle responsibility and authority—opportunities they might have waited years for, or never enjoyed, in the old centralized structure. Men of ability were in a fever of anticipation, hoping that they might be chosen for a post in one of the RHOs, where they could show what they could do. As the young men went off to service in one region or another, the Pru discovered how much talent had lain hidden under the layers of bureaucracy in Newark. "It's amazing how we were able to staff the RHOs," Louis Menagh, who had been an early and continuing—but discreet—critic of decentralization, conceded many years later.

Shanks had no difficulty finding an officer to head the Southwestern Home Office. As soon as Charles Fleetwood, the head of the Pru's Mortgage Loan and Real Estate Investment Department, heard about plans for SWHO, he asked Shanks, "Have you got a man in mind for the new regional office?"

"No," the Prudential president replied, "I haven't."

"Well," Fleetwood said, "how about me?"

He got the assignment.

SCENE AT A PUBLIC SCHOOL:

TEACHER—"Where is the Rock of Gibraltar?'"
Bright Boy (who reads the papers): "In Newark, N. J.
It is owned by the Prudential Insurance Company."

—*Life, December 29, 1898*

"The Rock," introduced in advertisements in 1896, was already appearing in magazine cartoons two years later.

Company began in 1875 as Prudential Friendly Society in basement of National State Bank at 812 Broad Street in Newark.

By 1892, Pru overflowed this structure, its fourth Home Office, at Broad and Bank Streets; another building was being added (where scaffolding appears at right of photo).

Pru's second Home Office (1878–1883) at 215 Market Street.

This structure, at 880 Broad Street, housed Pru from 1883 until 1892.

A gargoyle, one of many that adorned Pru's Newark buildings.

One of many extravagant touches, this archway mural shows "Prudence Binding Fortune."

Stained glass art and leaded glass, as well as rich wood paneling and vast expanses of marble, were intended to suggest stability and permanence.

Stone lions outside Pru's Home Office guarded the opulent interior.

The old Board Room, a setting of rococo splendor for men who rubbed shoulders with magnificoes like J. P. Morgan.

In earlier, more modest days, this was the President's Office.

John F. Dryden, guiding spirit behind Pru's founding, in buggy with his wife, Cynthia.

Allen L. Bassett, the first president (1875–1879).

Noah F. Blanchard, the second president (1879–1881).

Although Dryden's inspiration set Pru on road to greatness, he was its secretary, not head, for first six years. Dryden was Pru's third president (1881–1911).

Forrest F. Dryden, fourth president (1912–1922).

Edward D. Duffield, fifth president (1922–1938).

Franklin D'Olier, sixth president (1938–1946).

Carrol Meteer Shanks, seventh president (1946–1961).

Louis R. Menagh, Jr., eighth president (1961–1962).

Orville E. Beal, ninth president (1962–1969).

Donald S. MacNaughton, tenth president (1969–1970); chairman of the board and chief executive officer (1970–   ).

Kenneth C. Foster, eleventh president and chief operating officer (1970–1973).

Robert A. Beck, twelfth president and chief operating officer (1973–   ).

The Executive Office consists of chairman MacNaughton, president Beck, and these three executive vice presidents (left to right): Duncan Macfarlan, marketing; Fredrick E. Rathgeber, administration; Frank J. Hoenemeyer, investments.

Present Corporate Office, built in 1960, soars above trees of nearby Military Park.

Prudential's division of U.S. and Canada into regions: WHO, Western; NCHO, North Central; SWHO, Southwestern; SCHO, South Central; MAHO, Mid-America; CAHO, Central Atlantic; EHO, Eastern; NEHO, Northeastern; CDNO, Canadian.

Northeastern Home Office in Boston within Prudential Center: high-rise apartments, office buildings, a hotel, a shopping mall.

Head Office, Canadian Operations, in Toronto's financial district, at Yonge Street and King Street West.

Western Home Office, on Wilshire Boulevard in Los Angeles, floats on La Brea Tar Pits, whose museum, housing remains of prehistoric animals, is just off photo's left side.

Newest of Regional Home Offices: Central Atlantic, outside Philadelphia on the Pennsylvania Turnpike.

Eastern Home Office, in South Plainfield, N.J., to be occupied in 1976, shown in architect's sketch.

North Central Home Office, at Minneapolis, was victim of Frank Lloyd Wright's biting tongue, but civic leaders and newspapers hailed it.

Southwestern Home Office, at Houston, sold to cancer foundation. New Home Office to be in nearby Bellaire.

Mid-America Home Office, at Chicago, seen from Michigan Avenue facing north.

South Central Home Office, at Jacksonville, converted New Jerseyans into Floridians. Other side building faces river.

Prudential Building looms in distance as horse cars move slowly down Broad Street in photo taken in 1890's.

In early days, Pru was owned by stockholders, some of whom, like Dryden, made huge profits, inspiring muckraking cartoons like this.

Prudential's first agency outside Newark was in this building in Paterson, N.J.

In old days, this drying room served women when it rained.

Legion of typists took over after machines were introduced late in 19th century.

Mail room, where many Prudential executives traditionally began careers.

To Division Managers

    and Department Heads:

Gentlemen:

    When ordering lead pencils in the future, please state on your supply requisitions whether they are intended for Male or Female clerks, as a special pencil has been prepared for the exclusive use of each.

    The Prudential Peerless pencils for Male clerks.

    The Prudential Paper pencils for Female clerks.

    The Supply department will honor requests for a small quantity of enclosed holder for short pencils which we would like to have thoroughly tested in your department and report made on same as to their value.

        Very truly yours,

Segregation of sexes applied to recreation rooms, dining halls, elevators and even to pencils, as memo from turn of the century shows.

Life was real, life was earnest for clerks working calculating machines.

Tired Executive Becomes Inventor Of "Thinking Machines" and Business Delays Become Spectres of Past

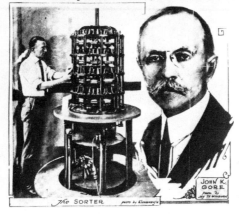

The SORTER

JOHN K. GORE

John K. Gore's work-saving inventions laid groundwork for later development of computers.

Prudential's ads over the years included "Prudential Girl" calendar pictures . . .

. . . The fleet steaming past Gibraltar . . .

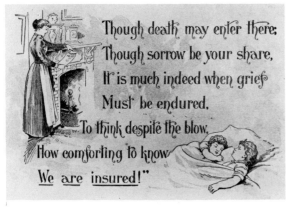

"Though death may enter there;
Though sorrow be your share,
It is much indeed when grief
Must be endured.
To think despite the blow,
How comforting to know
We are insured!"

. . . Grim reminders of human mortality . . .

. . . But always, "the Rock" remains, one of most widely recognized symbols in all business.

. . . Famed, hard-hitting television studies of modern history that provided basis for better understanding current events . . .

Protect all their tomorrows with Prudential life insurance. The same plan that makes your family's future secure can provide for your own retirement years. *See your Prudential Agent*

LIFE INSURANCE · ANNUITIES · SICKNESS & ACCIDENT PROTECTION · GROUP INSURANCE · GROUP PENSIONS

. . . Low-key messages designed to fit in with modern agents' professional approach to the underwriting of life insurance . . .

. . . Contemporary television comedy-drama in keeping with changing life styles . . .

Early promotional efforts were somewhat primitive, but effective.

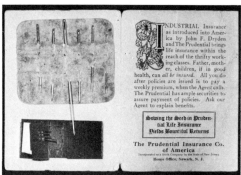

Pru chose to make pun on word "sew" when it distributed this promotional kit of needles.

"Hold fast to that which is good," superimposed on face of policy on calendar, was part of campaign to prevent policies from lapsing.

After World War II, Prudential advertised on TV programs like "Your Show of Shows," a 1950's favorite featuring Sid Caesar and Imogene Coca (shown here).

Jack Lemmon caused stir at Western Home Office during scene for award-winning movie, *The Apartment*.

In scene from another movie made at a Regional Home Office—this time, South Central —hideous Gill Man menaces Lori Nelson.

Family outings of Prudential employees association resulted in antics like this, on way to Asbury Park, where they swam and enjoyed boardwalk.

Employee beauty contests brought out entrants like this until feminist movement brought changes in 1970's.

Athletics included this employees' baseball team.

Runners, in sprint competition in 1920's, reflected the early stirring of a new attitude toward the role of women.

These swimmers posed during annual employees' outing at shore one year.

With a few employees, athletics became really important. Al Cicerone set records in AAU competition.

Board of Directors at the Time of Pru's Centennial

Orville E. Beal
Former President
The Prudential Insurance
Company of America

Robert A. Beck
President
The Prudential Insurance
Company of America

William T. Cahill
Counselor at Law—Partner
Cahill, McCarthy & Hicks

Fairleigh S. Dickinson, Jr.
Chairman of the Board
Becton, Dickinson & Co.

John E. L. Duquet, Q.C.
Canadian Advocate, Barrister
& Solicitor—Senior Partner
Duquet, MacKay, Weldon,
& Bronstetter

Margery S. Foster
Professor of Economics
Rutgers University

Burton G. Malkiel
Professor
Department of Economics,
Princeton University

James P. McFarland
Chairman of the Board and
Chief Executive Officer
General Mills, Inc.

Roger H. McGlynn
Counselor at Law—Partner
Lum, Biunno & Tompkins

Donald E. Procknow
President and Chief Execu-
tive Officer
Western Electric Co.

Robert M. Schaeberle
Chairman of the Board and
Chief Executive Officer
Nabisco, Inc.

Sydney G. Stevens
Former Chairman of the
Board
New Jersey National Bank

Some major figures in early days of Prudential (left to right): Edgar B. Ward, John K. Gore, Dr. Leslie D. Ward, Frederick L. Hoffman, Uzal H. McCarter, John F. Dryden. Men on Dryden's left (on right side of photo) played no significant role in Prudential affairs.

Harry S Truman, 33rd President of the United States, became Prudential policyholder in 1922, 23 years before he moved into White House. His policy application (right) was received three years after his 1919 wedding (above: Mr. & Mrs. Truman, who is at right, are surrounded by wedding guests). Special agent Rice Pendleton wrote that Truman had "a first class, well-stocked men's furnishings store." Acquainted with Truman for 10 years, Pendleton said he "is always smiling and seems to be in very good humor." On questionnaire, to query, "Do you intend changing your occupation?," Truman answered firmly, "No." Agent said of Truman's health, "He wears pretty strong glasses, but otherwise seems to be in the best condition." He was; he died fifty years later.

A native of Savannah, Georgia, Fleetwood had gone to the Georgia Institute of Technology, where he fitted his six foot one, 210-pound frame into a "Rambling Wreck" uniform as center on the football team. After graduating in the class of 1923 as a civil engineer, he went to work for a railroad, first as a draftsman and later in the field. "I was working with another civil engineer, a Cornell man, who had been all over the world and knew more about our profession than I could ever hope to learn," he once recalled, "but people weren't knocking doors down to hire engineers in those days. I found out that he wasn't making much more money than I. That was the point at which I decided that civil engineering was not for me."

As a result of that decision, Fleetwood went to work in the Atlanta mortgage loan office of the New York Life Insurance Company in 1925. Fleetwood traveled extensively throughout the South—for which his grandfather had fought during the War Between the States—doing business with his company's mortgage "correspondents," usually banks.

After his marriage Fleetwood was reluctant to continue devoting 80 per cent of his time to travel, so he accepted a position with a mortgage correspondent in Charlotte, North Carolina. There he produced and provided service on mortgages for a number of life insurance companies, including the Prudential. Early in the Depression Prudential began to set up a continent-wide network of mortgage loan branch offices, a harbinger of the company's later decentralization program. (Up to then Pru, like almost all other insurance companies, had been satisfied with the long-standing system of loan correspondents, a system which was still being used by many companies four decades later.) At that point Roger R. Rogers, the gruff Englishman who headed Pru's mortgage loan business, employed Fleetwood to handle "the two Carolinas and the two Virginias." His office was at Winston-Salem.

Fleetwood's success there led to a series of transfers to other offices: Kansas City, Philadelphia, northern New Jersey, and finally to the corporate Home Office in Newark. When Paul Bestor, who had succeeded Rogers as head of the Mortgage Loan and Real Estate Investment Department, retired in 1947, Fleetwood had been named to replace him. Three years later he volunteered to organize the new Southwestern Home Office.

As his principal aides, Fleetwood chose W. Jackson Letts, Thornton

W. Sterrett, Donald E. Bishop, and Robert W. Harvey. For Harvey, the Houston assignment was the key stage from which his career skyrocketed—until, near the very top of the company, it was destroyed in a tragic accident.

When he began searching for a suitable building site in Houston, Fleetwood took into his confidence two powerful men. One was former Governor William P. Hobby, president of the Houston *Post*, and a man with many other financial interests. Hobby's wife, Mrs. Oveta Culp Hobby, had been the first head of the Women's Auxiliary Army Corps (the WAACs) in World War II; from 1953 to 1955 she was a member of the Eisenhower Cabinet, as Secretary of Health, Education, and Welfare.

The other man was Jesse H. Jones, a Tennessean by birth who had moved to Texas and become one of the richest men in that state. Beginning in the lumber business, "he owned or came to own most of downtown Houston—hotels, a bank, a newspaper plant [the Houston *Chronicle*], a skyscraper, and other property," according to historian Edward Robb Ellis. Jones had been head of the Reconstruction Finance Corporation, a federal aid-to-business agency, during the Depression, and Secretary of Commerce from 1940 to 1945. His language was rough, his poker was deadly, and his dislike of Eastern financial institutions was unlimited. He welcomed the planned Southwestern Home Office as a new center of capital accumulation in the region.

Every day Fleetwood used to go to Jones's penthouse atop the Lamar Hotel for a drink with him. One day Jones said to Fleetwood, "I tell you what I'll do—I'll give you some land that I own right in the heart of downtown Houston."

When Jones pinpointed the property he was talking about, Fleetwood said, "I'll take it."

"Well," said Jones, twirling his glass of whiskey, "I'll *practically* give it to you."

In the end, Fleetwood purchased a 27.5-acre plot of woodland in Houston's South End, near the Shamrock Hotel, which had recently opened. The Texas Medical Center was also near the site, which was bounded on the north by Holcombe Boulevard, on the west by old Main Street Road, and on the south by Bray's Bayou. In fact, the medical center was so close that in 1974, when the University of Texas Cancer Foundation needed space adjacent to the center, Prudential agreed to sell its building and land to the foundation, making the property part of the medical center. Prudential then bought land at Bissonnett Avenue and Interstate Highway 610, in Bellaire, on which to build a new SWHO building. It was expected that the new SWHO structure would be completed and the old building vacated by Pru in 1977.

There were a number of features about the first SWHO building that attracted the attention of visitors. Of course it had many things to be found in other Regional Home Offices, including a lounge and a library for employees, a good-sized auditorium, a cafeteria, and a parking lot for employees' cars. But it also had a 75- by 42-foot swimming pool outdoors which could be lighted for night swimming. For art lovers, however, the highlight of the 18-story structure was a panoramic mural which covered 620 square feet in the rotunda. The mural was by the distinguished artist Peter Hurd—related to the Brandywine school of painting through his father-in-law, the celebrated N. C. Wyeth, although Hurd's subjects were primarily Western and his studio was at San Patricio, New Mexico. The Hurd mural, done in tempera over casein, was an interpretation of the slogan, "The Future Belongs to Those Who Prepare for It"—a Prudential slogan of somewhat nebulous origins. (One account has it that the company began pushing the slogan early in the second World War, fearing that a possible Nazi conquest of Gibraltar might turn its old slogan about the strength of the Rock into a sad joke.)

Fleetwood and his staff quickly won acceptance in the conservative but hustling business world of Houston. They loved Houston, and the feeling was reciprocated. In a typical outburst of civic booster sentiment, which was quite heartfelt, Fleetwood once said, "Here in East Texas we have everything for growth, prosperity, and human happiness. What more could anyone ask?"

Talk like that wasn't likely to make any enemies for Pru in Houston.

The Pru's impact on the economy, too, earned SWHO a permanent place of honor in the Southwest. Fleetwood had touched on this aspect of SWHO's operations in 1954, two years after the Houston office officially opened. In an article in a local periodical he wrote:

> Insurance money is mobile. For the good of our economy, it is essential that private capital be available for investment purposes in areas like Houston where rapid growth and development are taking

place. Frequently these areas do not generate adequate investment capital for their needs, and a transfer of funds from the older, more mature regions of the country should be made to meet their legitimate needs.

This function is accomplished by life insurance companies. One way to see the extent to which they have transferred funds is to compare their investments in different sections of the country with their policy reserve liabilities for these same areas. In the Middle Atlantic states [New York, New Jersey, and Pennsylvania], the companies have 69 cents invested for each dollar of policy reserve liability. In the west South Central region [Texas, Louisiana, Oklahoma, and Arkansas], investments run to nearly $3 for every dollar of policy reserve, and in Texas alone the ratio is a good deal higher.

These figures clearly demonstrate that life insurance companies do not siphon off policyholders' funds and concentrate them in the East or wherever their principal business office is located. Instead, these funds have been directed to those sections of the country where growth and development have created a need for capital to finance industry, businesses, homes, and farms.

Although Fleetwood's statistics were no longer valid 21 years later, the principle still held true: life insurance funds were mobile. Indeed, Fleetwood might have added that the Pru's decentralization had made the geographical spread of the company's investments far more meaningful.

In the spring of 1951—while the Southwestern Home Office building was being erected—the company announced that it would open another Regional Home Office in Chicago. There was some difficulty about a name for that operation because it was clear, even during the initial planning, that there would have to be at least two RHOs near the center of the U.S., and that some of the states usually lumped in the catch-all phrase "Middle Western" might have to be placed in SWHO or in another regional office that would cover the rest of the South. So the first name for the new operation was Chicago Insurance Office—a label which had the virtue, important in any large organization, of saying nothing at all while sounding impressive—the perfect ambiguity.

It had been the Pru's policy not to announce plans for a Regional Home Office until property had been acquired for the headquarters.

This made it less likely that the owners of possible sites would increase their prices, as they might well have done if they had known that a company with the Prudential's huge resources was the buyer. But finding suitable property in Chicago, in 1949—which was when the search began—proved unexpectedly troublesome.

The search was entrusted to Leo Sheridan, an independent real estate expert. Sheridan considered sites in Chicago's suburbs, in the Loop (the central business district), on North Michigan Avenue, on the outer Lake Shore Drive, and over the Illinois Central railroad tracks east of Michigan Avenue and north of Randolph Street, facing the northern end of Grant Park. Late in November 1949 Sheridan submitted a list of possible sites, but recommended the Illinois Central air rights as first choice.

A month later Shanks and several other senior officers of the Pru went to Chicago and visited each of the sites. The Illinois Central property was the last. They drove toward it up Michigan Avenue, bordering Grant Park. Several blocks away they could see a big beer outdoor billboard.

"I'm sold," said Shanks. After examining the site more closely, he said, "This is one of the most dramatic building sites in the country."

Not long before that, the Chicago *Tribune* had described the site as "probably one of the world's most valuable pieces of undeveloped city property." It had remained undeveloped, despite many attempts to devise building plans, because of the staggering legal and technical difficulties. As *Architectural Forum* said at the time the building was opened, "Not until a company with the resources of Prudential decided to build was anyone willing or able to go through the expensive process of acquiring title the hard way. This meant 18 months of negotiations. . . ."

The first documents involving the transaction—at the very beginning of the negotiations—were signed by Sheridan "on behalf of an undisclosed client." But the railroad soon became understandably concerned about whether the hidden buyer-to-be really was responsible and had the resources to carry through what was certain to be a monumental undertaking. It was mutually agreed that the identity of Sheridan's client would be disclosed in confidence to Federal Judge William J. Campbell, who was a personal friend of Wayne A. Johnston, president of the

Illinois Central, and Vernon Foster, the railroad's general counsel. Without disclosing the Pru's identity, the jurist assured his friends that they need feel no apprehension about the mysterious buyer's responsibility, resources, and reputation.

The principal negotiator on the part of the Prudential was James J. Brennan, who later served as the company's resident counsel in Chicago for nearly a quarter-century before accepting appointment as a judge. To the Illinois Central representatives, Brennan was known only as "Mr. Jim" until the deal was on the point of consummation. The negotiations were carried on in secret in an office that appeared from the outside to be unoccupied—suite 1307-A in the south section of the Insurance Exchange Building in Chicago. In a further effort to prevent accidental discovery, waste paper was collected and locked into a cabinet after each negotiating session. When the Prudential representatives traveled by train between Chicago and Newark, they never ate in the dining car together, and in Chicago they avoided being seen together in public places. "Never in the history of Chicago real estate," the *Tribune* said after the news finally broke, "has a major real estate deal been hedged about with such dramatic and successful secrecy."

"One of the greatest difficulties to be faced right from the start," Brennan said, "was the fact that the site had no adjoining streets—no method of ingress or egress at the air space level. At the various ground level elevations below the proposed building were located 21 suburban passenger and freight tracks of the Illinois Central and Michigan Central Railroads, [as well as] passenger platforms, which could not be eliminated; [and] a large freight house and a 15-story electric advertising sign, both of which would have to be torn down. Further, any proposed building would have to be erected over and adjoining the Randolph Street suburban station of the Illinois Central Railroad."

Another major problem was that the proposed building would have to be erected without undue interference with the operation of the railroad, with trains running as usual during construction.

There are several methods of transferring air rights. The path taken by the Pru and the Illinois Central involved "the conception and recording of the three-dimensional plat of subdivision," as Brennan explained it. In the deed to the property, reference was made by "individual lot number, not only for the air space conveyed [over the building site as a whole] but [also] for the areas in which caissons and columns for the support of the building were to be located.'' It was, in effect, as Brennan put it, a ''subdivision in the sky.''

''The principal objection to the subdivision method,'' Brennan said, ''is the fact that it is not . . . flexible. . . . Once the columns and foundations have been determined and their locations established and filed of record in the form of a subdivision plat, any changes in construction, even of several inches, may require an amended plat or a plat of re-subdivision to be made and recorded followed by supplemental deeds.''

An additional complication was that the railroad tracks, depressed below ground level, sloped upwards from south to north, and some of the tracks were curved and were at different levels, which made necessary the use of inclined rather than horizontal air-space planes bounding the various lots in the subdivision. Moreover, the lower level of the building had to be constructed at different elevations.

''The problem of air-rights construction above the Illinois Central tracks at the site in question was a peculiarly difficult one, and the city is indebted to the Prudential company for cracking this obstinate nut,'' wrote architectural expert Carl W. Condit in his 1974 study, *Chicago: 1930–70.* ''The difficulties arose from the need to define exactly the separate parcels of property at ground level for caissons and column footings and the space volumes below the basic air-rights plane needed to contain the lowermost columns, girders, and bracing elements, the parcels and volumes totaling 550 units.''

Many of the lots were so irregular in shape that there were no accepted scientific terms by which to label them, so Brennan spent many hours working with his wife, Catherine, drawing up descriptions of the geometric forms. When the final subdivision plat was filed in the Cook County Recorder's office, officials there said that the document, measuring three feet by twenty feet, was the largest ever filed there. It was certainly the most complicated.

When it was clear that the Pru would be able to reach agreement with the Illinois Central on the site, the name for the new center also emerged. The railroad, not long before, had published a book entitled *The Mainline of Mid-America,* so the Prudential people in Chicago suggested that the new operation be called the Mid-America Home Office (or MAHO for short, since the Pru is as addicted as the federal government to alphabetical contractions). The ubiquitous Admiral

Eubank liked the name, but the more conservative senior officers in Newark almost unanimously rejected it—until Eubank discussed the matter with Shanks, who proceeded to open the next Newark meeting on the Chicago project by saying, "The new name for this operation is Mid-America. Are there any questions, gentlemen?"

When Carrol Shanks, at a press conference on March 1, 1951, broke the Pru's 18-month silence to announce the establishment of MAHO, it was front-page news in the Chicago newspapers. As the *Sun-Times* pointed out, it would be "the first Chicago skyscraper to be built since the Field Building was put up at LaSalle, Clark, and Adams [Streets] 17 years ago."

At a dinner that evening in the Palmer House, Governor Adlai E. Stevenson—later to be an unsuccessful two-time Democratic candidate for President and then, in the 1960's, U.S. Ambassador to the United Nations—was the principal speaker.

"I am convinced," he began, tongue in cheek, "that our civilization has made at least some progress in 50 years. A Democrat can now rub shoulders with economic giants and not be accused of backsliding. I don't think that William Jennings Bryan could have gotten away with that."

Then he gave his blessing to the Prudential's program of decentralization:

"In another day—in the William Jennings Bryan day—finance and big business concentrated in the East. We see a healthy tendency toward decentralization of this economic power to serve the other great regions of our country in their own front yard. I cannot help but be enthusiastic about reasonable decentralization of big business just as I have so earnestly advocated local responsibility in my own field—that of government."

Ground was broken for the building on August 12, 1952, but construction took much more time than the Pru had to spend on its other buildings. The slow pace in the early stages reflected the necessity of interfering with the railroad's trains as little as possible. For example, each of the cylindrical caissons, varying in diameter from four to fourteen feet, had to be dug by hand, because heavy machinery could not be moved in. Each caisson was dug down to bedrock, about 100 feet below grade.

While construction was going forward, MAHO set up shop in a

building at 165 North Canal Street. "We froze there in winter and roasted in summer," George E. Beyer later recalled. His biggest disappointment, however, was the apartment the company had rented for him. Although it was on a street with "Lake" in its name—which led him to think that he would be living near the shore of Lake Michigan—the apartment was miles from the nearest body of water. But Beyer and the others didn't mind the inconveniences. "Everyone pitched in," he said. "It was really fun. Even the management people were in overalls at times."

Helen Warms recalled that the people from Newark "banded together" for a while. They felt like Easterners, outsiders. But then time and the friendliness of Midwesterners worked its way, and they felt themselves a part of Chicago. In a way, Mrs. Warms's life was bound up in the MAHO building. An underwriting approver, she was in charge of hostesses for the building's dedication, which took place December 8, 1955. A few days later, she got married. Her husband, Robert, also worked for the Prudential.

Incidentally, those who attended the dedication were given paperweights made of oak. An inscription on the paperweight said the wood "was part of the trestle erected in 1853 by the Illinois Central Railroad." The wood had "lain buried since the Great Chicago Fire of 1871" but "was unearthed in constructing" the MAHO building.

Most of those who were transferred to Chicago were happy with their assignment. But there were exceptions, of course. The classic story—a true account—is of a couple who were sent from Newark to the Western Home Office at Los Angeles. They didn't like Los Angeles, they decided, so they put in an application for transfer. Before long, they were sent to MAHO, at Chicago. After a few days in Chicago, they agreed that they'd never be happy there, so they returned to Los Angeles—before their furniture had even arrived in Chicago.

Morale was always high at MAHO, and credit for it was usually given primarily to the man who headed the office then, and for nearly a decade following—James E. Rutherford, one of the most widely known figures in the life insurance industry. He was also a rarity among Prudential executives, having been brought in from outside.

Born and raised on a farm in Arkansas, Rutherford sold real estate by day in order to pay for his law school classes at night. A University of Arkansas student who graduated at the head of his class, he was offered a job in a law office at $200 a month—less than he was making as a real estate salesman. So Rutherford continued working in real estate until that business fell apart at the end of 1930, during the early days of the Depression.

At that point a friend who was an agent for Penn Mutual suggested that Rutherford join his agency. Beginning in February 1931, Rutherford succeeded brilliantly as an insurance salesman, supervisor, and general agent. After several years he was transferred from Little Rock to Des Moines and later to Seattle. He left that city in 1942 to become the first executive vice president of the National Association of Life Underwriters (NALU), with headquarters in New York City at that time.

In January 1949 Rutherford received a telephone call from Carrol Shanks, inviting him to Newark for a chat. Rutherford found that Orville Beal, then head of the District Agencies Department and ultimately president of the Pru (during the 1960's), had pressed Shanks to bring the NALU executive into the Prudential organization. Before long, Rutherford was working as Beal's assistant in the District Agencies Department—although all of Rutherford's experience had been in Ordinary Agencies Field. But Rutherford was strongly people-oriented, and he could do his bit wherever he happened to be.

Rutherford had been with the Pru for only four years when he was named head of the Mid-America Home Office. An energetic outgoing man, he put his stamp on MAHO. It was characteristic of his management style that group tours of the building—which were frequent because of the interest in Chicago's first new office building in nearly two decades—always went through his own office, by his orders.

"Call me Jim," he told everyone he met. "I don't like to be called Mister. Jim is the name—call me Jim."

Soon almost everybody in Chicago, it seemed, was calling him Jim. He was involved in every sort of civic activity, and so were the men who served under him, including such leaders as Charles B. Laing, Raymond Cobb, and William Ingram.

Milburn P. Akers, an editor of the Chicago *Sun-Times,* apparently expressed the sentiments of a great many people when he wrote in his column one day:

> Men such as Rutherford get to the top. But they never forget those at the bottom. So they give of themselves in great measure to make their communities better.

Chicago is a better community because Rutherford lived and worked here.

For Chicago—as for Los Angeles and Houston earlier—the construction of a Regional Home Office by the Prudential had a galvanizing effect on the local economy. As architectural critic Carl W. Condit wrote in his book on Chicago's urban development, "Construction in the central business district [had lain] dormant [until] it was suddenly and finally shaken out of its slumbers by the erection of the Prudential Insurance Company's headquarters in 1952–55. . . . Although it is an emasculated variation on the skyscraper verticalism of the late Twenties, the Prudential served two valuable functions: it demonstrated the willingness of a major corporation to invest a large sum of money in its Chicago facilities, and it reminded the building and real estate interests that if any substantial demand for space appeared, there was nothing of prime quality available beyond 5,000 square feet. Moreover, the construction of the Prudential came shortly after a drastic revision of the Chicago building code in 1950 which substituted performance standards for the traditional specification of materials. It was a model for the entire country, and it eventually proved to be a potent stimulus to new construction. The revival of building in the Loop followed quickly after the Prudential's completion."

Before another decade was done, the Pru's MAHO was dwarfed by many taller and more imposing structures, up and down Michigan Avenue and throughout the Loop, but MAHO's construction had provided the lift that Chicago needed to begin its resourceful and daring postwar rebuilding.

And nothing could obscure the sight from Grant Park and the lake front of the Prudential name atop the building, visible for miles.

18/Of Sand and Snow

Besides Mid-America, two other Regional Home Offices—South Central and North Central—were opened in 1955. Inevitably, the competition for people to staff them was intense among the men designated to set up the new operations: James E. Rutherford, Charles W. Campbell, and Orville E. Beal. In fact, so many good men and women were siphoned off from the Corporate Home Office for the new ventures that the efficiency of operations in Newark—and throughout New England and the Middle Atlantic states—was jeopardized until the return of some Pru people to Newark.

During that time when the three senior men were vying for staff personnel, Campbell is reported to have said about Beal, "That baby-faced, blue-eyed so-and-so could steal the pennies off the eyes of a dead man."

There was some merit in the complaint. Beal's soft-spoken, gentle manner and his obvious and real concern for people at all levels, combined with a simple warmth of spirit that conveyed itself instantly, even to large audiences, misled many persons into believing that he could not be as demanding and as stern as circumstances might warrant. Nevertheless, Campbell's facetious comment came from a man who was, at the very least, Beal's equal in snaring promising young men for his own enterprise.

In its first two or three years Campbell's South Central Home Office (SCHO) had in its complement such men as Robert A. Beck, who rose to be president of the Pru; Duncan Macfarlan, who became an executive vice president; and Thomas Allsopp, John D. Buchanan, Jr., Donald R. Knab, Jack T. Kvernland, William P. Lynch, E. William Nash, Jr., and Clifford Whitcomb, all senior vice presidents 20 years later.

During the same period, Beal's North Central Home Office (NCHO) was staffed by a strong group that included Beal himself, of course (he ultimately became president and chief executive officer); Howard A.

Austin, Jr., Raymond W. Cobb, Harold E. Dow, Jack T. Kvernland (who was transferred there from SCHO in 1957), and Kenneth C. Nichols, all of whom subsequently became senior vice presidents; Donald S. Fuerth, vice president and associate general counsel; and such men as Henry E. Arnsdorf, under whom Pru's famous "Own a Piece of the Rock" promotional campaign was developed after he became vice president in charge of public relations and advertising at the Corporate Office in Newark in later years.

Campbell had a brief and insignificant head start on Beal: the announcement of what was then called the Southern Home Office was made on July 9, 1952, three months and seven days before the plans for NCHO were made public; but the Minneapolis operation was dedicated on June 21, 1955, only one month and fourteen days after the Jacksonville headquarters (which by that time was designated South Central in deference to the sensitivities of Ohio, which had been added to the region). Although the Mid-America Home Office had been announced a year and a half before SCHO, its building was dedicated six months after NCHO's edifice, construction having been handicapped by the difficulties in building over a continuing railroad operation.

The choice of a headquarters city for SCHO proved to be unexpectedly troublesome. Among Prudential officers, there was considerable sentiment for Atlanta, which was already on its way to a place of honor as one of the most progressive cities in the U.S. Charlotte, North Carolina, also had a number of advocates. But president Carrol Shanks's peripatetic assistant, Admiral Eubank, preferred Birmingham, which soon came to believe that it was certain to be the site.

Then Charlie Campbell entered the picture.

Only a couple of months previously, in June 1951, he had been elected a vice president of the Pru, but he had been recognized for several years as the company's peerless sales tactician. When he took over the Jacksonville Ordinary Agency in 1930, it was the smallest agency in the Pru; in 1941, it led the entire company in sales, and it covered all of Florida and a corner of Georgia. After Army service in the second World War, Campbell had been asked to take over the faltering Newark Ordinary Agency. Although surrendering the Jacksonville agency entailed a financial loss, Campbell accepted the new assignment. At that time, the Newark agency was writing $6 million of new business a year; Campbell set his goal, to be reached in 10 years, at

$25 million in new sales a year—and he and his agents exceeded that goal within five years. For five of his six years in Newark's Ordinary agency, his men won the President's Trophy, given to the company's outstanding agency (the only year they lost, the trophy went to an agency headed by a man Campbell had recruited).

A native of Alabama, Campbell was the grandson of a banker who had helped to raise the money with which Booker T. Washington started Tuskegee Institute in 1881 for the education of blacks. Campbell's heart always belonged to the South and, during the years in Newark, he had maintained a house at Atlantic Beach near Jacksonville. The house was damaged in a storm, but the Internal Revenue Service questioned Campbell's repairs to the property, so, late in 1951, he went to Jacksonville to settle the matter on the spot.

While he was there, visiting his old friends, he told them that the city should be making an effort to persuade the Pru to build its proposed regional office there. With Campbell's assistance, Jacksonville civic leaders prepared an impressive presentation of the merits of their city. At Campbell's urging, president Shanks, Admiral Eubank, and Valentine Howell, who had been elected an executive vice president in 1950, visited the Florida city. What they saw and heard made them realize that they might have been overlooking a site that was ideal for their purposes.

At that point, Louis Menagh, the company's influential vice president and comptroller, took a personal look at the proposed building site at Birmingham. As he walked around the property, he stepped into a deep hole, skinning his knee. Then his guide mentioned casually, "There are mines all over under here."

That did it. Menagh argued against Birmingham when he got back to Newark, and the other senior officers were ready to accept Jacksonville.

On July 9, 1952, the company announced that it was planning to build its South Central Home Office on land on the south side of the St. Johns River in Jacksonville, 15 miles upriver from the Atlantic Ocean. The site, between the Acosta Bridge and "the new Gilmore Street Bridge Expressway," the newspaper accounts said, included 1,100 feet along the river, where a promenade would be built. Less than eight of the property's 19 acres would be covered by the 22-story building; more than 11 acres would be landscaped to maintain the parklike openness of the Florida environment.

Seven months to the day after that announcement, Campbell was chosen to head SCHO. As his principal assistant he was given E. S. (Jack) Allsopp, a cousin of Thomas Allsopp. Jack was a real estate specialist, having started in that field in 1925 at the height of the Florida land boom. Four years later, still in Florida, he had joined the Pru's mortgage loan operations. When the company opened at Lakeland, Florida, the first insurance company office to handle mortgage loan delinquencies and foreclosed properties—that was early in the Depression—he was named manager. Later he had directed similar offices in Boston and Newark before being called into the Corporate Home Office.

While construction of the new building was still under way, the site was used as the setting for a number of scenes for a movie. Later two other films would use Prudential offices: 1960's *The Apartment*—a Billy Wilder work that starred Jack Lemmon, Shirley MacLaine, and Fred MacMurray as employees of "the Consolidated Life Insurance Company of New York"—was filmed in part at Pru's Western Home Office, a fact of which Pru's Angelenos were inordinately proud, despite the movie's bitterly cynical view of venality and morality in the business world. In 1968 *The Thomas Crown Affair*—in which Steve McQueen was a bank robber and Faye Dunaway played an insurance company investigator—made use of the Northeastern Home Office's Prudential Center complex in Boston.

The movie made at SCHO was entitled *The Revenge of the Creature*, starring John Agar and Lori Nelson. She played the unlikely part of an ichthyologist for whom a creature called "the gill man" developed a mad passion. A number of Pru employees worked as extras during the filming, some of which took place along the river bank near the cafeteria (later the cafeteria was moved into the main building and the separate building in which it had been operated was turned into a public restaurant).

At one point during the filming, which attracted crowds of curious onlookers, the actor who was playing the part of "the gill man" was being swept away by the current in the St. Johns River when one of the extras, John W. Johnston, swam to his side and pulled him to safety.

Another of the Pru extras, Robert L. Pettit, told a newspaper reporter, "Florida has made me nationally prominent."

Most of the Pru people who had been transferred from Newark to

Florida were equally happy; for them the joy was in the sun, the warmth, and the sand—although they didn't find what they expected when they first arrived in Jacksonville. When news of the SCHO establishment first broke, the number of Newark employees who volunteered for transfers was double the number of openings. In the end, 180 employees and their families—about 500 persons in all—were moved from New Jersey to Florida. At the same time, 237 young women and 33 young men who had been hired in Florida and sent North for training returned to their home city.

The special trains left Newark just at the beginning of the Labor Day weekend in 1953, when the temperature on Broad Street was 107 degrees. When they arrived in Jacksonville, the thermometer indicated only 88 degrees—and it was raining. For six weeks the rains continued. "Everybody kept telling us it was most unusual weather," one of that first group recalled many years later, reminiscing with other members of SCHO's large and active association of retired employees. "They said it was unusual, but the rain kept coming down."

But the rains stopped one day, the sun came out, and the New Jersey people settled down to become Floridians. Less than two years later a Newark newspaper sent a reporter down to Jacksonville to see how the transplanted Northerners were making out. Of the 180 families, he wrote:

"At first it was hard to leave their homes. Most of them took about three months [to get used to Florida]. Then they got 'sand in their shoes' and nobody interviewed wants to go home to New Jersey except one wife."

The headline over the long article: "Jacksonville Gains Strongest Boosters in Prudential Folks from New Jersey."

Jacksonville had won the devotion of the Pru people in spite of the inconveniences that afflicted them at first. During construction of the SCHO building, for example, employees worked in space rented in three buildings. "All three were well below Prudential standards," one SCHO pioneer, Albion U. Jenkins, Jr., recalled years later when he was a vice president at the Western Home Office. "In one of the buildings, if a 100-pound girl walked across the floor above, the ceiling would move. The buildings should have been torn down." Soon after SCHO's completion, all three buildings were demolished.

One building which, like the others, was not air-conditioned, despite Jacksonville's heat in summer, was near the tracks of a railroad that used coal. "We could keep the windows closed, and be hot, sweaty, but relatively clean," Jenkins said, "or open the windows and be a little cooler but covered with soot."

Nevertheless, to Jenkins and all the rest, "It was the kind of experience sufficiently far out to challenge the imagination of people." Most of the newcomers felt, as one of them said later, that they "were in on the ground floor." The sense of building something new and different, of taking part in the creation of a new enterprise, stimulated everyone. Throughout the company, the setting up of so many new Regional Home Offices had created a heady atmosphere that made those of an adventurous turn of mind eager to share in such a novel experience.

Typically, when Campbell had approached Maurice F. (Terry) Terbrueggen, manager of the District agency in Flushing, Long Island, saying, "How would you like to go to . . . ," Terbrueggen had interrupted him to say, "I'll go," before he knew that Campbell was recruiting him for SCHO.

Before the 1950's were over, Campbell was famous throughout the company for the high-powered marketing group he had assembled at Jacksonville. Frank J. Brennan, who rose to vice president at SCHO and was transferred to the Central Atlantic Home Office years later, was as representative as anyone could be of that disparate crew whose common characteristics were strength in sales management, driving ambition, well-nigh inexhaustible energy, and the extraordinarily high *esprit de corps* which Campbell had always been able to inspire in those he had singled out as having great potential for development. Brennan had been born and raised in New York, and the sound of Manhattan's streets never quite left his voice, although a quarter-century in the South overlaid it with an odd, rasping drawl.

The son of Irish immigrants, he had grown up in poverty; his father, who worked on the docks, was disabled by pleurisy, so his mother supported the family by working for the Metropolitan Life Insurance Company as a cleaning woman. Her son, too, worked for the Met briefly before World War II, "in the commissary and then screwing in light bulbs." After serving in the South Pacific during the war, he married Mildred Dupree, a North Carolina girl he had met during his

Marine training there, and settled down in Kinston, North Carolina (1970 population: 22,309). Brennan worked at a number of different jobs, most of them selling, before becoming a Prudential agent in 1949.

Brennan's decision to join the Pru must have come as a shock to his mother, who was piously loyal to the Met. "God bless Mother Met," she often said. In the early 1960's, when Brennan told her that the Pru was about to overtake the Met to become No. 1 in the insurance industry, his mother replied, "They wouldn't dare!"

Two years after becoming a Prudential Ordinary agent, Brennan qualified for the Million Dollar Round Table, an industry organization organized to lift the standards of agents and provide a forum in which they could exchange information on successful underwriting. Brennan kept selling more than enough to qualify every year after that; in time he was designated a life member. In later years Brennan was the only Pru executive who was both an MDRT life member and a Chartered Life Underwriter (CLU), the latter being the industry's highest professional designation in the marketing area.

In 1956 Brennan was enthusiastically applauded when he gave a talk in Washington, D.C., on opportunities in selling life insurance. Although he was a Catholic, Brennan's delivery of that kind of speech often had more of the fervor of a revivalist preacher, a technique extraordinarily effective in an industry whose salesmen must constantly fight internal battles against self-doubt and fear of rejection. In Brennan's Washington audience were William Lynch, who was then sales vice president of SCHO, and Duncan Macfarlan, who was executive director of agencies. Impressed by Brennan's personal record of achievement in sales, as well as by the leadership ability he had demonstrated in his speech, they called Brennan to Jacksonville to ask him to become manager of the Pru agency in Akron, Ohio. Brennan agreed to the assignment, and within a year his agency was one of the best in the country, winner of the President's Citation. The following year Brennan was transferred to SCHO in Jacksonville as director of agencies.

There Brennan worked closely with Robert Beck, who was also a director of agencies, and with their superior, Duncan Macfarlan, whose title was executive director of agencies (later the title "vice president, sales," was instituted for that rank). All three had to travel a good deal—so much that Brennan's mother told him she regularly lit a "big" votive candle for them because they were "flying all around." She said,

"I'll sure be glad when you all get steady jobs." At least Brennan said she'd said that, and who was to challenge the Hibernian tendency to make a good story better?

Working in a highly charged atmosphere, under a leader like Campbell who set high standards and accepted nothing but the best performance from his subordinates, pressures sometimes built up, of course; but Macfarlan, Beck, and Brennan managed to find constructive outlets for it—like a "cuss box" that once had $56 in it during a particularly trying time.

There was a good deal of camaraderie, too, among the three. They served as godparents for each other's children and they had an agreement that if one of them should die, the others would help the widow to settle his affairs.

Nevertheless, they were three wholly different varieties of men: Beck, self-contained, smooth, sweeping everyone along with his air of confidence; Macfarlan, gregarious, outgoing, fun-loving; Brennan, boisterous, loving the telling of good yarns in convivial company, eternally optimistic.

When SCHO was preparing to celebrate its dramatic leap from last place in production among the Regional Home Offices to first place, Beck wanted the place festooned with balloons, but Brennan thought they should have a spectacular display suggestive of star bursts.

"Damn it, we've got to have more dignity!" Macfarlan roared, as Brennan recalled it.

Of course, relationships like that among Beck, Macfarlan, and Brennan sprang up in every Regional Home Office—and in the Corporate Home Office in Newark, too, for that matter—but the great unifying factor in Jacksonville was the exhilaration of working for Charlie Campbell, "the Great Expecter," as many called him, because he expected the utmost from his people.

A great organizer and planner—a "management technician," as one of his successful "alumni" put it—Campbell did not have obvious leadership abilities. For example, he seemed remote to most of the clerical workers under him. Moreover, he was not the kind of speaker who sparks fire in an audience. But obvious or hidden, there was a high degree of leadership ability in Campbell, along with an uncanny faculty for detecting similar potentialities in others, often when those talents were apparent to no one else.

One day Campbell, Lynch, Beck, and Macfarlan were discussing a man under consideration for appointment as manager of an agency. Beck argued against the proposal, pointing out that the man's handicaps included an inability to deliver a speech effectively.

"How would you judge me on my speech presentation, Bob?" Campbell asked quietly.

The answer was clear, and so was the moral: if Campbell could be a strong and effective leader although he was a poor public speaker, so could the man under consideration.

Campbell "could recognize and develop ability in people of diverse types," C. Speed Veal, who worked for him for many years before becoming director of advertising and publications at the Corporate Home Office, told the Jacksonville *Times-Union and Journal* in 1968, when the newspaper was preparing a Sunday magazine cover story on Campbell. "Many executives have fixed ideas of the people they want but he hired many diverse types, for he recognized that the world is made up of many kinds of people."

The results of Campbell's knack for finding and developing talent were reported by the newspaper at that time, three years after his retirement: "A total of 40 men who were associated with him . . . have achieved the rank of manager or higher with Prudential. Ten of those associated with him . . . here have been promoted to vice presidents in the Corporate or other Regional Home Offices of Prudential. These include the top two men in . . . Boston [NEHO] . . . and the top three at Houston."

A half dozen years later, two of the five members of the company's highest management group—the Executive Office—were "Charlie Campbell's boys" (they were Beck, then president, and Macfarlan, executive vice president).

Of his legendary record of developing first-rate men, Campbell once said, "A man must be unselfish or else recognize that the best way to achieve a selfish objective is through unselfish means. Promotions create a vacuum, which is the strongest means of induction [that is, of drawing in new people of high potential]. One shouldn't stand in a man's way of promotion just to avoid losing a good man."

The fruits of Campbell's philosophy were manifest soon after the opening of SCHO on May 7, 1955—when the entire state of Florida, or so it seemed, turned out to celebrate the dedication of what was widely hailed as the tallest building in the state. Within five years sales in the ten-state region had tripled.

There was another effect, as the Jacksonville *Journal* pointed out in 1958:

> [During the previous year alone,] 107 meetings of local civic groups were held in the Prudential auditorium, with more than 28,000 people in attendance. Company employees are in service clubs, on the boards of charitable institutions, on volunteer fire departments, Boy Scout troops, Little League baseball, and many other worthwhile activities.
>
> Prudential has become a part of all phases of community life in the Jacksonville area.

In his emphasis on personnel development and on community service, Campbell was like Orville E. Beal, who was setting up the North Central Home Office at the same time that Campbell was founding SCHO. Otherwise, the two men were totally dissimilar, even in their origins.

Beal was born on March 11, 1909, in Monvue, Pennsylvania, a settlement so small that it does not appear on most maps. It is in Fayette County in the southwest corner of the state, close to the West Virginia border and about 50 miles south of Pittsburgh along the Monongahela River. He was the third of 12 children. His mother died when he was nine.

His father—to whom he was very close—was a Prudential agent. "He hated detail work, paper work," Beal said, "so from the time I was 13 I handled all of his account work for him, all through my high school years. In those days there were very few restrictions on driving a car, so when I was about 15 I began to drive the old Ford. My father never learned to drive a car so I drove him around his debit [sales and collection territory] holidays and summers, evenings and Saturdays, and so on. I took all his weekly accounts for him and balanced them and made the entries in his life registers. I attended staff meetings with him on Saturday mornings—that's when they were held in Uniontown—and so I got to know quite a little about the insurance business from his end even before I finished high school."

When he graduated from high school, Beal had no money to pay for college, so he took a job in the coal mines at nearby Nemacolin at 40 cents an hour. After three or four months, Beal left the mines for good, certain that he did not want to be a miner. The only other work with which he had any experience was insurance, which he liked, so he obtained a letter of introduction from his father's District manager in Uniontown and set off for the Pru's Home Office in Newark, where he got a job as a clerk. That was in 1926.

During the years that followed, Beal gradually rose through the ranks while attending Rutgers University at night. He earned his B.A. that way in 1937 and his M.B.A. in 1954, and was elected to Phi Beta Kappa, the honor fraternity. In 1964, when he was president of the Pru, Beal told a graduating class at the College of Insurance in New York City, "I know from personal experience what it means to work during the day and attend classes at night. I know what it means to squeeze reading assignments into all of the nooks and crannies of a crowded week—to read on buses—at lunch time—at recess periods—late at night and early in the morning. I know what it means to say 'No,' time after time, to party invitations—to give up weekends—to study on vacations—to struggle to stay awake in the classroom—to wonder whether all of this is worthwhile as you see other young people cruising along on their merry way."

In 1945 Beal was elected a vice president and two years later he was made head of the District Agencies Department. On February 10, 1953, when Carrol Shanks announced that Beal would be in charge of the new North Central Home Office (NCHO), Beal was head of public relations, advertising, and coordination of the Regional Home Offices with the Corporate Office.

From the beginning Beal was confronted with a major problem not of his making: a good many Minneapolis residents were angry at the Pru because it had chosen a site that was part of Minneapolis's treasured parklands. According to Marlin N. (Cap) Toussaint, NCHO's real estate investment specialist 20 years later, the site was initially chosen by Admiral Eubank and E. S. (Jack) Allsopp, although John Hibbard, who then handled real estate investments in the Twin Cities for the Pru, may have suggested it to them.

It is still all too easy to understand why other senior officers, coming out to look at the site proposed by Eubank and Allsopp, were taken with it. It was on a hilltop beside Wayzata Boulevard, an expressway that carries traffic straight west from downtown Minneapolis. The prop-

erty, consisting of 32 acres, only two of which would be occupied by the
NCHO building, lay between Brownie Lake in Theodore Wirth Park
and France Avenue South, which at that point is the city's boundary
with the western suburbs of Golden Valley and St. Louis Park. Because
that part of Wirth Park was separated from the rest of the sprawling park
by the expressway, it was used only as an archery range—although,
simply by existing as open space, it contributed to that atmosphere of
spaciousness and freedom that characterizes Minneapolis more than any
other large U.S. city.

On October 16, 1952, after several weeks of quiet negotiations
between the Pru and the Park Board, Shanks with his entourage attended
a Park Board meeting at which it had been planned that the project
would be announced. But the proposal ran into a snag: a two-thirds
majority (that is, 10 members) of the Park Board was needed to approve
the agreement, but only nine were ready to vote for it that day. Two or
three others said they favored it, but wanted more time to think it over.

The next day the mayor of St. Paul, on the other side of the Missis-
sippi River, invited Prudential's officers to take a look at possible sites
in his city, and they accepted the invitation. As they viewed property in
the company of St. Paul officials, the Prudential men were conscious of
the welcoming editorials appearing in that day's issues of the Minneapolis *Morning Tribune* and the Minneapolis *Star*. The *Tribune*
called the Pru's desire to build in Minneapolis "a harbinger of the
'golden era' ahead for the Upper Midwest." The *Star*'s editorial,
sounding a similar note, was headlined: "A Clear, Convincing Sign of
Better Years to Come."

Most city officials and business leaders were similarly eager to have
the Pru settle in their community, but there were many citizens who felt
otherwise, and they constituted an articulate opposition. One protested
that the NCHO building would "mar the park." Agreeing with him,
another said it would be "inappropriate" in an area that was "rustic,
urban, and beautiful."

Although he made no overt attempt to persuade the Park Board
members, Shanks certainly did not lessen the pressures on them when he
reacted enthusiastically to some of the St. Paul sites he was shown ("It's
a beautiful site," he rhapsodized at one place; "I just love rolling land")
and when he mentioned in an offhand manner that the company was also
considering sites in Omaha and Des Moines.

Two days after the first Park Board meeting, Shanks cancelled his offer of $190,000 for the Wayzata Boulevard site. In his letter he said that if the park commissioners wanted to make the company "a written proposal concerning this site, we will be glad to give it consideration."

A few minutes after the letter was hand-delivered, the Park Board voted to make an offer to the Pru to sell it the property it sought on the terms it had originally offered.

On November 5 a conditional sales contract was signed.

The following day the state Supreme Court dismissed a citizen's law suit which was intended to block the transaction. In the weeks and months and years that followed, the controversy gradually died down—so completely that even Frank Lloyd Wright wasn't able to rekindle it.

The famous architectural genius and curmudgeon had been invited to lecture to a local cultural society. When he arrived in Minneapolis in November 1956, little more than a year after the official opening of NCHO's building, his hosts took him on a tour of some of the architectural sights in the area. One of the first stops was the new Pru building. Beal greeted him at the door. What happened during the next few minutes must have strained even the tolerance of Beal, whose patience usually seemed inexhaustible.

Emerging from the car, Wright, then 87 years old and a colorful sight in a brown tweed coat with a high collar, wearing a shaggy felt hat which could not quite contain his bushy mane, looked about him, eyed the new building dyspeptically, and snorted, "To build a thing like this in a park is my idea of a poetry crusher with a capital P."

Of the design of the building, an irregularly shaped structure, four to ten stories high, Wright said, "This form [of building] had become international—a cliché. It has the standing at present that the old red brick building used to enjoy."

The most cutting blow of all came in the cafeteria, where Wright looked about him and commented, "I wouldn't gather from this that you really love your employees."

It wasn't that he didn't like anything. He expressed approval of the escalators. And in the kitchen he delivered a pat and a kick: "This kitchen is well done—an example of how far we have come with our civilization. Go out in front of this building and you see where we've failed."

Just before he got into his car to leave, Wright cast a parting stone: "This whole thing is a misadventure."

That must have been just the word Beal would have used to describe Wright's visit.

None of the original critics of the Pru's building could have taken much comfort from the great architect's comments, for in the course of his subsequent tour of the city he managed to flay Minneapolis because of a number of other local landmarks. Before departing from the city, he advised Minneapolitans to tear down the whole city and start all over —advice he had previously given to New York City and any number of other places large and small. But no city deserved that advice less than Minneapolis, a community of unique charm. What other city of its size (in 1970, a population of 434,400 in the city and 1,814,000 in the metropolitan area) could boast of 22 lakes within the city? There were 153 parks—almost nine square miles of parkland in a city of only 59 square miles. Moreover—as John Fischer pointed out in *Harper's* in 1969—the people of Minnesota, with "only two per cent of the country's population . . . have built the fourth largest university system, several excellent liberal arts colleges, a symphony orchestra respected throughout the world, the Tyrone Guthrie Theater, and three art galleries of distinction," and most of those institutions were in or near Minneapolis.

The charm of the city and the state were emphasized by Prudential in the publicity attendant upon the start of construction of the new building. At the ground breaking on May 8, 1953, Carrol Shanks—who had been assisted in the ceremony by the mayors of Minneapolis and St. Paul, both of whom had taken shovels in hand to turn over soil—said that, of all the Regional Home Office beginnings at which he had officiated, none was as gratifying to him as this, "because on this occasion I am in my native state."

Even before the ground breaking, other Prudential people had begun the migration to "the Land of 10,000 Lakes." Reign Bittner, who would be the personnel director, made a brief trip during the winter to reconnoiter. A few weeks later, in February 1953, Merrill P. Robinson, the new personnel manager for NCHO, arrived, rented a 20-by-20-foot office, room 612, in the Northwestern National Bank Building, and set to work with other recruiters who arrived the following week to begin hiring the 45 initial employees who would be needed when the first

NCHO operations started in temporary quarters six weeks later. The first person to be employed was a woman, Millie Swensen.

Another early arrival from Newark was Don Penn, who was to be manager of the Office Services Division. He learned to his "great surprise" on March 24 that he had been assigned to NCHO. "After informing my staff in the Personnel Division [in Newark]," Penn wrote at the end of the year, in a lighthearted memo to Beal, "I called Mrs. Penn, who responded to my message with a simple, 'Minneapolis!' "

Penn's memo, entitled, "I Was Decentralized: A Subjective History," provides some illustrations of the state of mind of the men and women who were starting NCHO, and of the kind of problems, big and little, they encountered.

On April 6, he recalled, he reported to the seventh floor of the North Building in Newark, where the NCHO team was being assembled and work was under way. Penn and his associates began preparing requisitions for supplies needed in Minneapolis, requested Robinson's recruiters to hire 12 clerks there, drew up floor plans, ordered furniture and equipment, and prepared a handbook of NCHO personnel procedures.

"Meanwhile, problems of a personal nature arose," Penn wrote. "My younger daughter, Patricia, had been squired by an ex-GI since his return from Germany. They had spoken casually of plans to be married in June of 1954. With the departure of her parents imminent, the young lady decided to accelerate plans for her wedding. Her engagement was announced on May 2 and the wedding date was set for August 15.

"May 8 was my last day in the [Corporate] Home Office and I left my friends with the feeling that I was totally unprepared for the task ahead."

His flight was pleasant, and he arrived at the apartment which had been rented for him by Vern Zook, who was to spend two harried years searching for apartments and houses for people transferred from Newark. At the apartment he was met by Harvey Mitchell, already a veteran of 24 years with the Pru, who had come out in March. For Mitchell, who was NCHO's assistant general manager, the move to Minneapolis was his first trip west of the Allegheny Mountains. Mitchell took Penn on a sightseeing drive around the city which became more exciting than intended when a severe thunderstorm with heavy hailstones struck the city, rocking the car, ripping a large sign off a roof of a downtown building, and flooding roadways. It was Penn's introduction to the wild storms which are one of the features of the North Central states.

That evening Penn and Mitchell visited Penn's assistant, Norman Loeffler, his wife, and their two-year-old daughter, who had preceded Penn to the Twin Cities. The Loefflers, Penn noted, "were the first complete North Central family [of the Pru] to arrive in Minneapolis."

On Monday evening, May 11—a week before operations were to begin—a trailer truck arrived from Newark with supplies, and Penn found that "the floor plans which I had so carefully drawn in Newark [were] immediately obsolete because the tilers were on strike and the space on the second floor which had been alloted to me for supplies was not completed." But there were other woes in store for Penn:

"The alley to the rear of this building [at 505 Nicollet Avenue, eight blocks of which have since been turned into a mall] separates us from the Federal Reserve Bank. On a Monday morning it is probably the busiest alley in Minneapolis. Through it must come all the Brink's trucks delivering weekend receipts to the bank. The morning of May 11 was no exception. It was raining. As our trailer truck completely blocked the alley, it was necessary to pull it away from the unloading platform each time a Brink's truck arrived. We caused quite a traffic jam and it was not a surprise when a representative of the Minneapolis Police Department arrived. In a friendly but firm tone, he informed me that I had 10 minutes to remove the trailer truck from the alley. Fortunately, the president of the Chamber of Commerce was able to extricate me from my predicament. With frequent interruptions, the unloading continued until it was completed at 4:45."

All that week Penn and Loeffler worked 14-hour days, trying to get the premises in fit condition for the people who would show up the following Monday, ready for work.

"One learns fast in such circumstances," Penn wrote. "It is impossible to set up a division in accordance with a floor plan calling for 50-inch desks when only 45-inch desks are available."

And so it went:

On May 18th, when NCHO began, an elevator got stuck between floors: "It was necessary to learn how to release a well-proportioned blonde elevator operator through the escape hatch, as well as to get the car back into operation. In both cases, we were successful. . . ."

"On the evening of May 17 the NCHO held its first social function, an informal picnic on the shores of Lake Calhoun. The gathering dispersed when the local gendarmes issued orders to extinguish the fire we had thoughtfully confined to a wire incinerator. . . ."

On June 15 the newly arrived Debit Policy Division began functioning, but the newcomers had not been warned about a problem with the plumbing. The result was that the third floor was flooded with water. Penn and the plumber argued over the probable cause. When it was found, it turned out that Penn had been right. "I had my reward when he generously informed me that I should have been a plumber. . . ."

A series of electrical failures led to a complete investigation of the circuitry in an effort to find a fuse that kept blowing. "Its location remained a mystery until . . . it was finally located in the dressmaking department on the third floor of the Penney Store [adjacent to the NCHO temporary offices]. Only then was it learned that the J. C. Penney Company had generously furnished the electricity for the lights, fans, and enunciators in the elevators for over three months. Two days later the line was transferred to a Prudential circuit. . . ."

On August 7 Penn flew back to Newark, on August 15 his daughter was married, and on September 1 he was back in Minneapolis with his wife and son.

In January 1954, when the south wing of the new NCHO building was completed, those employees who had been working at 505 Nicollet moved into their new, permanent offices. As work had expanded, other temporary office space had been rented in the Baker-Roanoke Buildings downtown, and the men and women who worked there made the move to Wayzata Boulevard later.

Some of the employees, like Curt Lefler, found themselves, to their surprise, missing the closeness that had existed in spite of—or perhaps because of—the primitive working conditions at 505 Nicollet. Others, like Curt Eastman, savored strange and often absurd memories: the personnel interviewer who hired Eastman seemed to be a complete authority on the Pru—but Eastman later discovered that the man had only been on the job two weeks himself.

When the new NCHO building was formally dedicated, on June 21, 1955—with Governor Orville L. Freeman and Shanks speaking at the usual ceremonies—1,100 of the 1,400 employees were men and women who had been hired locally.

After the dedication Beal intensified his efforts to win over those in the area who still resented the Pru for having built on that site. He invited the protesters in, listened to their arguments, went as far as he could to conciliate them. For example, a big red sign which had been erected on the building was taken down and put away permanently. The grounds and interior facilities, like the auditorium, were opened to community groups. The symphony orchestra gave a concert on the grounds.

"We even got two swans—Prudence and Rocky—for Brownie Lake," Henry Arnsdorf recalled. "When we invited the press to come out and watch when we introduced the swans to the lake, it turned out that neither of them wanted to go into the water. The newspapers had a lot of fun with that."

When Mary Erickson, a Pru employee, was crowned "Aquatennial Queen of the Lakes" in the summer of 1956, the company completed its integration into the community.

No one in the entire company had been better qualified than Beal to carry out successfully such a difficult job of establishing the Prudential as a good corporate citizen, despite the initial controversy. Patient, kind, humane, he sometimes seemed too good to be true. He was a deeply, and actively, religious man, but he did not push his religious convictions on others (indeed, two of the most important promotions that were awarded to his subordinates in later years went to agnostics). He had never taken a drink, but he was pleased when others enjoyed themselves at a cocktail party.

He was the right kind of man to represent the Pru in Minneapolis. He was also the sort of executive who—without putting unreasonable pressure on his subordinates—brings out the best in the men and women who work for him. "He often used to say," Arnsdorf remembered, "that 'every man is better than he thinks he is.' "

"Being part of the process by which people improve themselves is tremendously rewarding," Beal wrote a decade later. "I look for intelligence, industry, and the right attitude—an honest and constructive attitude. I look for men who are not lazy mentally or physically —and who have empathy toward others.

"Men are gauged by how they perform. A man must be willing to gamble on his own ideas. He has to lay himself on the line. This must be a day-to-day process, a way of living. If a man doesn't speak out, he lacks one thing a good executive must have—courage. A person stands for something throughout every day of his life and he shouldn't hold back and wait for the other fellow.

"I believe in helping other people to further their own development. I don't hesitate to put pressure on people with good potential to spend some of their time and money in this kind of investment in themselves. This part of my work I thoroughly enjoy."

Because of his quiet demeanor, the low key in which he handled even matters of crisis—"He never panicked when others would have," Donald Fuerth said—Beal's leadership qualities were sometimes obscured. But on September 20, 1955, they were fully revealed to a large and important audience.

It was the second day of a three-day "Management Conference" which was attended by all U.S. and Canadian employees of the rank of assistant general manager and above. The session was held in the gymnasium of the Gibraltar Building, which was crowded for the event. Beal was the last of several speakers to address the meeting that day.

He told his audience that after the dedication of NCHO that June he had spent a day or so a week, whenever possible, touring the various parts of his region. He had walked many debits with agents. He had sat with Ordinary agents while they talked with their clients. He had joined real estate investment men in discussions with businessmen and farmers about proposed deals. In short, he had gone back to the basics of the insurance business.

At that time, about one out of every six families had a Prudential policy. Speaking without a prepared text, Beal said that it was wrong for Pru people to take pride in that statistic. They ought to be thinking, he said, of the five other families "who don't have the protection of Prudential insurance."

Making the rounds with District agents, he said, he had been impressed anew by the remarkable rapport that almost always was apparent between the agent and the householders insured by the company. "People trust their Prudential agents," he said. He told of standing at a screen door with an agent and hearing the housewife within call out, "Come in and take the money yourself. You'll find it on the table." Beal and the agent walked in, took the money, and left—the agent calling out a farewell to the woman as he closed the door. She had not been in sight during their visit.

There was humor in Beal's speech, a sense of compassion for the agents, and a call for imagination in providing new kinds of protection for the people. Above all, Beal managed to convey his vision of what the Prudential meant to America.

When he ended his remarks, the audience gave him a thunderous, standing ovation. They wouldn't stop applauding—in a supreme act of lèse majesté, they gave him an ovation that far outstripped the applause that Shanks had received, and that, of course, is the ultimate corporate sin. But Shanks appeared not to resent it; indeed, he leaned over and told Beal that he agreed with the audience about the merits of the speech. Nevertheless, the unassuming Beal was "a little embarrassed" by the demonstration.

"It was obvious that all of the managers thought that Orville was *the* boy, that he really understood field experience," Raymond Cobb said, looking backward many years afterward.

That speech made Beal stand out as a leader. Combined with his record of achievement as head of NCHO and his previous accomplishments in other posts in the company, it showed him as a man who had still not had an opportunity to realize his full potential. Less than two years later, that condition was rectified. He was elected an executive vice president.

19 / Off with the Gargoyles!

It seems that some governmental body discovers a need to investigate the insurance industry every ten years, give or take a year or two. As the 1940's drew to a close, it was the turn of a House Judiciary subcommittee chaired by the head of the full committee, Representative Emanuel Celler, a Democrat from New York. Inevitably, the press and the politicians called it "the Celler Committee."

Prudential emerged from the hearings in excellent condition. When Morris L. Ernst, a liberal attorney from Manhattan, criticized the private placement of corporate bonds with insurance companies on the ground that the practice injured the investment banking business, chairman Celler, equally renowned as a liberal, broke in to say, "I have to take issue with that." He said he had checked into that matter, and in the previous six months the leading investment bankers had been "instrumental in placing with the big five insurance companies and a few other insurance companies upward of $550 million of first-mortgage bonds of gas transmission lines"—not to speak of the securities of many other industries—"and in every instance one of those investment bankers made a considerable amount of money."

When Ernst assailed the insurance companies for draining premium funds out of many areas of the country, Celler interjected, "It might interest you to know, Mr. Ernst, that the Prudential Insurance Company is creating [regional] divisions, and they are endeavoring to rationalize their activities so that moneys drawn from policyholders in a given section will be pumped back into that section." (Later in the hearings Leroy A. Lincoln, then president of the Metropolitan, insisted that his company had been the first to invest its funds equitably from a regional point of view; "I yield nothing to [Prudential] in that respect," he declared.)

On November 30, 1949, Carrol M. Shanks testified as the head of Pru. He chose to stand, ramrod straight, while giving his testimony.

188

One of Celler's first, tough questions dealt with a matter which had emerged as a vulnerable part of the company's operations in previous investigations—its lapse rate for Weekly Premium insurance (which originally was called Industrial insurance).

"[The lapse rates] are very consequential . . . are they not?" Celler asked.

"No," Shanks replied; "I think that the lapses are running fairly low. . . . When I have that figure I will give it to you, Mr. Chairman."

Subsequently Shanks did submit a table of lapse rates. It showed that only 4.8 per cent of the weekly premium policies in force at the beginning of the year had lapsed during the year. That figure meant that Pru had finally gained control over one of its most controversial problems. It had done so by recruiting better agents and by training them better.

A chart prepared by Sylvester C. Smith, Jr., the company's general counsel, showed that, comparing invested assets to policy reserves, Prudential was investing proportionately higher amounts of its funds in the Southwest than in any other region. The other regions, by proportionate investment emphasis, were ranked in this order: South Central, Western, North Central, Central Atlantic, and Eastern. Shanks summarized the principle of Pru's investments succinctly: "The West gets more money than we take out of the West. . . . The Southeast gets much more money than we take out of there, and that Middle South section also gets much more money than we take out." The same practice held true for the other, newer sections of the continent.

Another chart presented by Shanks indicated that the public's willingness to purchase additional life insurance tended to increase sharply during "hard times"—those periods when the economy suffered a recession or depression. For example, sales had risen markedly at the time of the 1921 recession. At the very outset of the Great Depression in 1929, sales of life insurance began climbing steeply, and they did not level off until 1932, which was the worst year of that terrible economic crisis.

Toward the end of Shanks's testimony, during a general discussion that included a number of members of the subcommittee and Shanks, chairman Celler happened to remark:

"I am a heavy holder of life insurance—I want you to know that."

"Prudential?" asked a subcommittee member.

"Prudential also," Celler disclosed reluctantly, as the hearing room was swept with laughter.

Despite—or possibly because of—the toughness of the investigation by Celler, who had won considerable attention as a critic of big business, Sylvester Smith was able to report later that the testimony elicited in the investigation "both with respect to the operations of the life insurance business as a whole and of the Prudential in particular has been quite satisfactory."

Before the Celler Committee completed its investigation, Prudential began the observance of its 75th anniversary, in 1950. On February 28 the company held a Founder's Day luncheon commemorating the birthday of its first president, Allen L. Bassett. Among the 225 persons who attended the event were 22 descendants of four former presidents of Prudential: Bassett, Noah F. Blanchard, John F. Dryden, and Edward D. Duffield.

Four months later war broke out in Korea. Reservists were called away from their civilian lives and the conscription of young men was stepped up; hundreds of Pru employees were affected as the number of men and women in uniform mounted sharply. Before the worst of the fighting was over three years later, 5,764,143 U.S. citizens had gone into service, and more than 54,000 lost their lives, while over 103,000 others were wounded.

Of course, many Prudential policyholders were victims of the conflict. One of the most poignant stories to emerge from the war involved one of the company's policyholders, a Marine corporal named Sidney Oehl, who was reported killed in action. Pru sent a representative to Oehl's father, Arthur, in New York City, with a check for the $1,300 in insurance which the company had issued on the young Marine's life, but the father rejected the money, refusing to believe that his son was dead. After a cease-fire was agreed upon in Korea, the impossible hope came true: Oehl came home after months as a prisoner of war.

At home Prudential was involved in another war of sorts—a conflict that caused, not bloodshed, but anguish, bitterness, economic loss, and mutual, if usually unspoken, regret on the part of many participants. That dispute was an 81-day strike of District agents—the largest and longest work stoppage by white-collar workers in the nation's history up to that time, according to the U.S. Department of Labor.

The roots of Prudential's labor problems stretched far back into the past. In the 19th century, when the company was founded, employees in almost all companies of any kind were treated with a mixture of kindly paternalism and unfeigned concern, on the one hand, and thoughtless arrogance combined with crude bullying, on the other. As the world advanced more deeply into the 20th century, employees in virtually every industry rebelled against the old, authoritarian ways of business. They wanted to be treated with more respect. They believed they had a right to lives of greater dignity than they had known before. Whenever possible, their jobs should include some degree of choice and judgment, however nominal.

Each industry adapted itself to these new concepts at a pace different from other industries. In many industries, change did not take place without labor conflict, which sometimes continued over several decades. Although the insurance industry was relatively slow to adjust itself to the new thinking in employee relations, change—when it came—was not accompanied by the prolonged strife typical of many industries.

For Prudential, the first encounter with unionization occurred in 1937, when attempts began to organize District agents in New York, Pennsylvania, and Wisconsin. In 1942 Pru signed its first union contract, covering District agents in the state of New York. Over the next seven years, the company's District agents were represented by either the United Office and Professional Workers of America, an affiliate of the Congress of Industrial Organizations (CIO); an American Federation of Labor (AFL) affiliate which later came to be called the Insurance Agents International Union; the International Union of Life Insurance Agents, an independent labor organization; or no union at all, depending on the area in which the agents worked. Finally, in 1949, the AFL union, which was an affiliate of the AFL-CIO a quarter-century later, won out over the CIO union in representation elections.

During the first month of 1951 a disagreement between the union and the company came to a head. Prudential found it necessary to suspend a group of agents in Pittsburgh. Four days later, on January 9, 2,300 agents protested the suspensions by calling in to report they were too sick to work. Three more days passed, and then 1,600 agents staged a wildcat demonstration outside the Corporate Home Office in Newark.

But the union, which had not sanctioned the work stoppages, helped to restrain the restive agents, and matters returned to normal—for the moment.

The following winter, contract negotiations led to the big strike, officially called by the union. The stoppage began on December 1, 1951, and did not end until February 20, 1952. It was the first—and the last—strike in Prudential's first century. Both sides learned, the hard way, that labor strife, while sometimes unavoidable, often exacts a far higher price than the participants expect.

For nearly three months the agents had to try to get along without their usual income. Wives and children did without. They suffered through a bleak Christmas and New Year's season.

For Orville E. Beal, vice president in charge of the District Agencies, the strike was a cause of considerable anguish. The son of an agent, he had always felt a special bond to the agents—who carried the message of family security to every hamlet and every crowded neighborhood on the continent. But now, during the strike, Beal was reviled by the pickets from time to time as he entered the Home Office.

The president, Carrol Shanks, was, of course, the primary target of epithets. There was an element of irony in this, for Shanks was politically a liberal, one of the relatively few top-level businessmen who had supported most of the social legislation of the 1930's—which included organized labor's Magna Carta, the Wagner Act, protecting union activity and the process of collective bargaining. Although Shanks, like Beal, had mixed feelings about the strike, he went out of his way to stand up to the pickets. Because he did not want them to think he was afraid of them, Shanks would have his chauffeur let him out two or three blocks from the Home Office, so that he could walk through the lines of pickets, his head high, as they sometimes shouted threats and insults.

But there were other occasions during the strike when pickets and Prudential officers exchanged friendly greetings and hopes that the impasse would soon be resolved.

When the strike finally came to an end, to everyone's relief, there were, inevitably, casualties and changes. One change affected Beal, who was transferred from the leadership of the District Agencies Department—where James E. Rutherford, whom Beal had brought into the company, took his place—to the top post in the newly created grouping of "Public Relations and Advertising, and Home Office

Coordination.'' Many Pru people felt that Beal's career had suffered a setback, but just two years later he was sent to Minneapolis to head the new North Central Home Office, where his performance was outstanding. The 1955 speech which catapulted him into an executive vice presidency, by demonstrating his leadership abilities and his capacity for instilling fervent loyalty in the field force, was given four years after the strike.

The strike in the U.S.—Pru's Canadian agents never went on strike; in fact, in only three provinces were agents ever organized, and since 1958 none of the Canadian agents has been represented by a union —impressed upon the company's management the necessity for good employee relations. An improvement in this area was in keeping with the general revolution which Shanks was carrying out throughout the company, so the strike might almost be said to have assisted his drive against the institutional inertia, bureaucratic stubbornness, and resistance by traditionalists which had slowed the pace of change in some areas.

Not long after the strike, Shanks told some of his men in top management that he wanted the company's field offices all over the country modernized, including the introduction of air conditioning. A few days later he was presented with a plan for air-conditioning every Prudential office in the U.S. and Canada over a period of three years.

"Three years!" he exclaimed. "I want it done in three weeks."

And in a matter of weeks it was done.

Shanks moved with equal determination in insurance matters. In health insurance, for example, Prudential had been active on a Group basis since 1925, but it was not until Shanks set up a Sickness and Accident Department in 1951 that the company began to sell health insurance on an individual basis. Individual health insurance was not in good repute at that time. Too many companies with low ethical standards were operating in that field. Those companies were adept at finding excuses for not paying claims. Policies were cancelled with reckless disregard for the policyholder's interests.

"I recall Shanks's saying, 'We will go into the individual health insurance business. We will go into it on the right basis. We will play the game the way it ought to be played, not the way those other companies do. And I think we can do a decent, profitable business,' '' Beal said many years later. "So we went into it, not on the basis of writing cancellable policies, but on the basis of non-cancellable health insurance. It was because of that decision that some companies had to quit selling their cancellable policies. The unethical companies began to pass out of the picture, while the major companies followed Prudential's lead in guaranteeing that individual health insurance contracts would be renewed.''

About the time that Pru was getting into individual health insurance, the question of public directors came to the fore. This issue went back to the Armstrong Committee hearings of 1905. The New Jersey counterpart of that inquiry—the Hillery Committee—had said in its report, ''Where the interests of policyholders are so great compared with the interests of stockholders [Pru then being a stock company] some directors should be selected more particularly charged with looking after the interests of policyholders, and who may be said to be in a sense their representatives in the board.'' Accordingly, a state law was passed in 1907 providing that the Chancellor, an independent judicial official presiding over matters in Chancery (that is, trial of issues in equity, rather than law), should appoint three persons to Pru's board of directors. The three appointees must be policyholders, but not stockholders.

As it turned out, the Chancellor's appointments over the years were men of notably high quality who contributed greatly to the company's welfare and progress. In 1943, when mutualization was completed and new legislation for the governing of the company had to be passed, the board of directors of Prudential urged that the new laws incorporate the concept of public directors which had served the company well for nearly 36 years. The Legislature concurred, and the Pru board continued to have three members appointed by the Chancellor.

However, New Jersey adopted a new constitution four years later, and the post of Chancellor was abolished, his functions being transferred to the Chief Justice. But in 1948 the legislature provided that the Governor should make the appointments to Pru's board—subject to the advice and consent of the state Senate. This was an idea which had been produced in the legislature, and nobody liked it. The Governor, Alfred E. Driscoll, liked his new power of appointment so little that he refused to exercise it. The following year the requirement for public directors was dropped from the law.

There matters stood until 1953, when the legislature enacted a new measure, increasing the company's board from 16 members to 23 (later upped to 24 when the chairman became chief executive) and providing for the appointment of public directors by the Chief Justice of New Jersey. There would be six public directors in all, one being appointed each year to a six-year term. Sydney G. Stevens of Princeton, a Trenton banker who was named a public director in 1953, was still serving on the board at the time of the company's centennial 22 years later, having proved to be one of the company's pillars of strength on many occasions over the years.

The 1950's also saw the widespread introduction of electronic computers and data processing equipment. In 1955 the first magnetic tape computers which had been ordered by Prudential were delivered to the Corporate Home Office. But Pru's involvement with computer systems went back to much earlier days. In fact, at least one authoritative text, *A Computer Perspective,* by the office of Charles and Ray Eames, published by the Harvard University Press, traces Pru's role in the development of computer technology all the way back to the 19th century, to John K. Gore, the company's actuary.

Gore, the Eameses wrote, could see that "Prudential, with its extensive statistical departments, desperately needed a mechanical way of handling data." To meet the need, Gore drew up plans for a perforating machine and a card sorter, and his brother-in-law, a mechanical engineer, used the Gore concept to create machines which, installed in 1895, were "used well into the 1930's." Gore's early machines are on display in Prudential's historical museum.

In 1944 the first modern digital computer, the Mark I, was completed at Harvard by the International Business Machines Corporation (IBM), and within three years Prudential was testing the adaptability of such equipment to the life insurance business. Henry W. Schrimpf, Jr., of Pru's Methods Division, in a memorandum to E. C. Berkeley, chief research consultant, dated July 11, 1947, reported on "Ordinary Insurance Premium Billing—Trial on Harvard's Sequence Controlled Calculator (Mark I)." Schrimpf was enthusiastic about the results. "We have been discussing for some months a certain type of electronic sequence-controlled calculator for premium billing and other insurance company work," he pointed out. "Our experience in this trial convinces us that such a calculator will work."

Not long after that, Pru placed an order for an electronic computer with the Eckert-Mauchly Computer Corporation, which developed

UNIVAC. Prudential's board of directors was told in 1949 that Eckert-Mauchly had "made considerable progress during the year" and "successfully completed two special purpose computers," but the board was warned that it would "be quite some time before we can look forward to delivery of our machine, which is considerably more complicated because of its adaptability to various kinds of problems." During the following year, the accidental death of Eckert-Mauchly's principal backer triggered a number of problems that led to cancellation of Pru's contract in 1951.

As a result, Prudential turned to IBM, which in 1955 delivered a model 702 and a model 650 to the Corporate Home Office, in addition to a model 650 to the Canadian Head Office—the first of three generations of computers over the next 20 years. By 1967 Pru had 52 electronic computers "going full blast, around-the-clock for the most part," in the words of A. Douglas Murch, Toronto-born head of Pru's Computer and Insurance Services Department at the Corporate Home Office.

During the last half of the 1950's, the Planning and Development Department—which was itself one of the modern management concepts, common in other industries, introduced into Pru by Shanks—was staffed by many brilliant men, headed by Charles B. Laing. Among his assistants, many of whom went on to important posts at Prudential, were Thomas Allsopp, Floyd H. Bragg, Robert W. Harvey, R. Morton Darrow, and Joseph M. Savage. As the person directly in charge of computer developments, Savage played a leading role in helping Prudential to establish its leading position in the insurance industry in the use of computers to help overcome the enormous mass of paper work, according to his associates' recollections. In later years, at the Mid-America Home Office to which he had been assigned in 1964, Savage himself said of that golden time in the 1950's, "During those years, we were constantly disciplining our systems and always reaching into the manual systems in order to convert additional operations to electronic data processing."

In 1956 a major controversy arose over which computer models should be used in the Regional Home Offices. Laing's men argued that all the RHOs should be equipped with IBM 705's, which would be big, second-generation computers. Louis Menagh, the comptroller (and an increasingly powerful figure in the councils of top management), felt strongly that the 705's, which were not yet available but soon would be, were too expensive and that the volume of work for each machine would not justify the cost. The result of the dispute was a compromise: the Corporate Home Office and some of the RHOs used 705's, which were installed in 1957, and the others used 650's. Because the systems for the two generations of computers were not compatible, communication of data between some of the RHOs was impossible by electronic means. By the early 1960's it had become clear that the computer systems of the company had to be standardized and coordinated into a rational continental system, and the long process of achieving that end was begun.

While the controversy raged, however, it reached levels of passion that belied the public's impression that life in the world of large corporations is always routine and dull. Although Laing and Menagh apparently did not share in the intensity of feelings, some of their subordinates did, and in a few cases the disagreement left a certain amount of bitterness. Twenty years later there was still suspicion here and there that careers had been stunted by the clash. "A lot of people got chopped up in that affair," one of the survivors said.

Which side was right and which was wrong was difficult to determine after many years had passed. It was true that some of the RHOs had not had a sufficient volume of work to justify 705's in 1957, as Menagh held—but many companies in those days (and Prudential itself, from time to time) let smaller businesses use their computers on a leased-time basis in order to put the equipment to maximum use and render it more economical. On the Laing side of the argument, it was clear, even in the 1950's, that a standardized system would facilitate communication among RHOs and enable the company to plan rationally for the future. But in the 1970's, there were some Pru computer people who felt that Menagh's position had been the most logical for that time. Yet Menagh's most gifted aide, William Chodorcoff, later an executive vice president, agreed with the arguments of Laing's men. As Alexander Pope said, "Who shall decide when doctors disagree?"

During the same year in which the first magnetic tape computers were being delivered to Pru, another development occurred which would have similarly far-reaching consequences for the company. The annual report to the president from the Law Department for 1955 included this sentence: "In the [Corporate] Home Office seven new lawyers were added to the staff, including . . . Donald MacNaughton as associate counsel." Fourteen years later, Donald S. MacNaughton would become the head of Prudential.

Born in the factory city of Schenectady, New York, on July 14, 1917, MacNaughton grew up in a household that was middle class in terms of mores, but poor from an economic point of view. Both parents were immigrants from Scotland. His father worked in the shops of the General Electric Company. As a teen-ager during the Depression, Don MacNaughton got up before dawn to deliver newspapers in order to earn a little extra money. That work established a lifelong habit of early rising.

In high school young MacNaughton, unusually tall for those days —he eventually reached a height of six feet four inches—was a star on the basketball team. It was his coach who first encouraged him to think of going to college. Because of his grades, which helped him to be chosen class valedictorian, he was able to win a full academic scholarship to Syracuse University. He wanted to go to law school—but that meant post-graduate work, and he had no money, so he majored in history and education.

"The only thing I could do was teach," MacNaughton later recalled. In the fall of 1939, the year of his graduation, he took a job teaching history in Pulaski, New York, near the eastern end of Lake Ontario and not far from Watertown. He also coached the school's basketball team. On the side, for $30 a game, he played basketball with the Syracuse Nationals, a professional team affiliated with the National Basketball Association.

Two years after leaving college, MacNaughton married one of Pulaski's first-grade teachers, Winifred Thomas. A few months later —three months after Pearl Harbor—he enlisted in the service. After officer's training at Miami, he was sent to the Pacific as a flight controller in the Air Force (then the Army Air Corps).

With the end of the war in 1945, MacNaughton, along with millions of other young men and women, was released from service, and he went back to teaching at Pulaski. But he was no longer satisfied with his life there. Like other young men, his horizons had been broadened by his wartime travels. And like so many others, he had a new and higher estimate of his true value as a person.

"I thought I was capable of doing more than I had been doing in

Pulaski," he said. "And I resented the fact that I wasn't getting any extra pay for coaching basketball. I worked damned long hours at coaching. We had the best team in that area because we worked harder at it than anybody else did."

To the school board, MacNaughton presented an ultimatum: pay me more money or I'm leaving. Goodbye, said the board, which obviously had not yet realized that the postwar young men were quite different from what they had been when they left for war service.

Now MacNaughton entered Syracuse University's law school, using the benefits of the GI Bill of Rights, which he continued to praise for the rest of his life as one of the greatest moves ever made by the U.S. government. "It was also the best investment the government ever made, as far as I'm concerned," he said. "They gave me $90 a month and look what I'm paying the government in taxes now!"

Although $90 would go much further in the late 1940's than it did 30 years later, it was still insufficient to support a family, and the Mac-Naughtons by then had a son. So Winifred went back to teaching to help carry them through the accelerated law course, which required Mac-Naughton to continue his studies during the summers. After two years he completed his work, passed his bar examinations, and began practice in Pulaski.

About six years later, MacNaughton, then a partner in a small but prospering Pulaski law firm, was talking with a law school classmate, George Klein, who had gone to work for the State Insurance Department. Klein urged, as he had often done before, that MacNaughton take a post with the department. Believing that a stint with the department might help bring business to his Pulaski law firm afterward, MacNaughton this time went along with the idea. After all, Thomas E. Dewey was the Republican Governor, and he was certain to be re-elected in November; so MacNaughton, accepting appointment as Deputy Superintendent (that is, Commissioner) of Insurance in June 1954, knew he would have at least four and a half years on the job, if he wanted to stay that long.

Unfortunately for MacNaughton—or perhaps fortunately, as things turned out in the end—he was not privy to the plans of Governor Dewey. In late summer Dewey announced that he would not run for re-election. With the unbeatable Dewey out of the race, the election was won by Averell E. Harriman, a Democrat. That meant that most of the state appointive offices would be filled by Democrats. Republican MacNaughton, only six months on the job, surely would be ousted. Suddenly his future was clouded.

During his relatively short time in the State Insurance Department, MacNaughton had already received a couple of job offers. MacNaughton told a friend, Julius Sackman, the head of the department's Life Bureau, about each of the offers, but Sackman advised him not to accept them. In the succeeding weeks, MacNaughton received invitations to go to work for a number of other insurance companies, but Sackman still advised him against accepting any of them.

"If you want to get into the insurance business," he told MacNaughton, "go with either the Metropolitan or the Prudential. They're the best."

One night, while mulling over the latest offer he had received, MacNaughton telephoned Robert Dineen, whom he knew well. Dineen, who had long been head of New York's Insurance Department, was then with the Northwestern Mutual Life Insurance Company in Milwaukee. MacNaughton told him he had just about decided to decline the latest job offer and go back to his law practice in Pulaski.

"Don't make any decision yet," Dineen advised him.

Dineen said he had just written to Sylvester Smith, general counsel of Prudential, urging him to grab MacNaughton for Pru.

A few days later, MacNaughton crossed the Hudson for an interview with Smith, during which he was offered a post with the company. When MacNaughton returned to Manhattan, he told Sackman about the offer from Pru.

"Now you're talking!" said Sackman. "This is the offer to take."

At first MacNaughton was assigned to work with the Pru's Sickness and Accident Committee, which supervised the individual health insurance operations of the company, because this was a field which Prudential had only recently re-entered.

Then MacNaughton worked as an assistant to Alexander Query, the company's mercurial, theatrical, and rather dashing associate general counsel who was responsible for matters involving insurance regulation (except for relations with New Jersey authorities and with Congressmen and other public officials in Washington, D.C., which were handled by Richard J. Congleton, an old hand at politics).

"It was the best kind of job I could have gotten," MacNaughton said later. "All Pru's problems came to our attention. We were in Group insurance one day; we were in Industrial insurance; we were in agency problems; we were in investment problems. Any matter that became a serious problem at the regulatory or legislative level involved us. So it was the best way in the world for me to learn about Prudential in a hurry.

"I loved the job. We worked all hours. I don't think I took a vacation during the first four or five years. The job itself seemed like a vacation. It was such an exciting job."

In 1957 Query replaced Beal—who had been elected executive vice president—as head of the North Central Home Office in Minneapolis, and MacNaughton was promoted to Query's old position. It was an especially sensitive job at that time—the insurance industry was under attack by the Federal Trade Commission because of some assertions in the advertisements of certain companies. An industry committee had been formed to draft model legislation which would govern health insurance advertising. Valentine Howell, who had been one of Pru's two executive vice presidents during the 1950's (the other was Harold Stewart), was a member of the committee, and MacNaughton worked with him, attending committee meetings and sketching out the company's position.

"He was a good man to work for," MacNaughton recalled, "because he let you make decisions at meetings he didn't attend. He wasn't one of those guys who expects his men to say, under those circumstances, 'Well, I'll go back and see what the boss says.' He gave me my head."

As a result of Howell's willingness to give MacNaughton a free hand, the latter played the leading role in drafting the legislation for the industry. It was generally agreed that MacNaughton had done an exceptionally good job with the delicate assignment. Inevitably, his stature in the company and in the industry grew. There were already some in middle management at Pru who were speculating how high he might eventually rise.

The environment in which MacNaughton worked was rapidly changing. Shanks had come to the conclusion that the Prudential buildings erected by John Dryden's command at the turn of the century epitomized the old, stodgy, prewar company, not the modern, efficient organization Shanks had been building for a decade. Therefore, in 1955—the same year in which MacNaughton joined the Pru—a

Newark newspaper reported that the Main Building, a "mixture of Romanesque and Gothic architecture," was "finally to be razed after dominating the heart of Newark for more than 60 years." The news item said that the building, "put up by the late John F. Dryden, founder of Prudential, as the culmination of his dreams as to the kind of home office his company should have, is giving way to a $20 million redevelopment project" which would be highlighted by "the dream of a new century, a 24-story white-marble tower building as plain in design as the old building was elaborate."

For nearly a decade the air around the Corporate Home Office in Newark was thick with the dust raised by demolition crews and builders, for the old North Building in 1962 was also torn down. With the destruction of the old buildings went the marble floors, the dark Mexican mahogany and the carved black oak paneling, the ceilings covered with murals and gold leaf, the walls six feet thick. The demolition, supervised by E. D. Stern for the Cleveland Wrecking Company, attracted a good deal of attention throughout the U.S. One night, on a telecast of the NBC Evening News, anchor man Chet Huntley told his viewers:

> Though leaving no stone unturned, [Stern] has become a part-time art dealer, and during the past year he has sold about 260 gargoyles, wrenched from the crumbling walls [of the old Prudential buildings in Newark]. His customers have ranged from prosperous businessmen to schoolteachers, like this lady who bought a sinister 600-pound number for about $40 because she "always wanted one."
>
> The company warns that these are merely decorative pieces, although they were imported from Europe. Gargoyles are really horrible-looking rain spouts, designed to ward off evil spirits while carrying water from the eaves. But the folks impulsive enough to plunk down cold, hard cash to cart these grotesque creatures home are certainly entitled to call them gargoyles.
>
> The people who buy gargoyles place them on the floors of their living rooms as combination conversation pieces and things to stumble over. Others put them in their gardens to cheer up the flowers. At any rate, the supply of gargoyles is running low. Last week, Mr. Stern's stock was reduced to 30 when a lady stopped and purchased one to send as a valentine.

When the rebuilding was finished, Pru's executive offices were in its new Plaza Building, fronting on Broad Street between Academy and Bank Streets. Behind the main 24-story tower was a seven-story wing. The rest of the block to Halsey Street was occupied by a shopping mall one story high. The Gibraltar and Washington Street buildings were still full of Prudential employees, and they were connected with the Plaza Building by a tunnel. Across Bank Street, where the old Main Building had stood, was an office building housing a bank.

But many Prudential men and women—including a goodly number who were otherwise wholly in sympathy with Shanks's modernization of the company—mourned the passing of the opulence that had, for so long, symbolized Prudential.

20 / 'It Drives You Nuts'

While Prudential men and women were scattering across the country, setting up Regional Home Offices, the same blaze of creativity which drove them with astonishing ardor had touched off the imagination of those who remained in Newark. In no area of the company's activities was this more visible than in Group life and health insurance and Group pensions. And in none of the Prudential's activities was improvement needed more.

For nearly half a century Pru had displayed an ambivalent attitude toward Group. It had been involved in Group or Group-like activities for a long time. In 1898 it had written 150 Whole Life policies on married couples employed by Montgomery Ward and Company in Chicago; the employer had handed out the policies as Christmas presents. A short time later the Ithaca (N.Y.) *Daily Times* insured all its employees with the Pru. For technical reasons which need not concern us now, neither of those wholesale policy issues was a true Group case in the modern sense. But the two did indicate that the Pru was interested in covering many policyholders in one transaction—as it should have been, for the economies in such an arrangement were obvious.

The first true Group policy was issued, not by the Pru, but by the Equitable Life Assurance Society, which covered the 121 employees of a leather company in 1911. Like John Dryden with Industrial life insurance, the Equitable had copied an idea conceived by an English life insurance company. Ironically, however, the Equitable's first really big "case," as Group clients came to be called, was the same company which had favored the Pru a few years earlier—Montgomery Ward. In 1912 Montgomery Ward entered into an agreement with the Equitable under which about 2,000 employees were covered for life insurance, disability benefits, and old-age pensions.

Within the Pru, John K. Gore and James F. Little worked out the actuarial and technical problems for issuing Group policies, and on August 21, 1916, the company's first Group life insurance policy —designated No. G-1001 (undoubtedly numbered so to suggest that the Pru had long experience with this new kind, with 1,000 other policies previously issued)—was written, covering employees of McCormick and Company of Baltimore. For some reason, the policy remained in force only nine months, but by that time other Group policies were being issued.

For nearly 30 years after that the Pru, stumbling and bumbling in its efforts to cope with Group, lagged far behind the other leading life insurance companies. One example of the company's ineptness in that period was provided many years later by the gifted Scotsman, Edmund B. Whittaker. Although he was not associated with the Pru during that early, dismal era of Group, he studied the company's past activities —after he became responsible for Group in the 1940's—in order to learn from the mistakes of the past. Whittaker said, "For the first ten years of Group endeavor we did not write Group health and accident insurance, but combined with the Commercial Casualty Company of Newark, [which] wrote the health. We had no casualty claim department at the time, and it was felt that this was the most economical method of handling the combined package. However, it turned out to be a great mistake, as the retentions of the Commercial Casualty were so high that nobody would buy the combined package."

Despite its generally dismal Group record in those fallow years, the Prudential did introduce some innovations then, including one new variety of Group insurance which ultimately assumed enormous importance in the economic life of America. In the late 1920's it became, apparently, the first company to put into general use certain low-cost, administrative procedures which could be handled by the employer-client, thus eliminating detailed record-keeping by the insurance company. Another innovation by the Pru was the use of a draft book which was placed in the hands of the employer-client as an inexpensive, quick way of processing Group accident and health claims.

The new variety was Group creditors insurance; that is, insurance on the lives of borrowers to cover payment of loans in case of death, thus freeing their families from the burden of that debt. The Individual form of creditors insurance was conceived in 1917 by Arthur J. Morris of

Norfolk, Virginia, in order to protect cosigners and debtors who borrowed from his Morris Plan banks. But it was not until 1928 that Group creditors insurance came into being.

"Unlike its predecessor [individual creditors insurance], the Group approach was the product of the vision and thinking of not one, but of three men," according to *An Analysis of Group Creditors Insurance*, an M.B.A. thesis presented to the University of Southern California by James B. Jacobson, who later became head of Pru's Group Insurance Department. "In 1927 Reynolds Pomeroy, a prominent New York insurance broker and close friend of Roger Steffan, an officer of the National City Bank of New York [now the First National City Bank or, in its own advertising jargon, Citibank], conceived the idea of covering all of the bank's personal loan borrowers under a blanket Group policy. Steffan, being a progressive officer of a progressive bank, was readily receptive to the idea. Pomeroy, like Morris, presented his idea to various New York life insurance companies, all to no avail. . . .

"In due time, Pomeroy met James Little, vice president and actuary of the Prudential. . . . Little, a creative thinker of extraordinary ability, accepted the problem as a challenge to formulate a Group coverage for a new field."

During the next decade, the eight other companies which became, with Prudential, the leaders in Group creditors insurance entered that field one by one.

But Group creditors insurance was the exception that proved the rule: in general, Prudential showed an inability to grasp the opportunities in Group insurance and pensions before the second World War. Indeed, after the death of Fred Tasney in 1925 there was no Group vice president (the title would now be senior vice president).

"As always happens when there is a divided responsibility, nothing got done," Whittaker wrote in a 1957 memoir. "During the years prior to 1934 we passed up cases such as General Motors, which was offered to us, and we lost out on General Electric, Westinghouse, and a great many other large cases. We would certainly have had our share if we had had a single dynamic organization, but Group Sales [was] always the second extra job of the Industrial or Ordinary Agency vice president, who was concerned primarily with his own line of business, secondly with advertising, and Group was a poor third. Even if he had had the time to pay attention to Group, he had no inclination, was much too old to learn, and did not believe in it anyways."

At one point during the 1930's, Whittaker said, there were two separate—and competitive—Group sales field forces. "There was no liaison between the two," he said, "and on occasion both of them called on the same case on the same day. Neither [of the two Group sales heads] would ever leave his office for fear the other would put one over on him. The results were, of course, disastrous, and the Prudential was a miserable fifth or sixth in production for the five years preceding 1943."

That was a key year, for Group as well as for the other branches of the company—the year in which Carrol Shanks became the effective head of the Pru. He decided that the company should either compete aggressively in the Group insurance business or get out of that field entirely (as it had done with respect to Group pensions in 1940). The responsibility was handed to the Actuarial Department, headed by Valentine Howell. Whittaker said, "I shall never forget my dismay when Val called me in one day and said, 'Ed, we are in the sales business. The Colonel [Franklin D'Olier, then nominally head of the Pru] and Carrol have decided to consolidate all Group operations except Claim in one unit and put it under me, and you are going to run it.' "

In vain Whittaker protested that he knew nothing about sales. He'd better find out, Howell replied.

It seemed like a singularly unpropitious time. Because of wartime restraints and shortages, people were buying very little on installment plans, and the war-created full employment plus overtime wages in many industries had sharply reduced the demand for loans; so Group creditors insurance—the only area in which Prudential was the leader—had diminished painfully in volume.

On the other hand, the revival of industry from the Depression of the 1930's, the ruling by the Internal Revenue Service that Group insurance premiums were an ordinary business expense for employers, and—most of all—the finding by the government that such premiums were not inflationary and therefore were exempt from wartime controls on wages, prices, and profits—all these factors created a climate highly favorable to the efforts of Whittaker's salesmen, who became known as "Group representatives." With Group insurance premiums permitted while most pay increases were prohibited as inflationary, a clamor arose on the part of almost every union, in contract negotiations, for inclusion of the premiums as a contract benefit; it was, after all, one of the few new benefits that the unions could demand without defying the government and appearing to weaken the patriotic war effort. Moreover, many employers were not only willing, but eager, to pay the premiums, for they could not offer higher pay or other inducements to attract and hold high-quality labor, but liberal fringe benefits might do the trick.

Thus, the Pru's newly reorganized Group operations began to prosper in 1944, the first full year under Whittaker's leadership. Of the seven large companies writing Group life, only two showed an increase that year, and one of the two was Prudential.

One of the reasons was the receptivity to new ideas which was already being demonstrated by the Group people of Pru. For example, the insurance laws of most states prohibited the writing of a Group policy covering fewer than 50 lives, a barrier that snarled union-management negotiations in a number of industries. But Martin E. Segal, then an insurance broker and later head of an actuarial organization, conceived a solution: the insurance company could issue policies directly to the union if the bargaining agreements provided for a percentage of the payroll to be turned over to the union for this purpose. Whittaker welcomed the idea, and it quickly brought a great deal of new business to the Pru.

In 1945 the Group business was in an unsettled state because of the reconversion from a wartime to a peacetime economy. Pru's Group life insurance in force was reduced by $93 million (although that was only four per cent of the amount in force at the beginning of the year), and most of the reductions came from cutbacks in the aircraft and munitions industries. Nevertheless, the company—which had been in sixth place in 1943 and fifth in 1944—rose to fourth place in production of new business among companies writing Group life insurance.

That year was a landmark for Prudential in another way: in 1945 it reentered the Group pension business after an absence of five years. It was not the best of times for such a move. "From 1945 to 1949 the rate of growth of new plans fell off markedly," Joseph J. Melone* has

---

* At the time he wrote this in 1963, Melone was assistant professor of insurance at the University of Pennsylvania's Wharton School of Finance and Commerce. He later joined Prudential and became a vice president.

written. "During this postwar period, employee interest centered upon cash wage increases in an attempt to recover the lost ground suffered during the period of wage stabilization [the wartime years]."

Despite the handicap of bad timing, Prudential moved ahead rapidly in the Group pension field. In 1945 Group pension earned "considerations" (that is, money paid in to the company, like the premiums paid on insurance policies) of $44,069,000. Five years later they came to $121,219,000. In 1955 they amounted to $194,692,000.

By 1946 America was getting back to the usual comforts and tensions of peacetime. But for the Pru's Group people, one wartime problem remained. During the war the company had insured the thousands of people working on a highly secret government operation at Oak Ridge, Tennessee. After the city of Hiroshima, Japan, was destroyed by a single atomic bomb on August 6, 1945, and the city of Nagasaki by another, more powerful bomb three days later, the U.S. government disclosed that the key work on the atomic bombs was being carried on at its Oak Ridge plant. "The experience throughout the war [at the plant] was exceedingly favorable [from a life underwriter's point of view]," Whittaker reported in his 1946 annual Report to the President, "but as a condition to continuing this particular policy under our normal type of administration, we informed the War Department [now the Department of Defense] that we intended to build up a suitable catastrophe reserve."

That was the year in which the Group Insurance Department was established as a separate entity, with Whittaker elected vice president in charge of it (vice president then being the equivalent to the later rank of senior vice president). Edward M. Neumann, his top assistant, was promoted from assistant actuary to associate actuary.

From the beginning, Whittaker had put special effort into recruiting—and, when he felt like it, stealing—the most qualified and talented people he could find. And he found them—men like Alan M. Thaler, later a key person in the development of Major Medical coverage and other pioneering concepts; Meyer Melnikoff, one of the most original minds in the Group business, who came to head the Group Pension Department in later years; Kenneth C. Foster, who ultimately rose to president of the company; and far too many men of extraordinary talents to list here.

In recruiting talented young people, Whittaker used to say, "If I were a young man starting out with an insurance career, I would certainly pick

. . . Group . . . both for potential and for the fascinating nature of the work. It drives you nuts, but nobody wants to get out of it.''

One measure of the success of Whittaker's heavy emphasis on getting and developing talented people was the fact that in 1974, on the eve of the company's centennial, three of the nine Regional Home Offices were headed by men who had emerged from the Group business —Kenneth C. Nichols, Eastern Home Office; Richard G. Merrill, Southwestern Home Office; and James B. Jacobson, Western Home Office—a record all the more remarkable because the total number of employees in Group Insurance in 1974 was 3,256 and in Group Pensions 948, for a combined total of 4,204 in a company whose employees numbered about 60,000.

Whittaker's wiliness and his somewhat prankish approach to the solution of problems, especially if they involved corporate protocol, was illustrated by the manner in which he swept Ken Foster into his department. In 1953 Foster was head of administration in the District Agencies Department, and his office was next to that of James Rutherford, the head of District Agencies. One day Whittaker dropped in on Foster and asked him if he'd work for Whittaker if Foster were transferred to Group. Of course, said Foster—assuming that Whittaker had just come from discussing the matter with Rutherford in the adjacent office and that Foster was only being asked his attitude as a courtesy.

In fact, Whittaker had not even hinted at such a move to Rutherford. But immediately after leaving Foster's office, Whittaker went to Carrol Shanks and said, in effect, Foster says he'd work for me. Can I have him? Certainly, Shanks replied.

A short time later, Rutherford discovered—from Foster—that one of his best men had been filched from under his very nose. Rutherford appealed to Shanks in an effort to block the transfer, but it was too late. Shanks tended to make snap decisions, and, once made, the decisions were rarely reversed by him.

As it turned out, the shift of Foster into the Group Insurance Department was a bit of providential timing for the Pru, although it caused headaches, if not ulcers, to some people over the next nine years.

The good fortune was that Foster greatly strengthened the management of the department at a time when Whittaker's problems with alcohol were just beginning to affect his performance as an executive —although, up to a few months before his death, Whittaker continued to provide spirited leadership to his devoted followers. Knowing of the decline in Whittaker's health, executive vice president Valentine Howell believed it essential that Foster stay in Group during what was likely to be an increasingly critical period.

The headaches and ulcers developed as it became increasingly apparent with the passage of time that there was a basic clash between Foster and Neumann, Whittaker's principal assistant, a tall, bespectacled, distinguished-looking man who was regarded by his subordinates as "very bright but opinionated." The distaste between Foster and Neumann grew into a feud of memorable proportions, a clash remarkable for the fact that Neumann was, until Whittaker's death in 1958, officially Foster's superior and undeniably higher in rank, as a vice president, than second vice president Foster. Nevertheless, throughout those years—and for four years after Whittaker's death—the feud kept tensions in the Group operations at a high level. Paradoxically, each of the two principals—Foster and Neumann—tended to spend a good deal of his time in office conferences with people who worked for the other. (It says a good deal for Whittaker, Neumann, and Foster—and all the rest of the people in the department—that Pru's Group operations made such giant strides despite such diversions.)

After Whittaker's death, Group was divided into two departments: "Group Actuarial and Underwriting Department," headed by Neumann; and "Group Department," run by Foster. The areas under Foster included Group Insurance, Group Sales and Service, the three Group geographic regional divisions, and three Group Pension divisions—Actuarial, Administration, and Issue. The organization chart for that time indicates that two of the divisions under Foster (Group Insurance and Group Pension Actuarial) were formally assigned to Neumann's department but were, in fact, "under administrative direction of the Group Department." It was a mish-mash that made little sense to anyone.

When Whittaker was on his death bed, Foster was summoned to Shanks's office and informed of the proposed division of Group responsibilities. Shanks also told him that he was being elevated to the rank of vice president—the same rank as Neumann.

Understandably, the news gladdened Foster, until he noticed, with mounting uneasiness, that Shanks's knuckles, clenched on the arm of his chair, were turning white—a well-known sign that his temper was rising and he was struggling, probably in vain, to contain it. Shanks talked about Foster's new responsibilities and opportunities—the knuckles getting whiter all the while—and then he turned to the matter of personnel. By this time Shanks's knuckles were dead white and Foster—promotion or no promotion—was quailing inwardly.

"Ken," Shanks said, "you've got to change in your ways of handling people. You've got a quick, hot temper, and people are afraid of you. Now, that's not good. That's not a state of affairs beneficial to you or the company."

Then the pressures which had been building up inside Shanks broke through.

"Damn it, Ken," he roared, pounding his desk for emphasis, "you've got to control your temper! You've got to stop frightening people!"

Obviously, Shanks was wholly unaware of the apprehension caused among most Prudential people by his own displays of temper.

Even before Foster's transfer to the Group operations—from the very beginning, in fact—Whittaker's policy of manpower development began paying off in measurable terms. In 1949, for example, after little more than five years under Whittaker's leadership, the Group operations were setting spectacular records. "For the first time in the history of the Prudential," he wrote in his annual departmental report for that year, "our Group life insurance production exceeded that of any other company, and by a very large margin. Our 1949 Group life volume of $589 million is not only the largest ever written by the Prudential, but is the largest ever produced in one year by an insurance company."

A major reason for the astonishing Group success at that time was the Pru's pre-eminence in Group creditors insurance. The 1949 results, for example, were strongly affected by the business received from two new accounts, one a national consumer credit organization, the other the financing arm of one of the biggest automobile manufacturers.

In succeeding years Pru's leadership in Group creditors insurance reached a point at which the company had more than half the market for that form of coverage in the U.S. Then the Pru's share of the Group creditors insurance market began to drop until, by the time the company celebrated its hundredth birthday, the Pru share was below 10 per cent. The biggest reason for the decline involved the question of "reverse competition." This refers to the fact that the creditor can pass the premium charge on to the borrower, but can keep the dividend paid by the insurance company. The higher the premium rate charged by the insurer, the higher the charge to the borrower, and the greater the dividend. So creditors tended to shop for insurance that had high rates. Prudential refused to charge the unconscionable rates demanded, but many competitors took a more indulgent view of the practice—so a good deal of Group credit insurance went to them.

A significant innovation of the 1950's in which Pru played a leading role was Major Medical insurance. Traditional hospital and surgical insurance developed on so-called first-dollar basis which paid a lot of small claims. But payment often depended on whether the insured person was in the hospital. Moreover, that kind of insurance carried specific limits—often too low—for the number of days of hospitalization, the type of surgical procedures, and so on. Major Medical, as the name implies, was developed to cover all, or a large part of, truly major expenses which could ruin a person and his or her family (for this reason, Major Medical was often labeled "catastrophe coverage" when it first appeared). But Major Medical was not intended to cover small claims which might be difficult but would not be ruinous.

Whittaker himself became acutely aware of the limitations of the traditional insurance when his daughter had rheumatic fever, which kept her out of school for two years. "Though I had hospital insurance and surgical insurance," he said, "I collected nothing because my daughter did not go to the hospital or have an operation. We were able to take care of her at home, but the expense was considerable." Many heart cases, he pointed out, fell into the same category.

In 1949 another insurance company had issued, on an experimental basis, a policy to cover catastrophic illness or accident. That policy included a deductible amount, to eliminate small claims, and what insurance men call "a coinsurance factor"—meaning that the insured had to pay part of the bill (the theory behind coinsurance being that the policyholder thus had a stake in keeping the cost down). Many insurance companies began trying to shape similar, but better, policies.

It seemed to Whittaker and to Alan M. Thaler, the assistant whom he put in charge of the development of Major Medical coverage, that there were two weaknesses in the pioneering company's initial, experimental effort. The first was the deductible factor, which had been calculated on the basis of each separate illness. The Prudential people believed that the deductible should be based on the individual or the family's medical expenses in a year.

The second weakness perceived by the men at Pru was statistical. The premium rate had to be soundly based, had to truly reflect the risk, for an employer that instituted a Major Medical plan was going to run into trouble from his employees if the employer tried to abandon it. So the premium rate had to be as close to the mark as possible from the very beginning—despite the lack of adequate health cost statistics. To meet that lack, the task force at Pru decided to conduct a survey of the medical expenses of a segment of Prudential employees. Questionnaires were sent out to all employees at assistant manager rank and above. The survey also included employees in those levels who had retired during 1949 and 1950, the two years under study. "This was done," Thaler explained, "since it was felt that in some cases impaired health might have been the reason for retirement." Even those who had died during the years under study were included. "An attempt was made to reconstruct the medical expenses of such persons, at least for their final illness," Thaler recalled. Of course, the survey covered not only the employees themselves, but also all of their dependents.

The questionnaire survey provided a sound basis for constructing premium rates. It also uncovered some hitherto-unknown facts about medical costs. For example, the survey—which covered 5,000 Pru employees plus their families—showed that costs varied sharply from one part of the country to another: the West was most expensive, followed by the North East, the North Central, and the South, in that order. Another discovery was that surgical and home nursing costs rose dramatically with each step-up in family income.

At the 1951 gathering of the Society of Actuaries, Thaler reported on the survey, provided charts of statistics which had emerged from the study, and discussed Prudential's own Major Medical plan, which had been based on it. In the subsequent discussion, his fellow actuaries were generous in their praise of the study and his presentation. One actuary said, "The smaller companies such as ourselves should be very grateful to these larger companies like the Prudential for making their studies available to us. Unfortunately, we do not have enough experience ourselves to devise our own rates and have to base our rates upon the experience of these larger companies."

Most of the Group business being written at the time involved large numbers of employees—in the hundreds or thousands or even tens of thousands—covered under one policy. However, there clearly existed a large market of much smaller groups which was, so far, untapped.

Many agents felt that, as Group insurance covered more and more people, those who were covered by Group policies might feel they didn't need individual policies. In fact, the insurance industry as a whole had opposed Social Security in the 1930's for precisely that reason —only to find that Social Security made people more insurance-minded than they would otherwise have been. The same thing happened during the 1950's and 1960's: the enormous expansion of the Group insurance business may have contributed to the selling of even more individual insurance. But many agents could not bring themselves to accept this fact. Perhaps if they were able to sell Group insurance to their own clients, they might have a more positive attitude toward Group.

Thus was born the "Employee Security Program" (thereafter referred to within the company by its unfortunately metaphysical initials: ESP). The prime responsibility for its design was Thaler's. The life and health coverages were similar to those provided under Group policies for larger employers, and the program was developed on the basis of administrative and sales methods which were expected to produce premium costs only slightly higher than those of large-group employers. In order to conform with regulations limiting Group sales to 10 or more—ESP could cover a group as small as four—the Pru asked a few key health questions, thus technically treating the coverage as Individual insurance, since such questions were excluded from Group underwriting. The policies themselves—the actual documents—were even designed to look like individual health policies, which the agents were used to selling. When it was introduced, late in 1955, ESP quickly established itself as a strong Prudential product.

A decade later Pru set out to design new coverages for small groups. The idea and the decision came from John K. Kittredge; under his direction Martin D. Vogt headed a task force that carried out the job.

In the long procession of uncommon men and women who have been associated with Prudential since its beginning, Kittredge surely deserves a special place. Despite the handicap of a left hip that was fractured at the age of six and left him lame, Kittredge was graduated *magna cum laude* from Williams College in 1948, with election to Phi Beta Kappa. At Prudential, Kittredge became an actuary and quickly established a reputation during the 1950's as one of the brightest young men in the company. Apart from a two-and-a-half-year stint at the Mid-America Home Office at Chicago, his assignments kept him at the Corporate Home Office. During the 1960's, he often juggled several responsibilities at once. Toward the end of that decade, just after he had received approval to go ahead with the design of new small-group coverages, he was injured in an automobile accident. This time his right hip was dislocated.

"I went to visit him in the hospital," Vogt said. "I know he was in a lot of pain and discomfort, but he was already having work sent out from the office to him."

Kittredge told Vogt, "Let's go to work right now on that small-groups project."

He handed Vogt a big brown envelope in which he had received some materials from the office, and Vogt started taking notes on the envelope. Before he left the hospital room, Vogt had a list of 25 or 30 things that needed to be done.

Vogt and the task force, under Kittredge's direction, designed two new, improved small-group packages to take the place of ESP: the Group Security Program (GSP), initially including groups of 10 to 34 persons, the latter number later being raised to 49; and the Employee Benefits Program (EBP), for groups of two to nine persons. Both programs were managed, with respect to record-keeping, out of the South Central Home Office, which consistently had maintained the lowest operating costs for its administrative functions. GSP was first introduced in some states in the spring of 1970; EBP, a year later. They were immediately successful. As special agent Arthur Murray of Baltimore's Center City Agency said after GSP had been on the market for a year, "When GSP came out, I knew right away it was going to be a honey of a plan. I think mine was the first proposal to reach the Home Office." Like other agents around the country, Murray liked GSP and EBP because they were flexible and comprehensive—and because they met a deep-felt need in the community.*

---

* Still later, the Actuarial Department, under senior vice president and chief actuary Jack T. Kvernland, extended the rationale underlying GSP and EBP to the development of an *individual* health insurance policy, the Coordinated Health Insurance Program (CHIP), which was sold by District and Ordinary agents. As the company's manual for the field forces put it, CHIP "offers individuals and their families an up-to-date plan of major medical coverage of the type usually available only under Group insurance plans. Prudential has never before made this type of medical care coverage available on an individual basis. Furthermore, we are not aware of any other companies making such coverage available on an individual basis." Understandably, the public reacted to CHIP with enthusiasm, buying its protection in great numbers.

Among the other new coverages that emerged from the Group operations in the company's fourth quarter-century two had special importance. The first was a plan that provided benefits for Long Term
Disability—usually about 50 or 60 per cent of the disabled person's base
earnings. Richard J. Mellman, working with Kenneth C. Nichols, an
up-and-coming young man who would one day head the Group Insurance Department, put the program together, and Nichols followed
through on its implementation.

The second important coverage was a program of Survivor Benefits.
Early in the 1960's Nichols had become concerned with the plight of a
spouse and children left with only the death benefit under the basic life
insurance plan if the breadwinner died. Survivor Benefits, designed by
Gil Noren but strongly advocated by Nichols, provided additional
monthly income payments for a given period of time to help ease the
burdens of adjusting to a new way of life. It took some time for the
concept to win acceptance, but in time it became a significant part of
Pru's Group products.

There were many other developments late in the 1960's and during
the first half of the next decade, of course—like Dental insurance—but
the long-term significance of those developments would not be clear
until the latter part of the decade, at the earliest.

One thing was clear: Group life and health insurance had come a long
way from the early, uncertain days. It was now a mature operation,
staffed by highly skilled professionals, that made a significant contribution to the company's stature. In 1974, Group Insurance celebrated the
imminent centennial by achieving the best sales year in the history of the
industry with continued excellent earnings results. The volume of new
Group Life cases was $4.7 billion—267 per cent of the figure for the
preceding year—and for the first time in at least a decade the volume of
new cases exceeded the additional issue production from in-force cases.
The overall Group Life production in 1974 was $12.2 billion. Group
Health premium sales also set a record, increasing by 42 per cent over
the previous year to $135 million.

The road to that achievement had been blocked, to some extent, by
the somewhat unreal division of responsibilities between Foster and
Neumann in the late 1950's. That contretemps was not resolved until
after Louis R. Menagh succeeded Carrol M. Shanks as president of Pru
on January 10, 1961. Foster lost no time in pointing out to Menagh the
inherent difficulties in the organizational structure as it had existed for

several years. As a result, on April 1, 1962, Group activities were assigned to two new departments: Group Insurance, which handled all aspects of Group life and health insurance; and Group Annuity, which was responsible for all Group pension operations (in the 1970's that department's name was changed to Group Pension).

Henry E. Blagden, who had been working with Neumann all along, was given responsibility for the actuarial, underwriting, and contract functions of the new department, and Meyer Melnikoff was transferred from the Planning and Development Department to take charge of pension sales, service, and administration. After Neumann's retirement in 1966, Melnikoff succeeded him as senior vice president in charge of the department.

A quiet, reflective person who nevertheless enjoyed the give-and-take of practical business discussions, Melnikoff had worked for a year as a high school teacher of mathematics before joining Pru as an actuarial trainee in 1939. After serving as an officer with the Army Signal Corps in the Philippines during World War II he had returned to the company to begin a steady rise through the ranks. Early in his postwar career he had made himself an authority on pension plans of all kinds. In 1955 Melnikoff and J. Edward Day of Pru's Law Department (later head of the Western Home Office, which he left to become Postmaster General of the United States) jointly prepared one of the company's opening salvos in what was to become a hard-fought campaign, an article in the *CLU Journal* entitled "The Variable Annuity as a Life Insurance Company Product."

A variable annuity is a contract which provides that the payments to the annuitant will vary from month to month, depending on the results of the investment of the annuity's funds in equities—primarily common stocks. This contrasts with the traditional life insurance company annuity, which provides for a fixed-dollar payout.

The variable annuity concept emerged as an attempt to cope with the long-term inflation which had been eroding the value of the dollar and thus causing severe difficulties to many retired persons. In 1950 William C. Greenough, of the Teachers Insurance and Annuity Association, carried out a study which indicated that, over the previous 70 years, income from combined fixed and variable annuities would have provided a total income that would reasonably have retained its purchasing power, thereby resisting the effects of inflation. As a result of his report, his organization established the College Retirement Equities

Fund as a sister institution, to permit college teachers to allocate up to 50 per cent of their premium payments to the purchase of equities in a common pool.

For national life insurance companies like the Pru, the road to variable annuities was not so simple; it was blocked by legal obstacles at the state and federal levels and by the opposition of more traditional life insurance companies and important groups in the securities industry. As *Business Week* put it in a cover story on Prudential in 1958,

> Prudential's Shanks is the moving force behind a massive effort to offer variable annuities to the public at large via the nation's roughly 200,000 life insurance salesmen (about 29,000 to 30,000 of whom sell Pru policies).
>
> To do this, he must eventually overcome the dogged opposition of a large and powerful segment of the financial world: the Securities and Exchange Commission, the Investment Bankers Association, the New York and American stock exchanges, the National Association of Securities Dealers, the National Association of Investment Companies—plus a formidable group of opponents within his own industry, led by Frederic W. Ecker, president of the Metropolitan Life Insurance Company.

Shanks argued that there was "a good possibility" that the inflationary spiral would continue indefinitely, depleting the income of persons who had retired on fixed-dollar programs.

Ecker, on the other hand, asserted that there had been "little inflation other than during war, and in periods immediately following war." He also pointed out that there had been periods—few but sometimes lengthy—when the cost of living rose while stock prices fell.

While the debate—and the innumerable legal and legislative battles—dragged on, the public made its own decision known in that ultimate forum, the marketplace: an increasing number of pension funds which had been managed by insurance companies were shifted to banks which were free of the legal restrictions limiting insurance companies' investments in equities. (However, most of the pension funds which were moving increasingly into equities continued to pay benefits on a fixed-dollar basis. This meant that if the expected increase in return was realized, it would not help the pensioner but would reduce the employer's pension costs.)

One major impediment to Pru's selling of variable annuities, the company felt, lay in the regulatory requirements of the Securities and Exchange Commission, which insisted that Prudential was subject to its jurisdiction. Pru asserted that it was exempt from SEC regulations governing the sale of variable annuities, and the issue was fought all the way to the U.S. Supreme Court, which ruled that Prudential was not exempt. At that point the SEC, having won its court fight, relaxed its regulations somewhat. The commission authorized the Pru to sell variable annuities to the retirement funds of corporations, with certain minor limitations, and to self-employed persons. But Shanks, by that time, was no longer at the head of Pru.

By the summer of 1967, the *Wall Street Journal* was able to carry an article headlined: "Variable Annuity Policies are Becoming Darling of the Life Insurance Industry." In the course of the lengthy report, the newspaper said, "Even one of the most conservative of the major insurance companies, Metropolitan Life Insurance Company of New York, has apparently found the lure of variable annuities irresistible. This year, it was learned, the Met began negotiating variable annuities with its Group clients. . . ."

However, a half dozen years later the variable annuity no longer appeared as attractive as it had been. Double-digit inflation had joined with a prolonged stock market slump to batter what had been intended as a protection to retired people. The economy was in a state rarely experienced before in America. Over the long pull, it was possible —even probable—that the trends found in Greenough's 70-year study would continue to hold up. But retired people cannot feed themselves today on tomorrow's probabilities, and many companies felt compelled to put a floor under variable annuity payments to retired employees. Prudential's own retired men and women received such protection from the company for a limited period.

During the 1950's and the 1960's there were many other far-reaching changes in the Group Pension business. In 1951, 80 per cent of the company's funds in that area were held as reserves for annuities purchased for specific individuals; only 20 per cent represented funds held on a collective basis, not allocated by individuals. Twenty years later the collective funds were about equal to the individual reserves.

Before and for a decade after World War II, "pension plans generally employed an insurance company to furnish a full package of retirement plan services, including investment of funds, actuarial work, plan design, record-keeping, employee communications, and payment of benefits,'' Melnikoff once recalled. But ''the 1950's began a trend toward unbundling of pension plan services.''

There were many other changes taking place during those years—in law, society, business, trade unions, and, most of all, attitudes—that altered the Group pension business sharply. As Melnikoff once put it, Pru's pension people basically dealt in ideas.

''Many years ago in the early days of our business,'' he said, ''the ideas in many cases were simpler—such as the mere concept of a pension plan and its advantages to the employer. In those days, the establishment of any pension plan required salesmanship with missionary zeal.

''Such simple idea sales may occur today, but largely in smaller companies. The idea of a pension itself is now well accepted and pensions are bargained for by unions, so that the creation and design of a basic pension is unlikely to be an important factor in many large cases today. [Nowadays] ideas, to be helpful to sales, must involve concepts which have not yet received widespread acceptance—such as the multi-collective bargaining unit structure of the [Prudential-managed pension fund of the] Western Conference of Teamsters or the variable annuity structure of the New York City teachers' program.''

Many of the new ideas of the postwar quarter-century did not necessarily originate with Pru, but most of the better ideas were quickly adopted, refined, and developed by the company.

In the development of new concepts, Melnikoff and his aides found themselves working ever more closely with Prudential's investment experts, helping to devise investment alternatives for pension funds. One result of this search was PRISA, the company's Property Investment Separate Account, which was established to give pension plans an opportunity to diversify their investments by putting a portion of their funds in property, to supplement the income from stocks and bonds. PRISA was attractive to pension funds for several reasons: if inflation continued, real estate values were likely to appreciate sufficiently to provide a hedge against a troublesome bind; property offered a relatively high current yield; PRISA offered diversification both by property type and by geographic location; and it was managed by Pru's own Real Estate Investment Department, including approximately 300 specialists in nearly 100 cities, in addition to a Corporate Home Office staff with an outstanding record for investment returns. So it was understandable that by the fall of 1974, Melnikoff was able to report that "the roster of our PRISA contract-holders includes 20 of the top 100" industrial corporations listed in *Fortune* magazine's annual survey of U.S. companies.

Another arrangement useful for many pension funds was one in which the pension plan's money was put into the investment fund of Pru's Variable Contract Account. As needed, withdrawals could be made to buy fixed-dollar annuities for retiring employees. The amount of the pension benefit paid to a retiring employee was set by the provisions of the pension plan and was not measured by the investment experience of the investment fund.

About the same time—early in the 1960's—Prudential began offering Non-Participating Contracts. These were designed for employers who wanted to fund a pension obligation on a basis which provided for the lowest guaranteed initial cost, with no future dividends or experience credits. Among those who found merit in such contracts might be employers who were going out of business but wanted to buy the benefits accrued to that time for all the employees. Pru's Group pension experts offered nonparticipating contracts to cover terminated pension plans, retired persons living under continuing plans, and maturity funding of profit-sharing plans. In 1962, the first year in which the company offered such contracts, one of the contracts issued by it involved "a single consideration of more than $12,500,000," according to the department's Report to the President.

Four years later some alliteration-mad people put together the company's Flexible Funding Facility for clients who wanted not only freedom as to the timing and movement of contributions, but also complete flexibility in the use of Pru's annuity facilities. Under FFF, clients could achieve the kind of investment mix they wanted, including equity, deposit, short term, and property accounts.

A few years earlier the pension business had begun to benefit from a number of events. In 1959 insured pension plans, which had suffered a tax disadvantage as compared with trusteed plans, won a break when they were given partial federal income tax relief. Three years later the capital gains tax imposed on life insurance companies in 1959 was removed from all qualified pension reserves based on a separate asset account.

Inflation had become a persistent problem in the years that followed

World War II. Its impact was apparent in interest rates, including bonds. Indeed, investments of all kinds were returning yields far above the prewar levels. But insurance company annuity rates reflected the rate of return on the entire portfolio, which included many securities purchased years earlier when yields were much lower. Within the insurance industry, a number of people—including Pru's pension specialists—began to advocate what came to be called "investment year" interest methods for crediting interest to Group pension general account clients. After two years or more of study within the company, the board of directors, in 1961, authorized the use of the "investment year" system, which reflected the higher rate of return on new money and thus benefited pension clients. However, New York's insurance regulators challenged Pru's right to employ the new method, and it was not until 1963 that it was possible for the company to begin using the new method for dividend purposes in its Group pension business.

Despite its small staff—less than 600 in the Corporate Office and perhaps 100 in the Western Home Office, plus a field force of a couple of dozen persons scattered across the country—Pru's Group Pension Department had grown into a very important part of the business, starting from those World War II days when the company wrote no Group pension business at all. By the company's reckoning, it was in first place among life insurance companies in new business written in 1974. In terms of assets, by the latest reckoning Pru's Group Pension operations were No. 1 in the life insurance industry—indeed, only two other institutions, both New York banks, had more pension assets than Prudential.

Of course, the giant strides of the Group Pension Department had been made possible, in significant measure, by the outstanding yield record developed and sustained over the years by the investment departments (see Chapter 22).

But the Group Pension achievements were impressive by any measure. At the end of 1951, nine per cent of Prudential's total assets represented Group Pension reserves. By the end of 1974, that figure had tripled to over 27 per cent. Indeed, during most of the years since Prudential's assets topped those of the Metropolitan, Pru's Group Pension assets had given the company the edge over the Met.

There were always problems—there always would be. In 1974 a federal law to reform abuses found in the administration of some pension funds in the U.S. created complications for life insurance companies, employers, labor unions, trade associations, and even the federal officials who would have to put the new law into effect. But Pru's Group Pension people would handle that problem, and the next, and those that followed.

The men and women of Group—both Insurance and Pension —thrived on difficulties and on the unexpected. That was the nature of the business.

They tell of the time when Louis Menagh, not yet president of the company, was accosted in the hall by another Pru officer.

"What's new in Group?" the man asked.

"I don't know," Menagh replied. "I just got back from lunch."

21/The Agonizing Duel

There are some men and women to whom bizarre and unusual things happen more frequently than occurs with the ordinary run of people. Or perhaps they just recount their adventures—real or imaginary—in a more colorful way. Whatever the explanation, there are such people, and one such Prudential person, during the last quarter of the company's first century, was an officer whose legal name was Maurice F. Terbrueggen, although nobody ever called him anything but Terry. Some of the incidents in which he was involved were the stuff that legends are made of. Most of them took place when he was manager of Pru's Brooklyn office, which covered the waterfront, among other areas. That was right after the second World War.

"We had a new, inexperienced agent, a recent immigrant whose native language was German," Terbrueggen recalled. "Unfortunately, he had not mastered the English language very well yet. Even more unfortunately, his territory consisted almost entirely of Italian-Americans, many of whom spoke only broken English. Somehow, he managed to communicate just well enough to sell a fair amount of insurance."

One day a policyholder on that debit came into Terbrueggen's office to file a death claim. Dolefully he told Terbrueggen that his "Rosie" had died.

After murmuring the proper expressions of sympathy, Terbrueggen learned that the German-speaking agent had insured the Italian-speaking man, his wife, and their children, including the lamented "Rosie," who had attained only the tender age of nine at the time of her death. Terbrueggen had no way of knowing what her weight and height had been at the time she was insured, three years earlier—probably the agent had simply written "Normal," a practice that was permitted in those days on Weekly Premium policies covering children under 15 years of age.

225

"When did she die?" Terbrueggen asked the bereaved policyholder.

"Just yesterday," he replied mournfully.

"Had she been sick long?" Terbrueggen probed gently.

"No," the man said. "It was accident."

"How did it happen?"

"She was hit by a car."

"Crossing the street?"

"No. She was pulling my wagon."

"Rosie," it seemed, was the man's horse.

"As far as I know," Terbrueggen said 30 years later, "it was the only time Prudential ever insured the life of a horse."

In insurance, as in other fields of activity, Brooklyn was different from almost any point of view.

Terbrueggen's district included neighborhoods which had spawned Murder, Inc., in the 1930's and would be home to some of the most notorious gangsters of the postwar period. Processing an endless stream of death claims covering men whose bodies had been dumped out of cars, found in the trunks of stolen cars, tossed into the East River, or fallen in the street after gun fights, Terbrueggen came to the conclusion that his agency must have the greatest number of homicide claims in the U.S.

One day Terbrueggen got a call from some gangsters who told him that one of his agents had been taken out to sea and would be tossed into the ocean 20 miles from shore because he had confused the mobsters' followers about the insurance protection they were entitled to under a Prudential policy issued to an organization which, it developed, was controlled by the hoodlums. Dashing over to the organization's offices, Terbrueggen reassured the dissidents that they did have all the protection their leaders claimed to have bought. His agent, he told them, had been mistaken. Later that day the agent, chastened by his narrow escape and with an appreciation of the hazards of life unusual even among insurance agents, was set free.

Terbrueggen's experiences became legendary because they were unique. But whenever agents gather and exchange stories, it becomes apparent that the unusual and the unexpected are a part of the life of virtually all life insurance agents, regardless of the sales organization in which they work.

In Prudential, there are two separate large sales organizations. By far the largest, in terms of personnel and sales, is the District Agencies Department, which sells Ordinary and Monthly Debit Ordinary insurance and collects the premiums for Weekly Premium policies still in force. (Ordinary insurance, issued on an individual basis, is sold in face amounts of $1,000 or more, the premiums being paid by mail. Weekly Premium is the customary name today in the Pru for the Industrial insurance which gave the company its start, although no new Weekly policies have been sold since 1968. Monthly Debit Ordinary is like any other Ordinary life insurance, except that the premiums are collected by the agent.) The Debit system of insurance was intended primarily to serve low- and middle-income groups. By the end of 1974 there were 27,568 employees in the Pru's District Agencies Department—of whom 19,734, engaged in selling policies and collecting premiums, were designated as *agents*.

Their counterparts in the Ordinary Agencies Department were called *special agents:* there were 4,415 of them at the end of 1974. The primary charge of the Ordinary Agencies is to serve middle- and upper-income groups, as well as the business insurance and estate conservation markets. Supporting the efforts of the special agents were 2,043 employees of the Ordinary Agencies Department.

In both organizations, a large portion of the responsibility for recruiting, training, and developing agents—agents who would become successful career underwriters—was borne by middle management in the field. This vital role in the growth of the two departments was filled by *sales managers* in the District Agencies and *division managers* in the Ordinary Agencies. They were regarded by Prudential's top marketing executives as "the backbone of the sales effort," as one memorandum put it.

Agents—whether District or Ordinary—often feel that they are insufficiently appreciated, and there is some evidence to support that suspicion. Most of the textbooks and other literature dealing with insurance concern themselves primarily with actuarial work, regulation, investments, administrative matters, and other lofty matters, while ignoring the practical, professional, and ethical problems faced by the agents. Indeed, one multi-volumed work devotes not a single chapter to the work of agents. Nevertheless, the agents are the most important people in the insurance business. They are the front-line troops on whom everything else depends.

"It is not, after all, the Shankses and the Beals who have made Prudential what it is," *Fortune* magazine commented in 1964. "Those billions in premiums have to be sweated out of the consciences of the people in what is still the most agonizing person-to-person sales duel on the American scene. The root strength of any life insurance company lies in its agency force. . . ."

Since the days of Dryden it has been recognized that life insurance is not simply bought—it is sold. Passive marketing systems, which made life insurance available to those who chose to go to an institution to buy it, have never been more than a negligible factor in total life insurance protection, as shown by official statistics. Ultimately, everything depends on the individual man or woman who presents the client with a program designed to protect his or her family in case of death or illness, to plan for the costs for a college education, or to prepare for other future needs, including retirement. Almost always, it comes down to the individual agent who works with business men and women, helping them set up Group health and life insurance programs, pension funds, and protection for their company against the possible financial consequences of the loss of a partner or other key executive. Thus it is, in the final analysis, the agent who provides millions of people with insurance protection and, indirectly, makes available the capital needed for a significant portion of the economic prosperity of the country.

Moreover, there is no reason to think that the importance of the individual agent will diminish in the foreseeable future. As Donald S. MacNaughton said in 1969, despite government-provided benefits, mass merchandising, and the increasing competition from other financial institutions, "The future for the sale of individual life insurance products by individual salesmen is bright. It will *always* be necessary to persuade people to buy and pay for the proper amount of security for their families. I doubt that mass coverage and mass techniques will *ever* fill the need so long as we continue to live under a free-enterprise system."

When *Fortune* referred to the marketing of life insurance as "the most agonizing person-to-person sales duel," it was not engaging in hyperbole. Dealing as the agent does in intangibles, it requires real courage on the agent's part to keep ringing doorbells, opening office doors, and facing strangers, day after day, all day long—and very often in the evening and over the weekend. Despite the air of confidence that agents always try to project, they are frequently beset by the fear of rejection. Somehow, by each in his or her own way, that fear is overcome, and the relentless process of uncovering leads, meeting prospects, preparing insurance programs, and selling is carried on.

Given the tensions and the pressures, the self-doubts and the need to find inner resources of strength, it is inevitable that agents should often find themselves taking advantage of all manner of circumstances to close a sale. In Sioux Falls a special agent, Earl Snyder, waited on customers to help out a drive-in restaurant owner who was suddenly overwhelmed with business, then sold him a policy on his 15-year-old son. When a young man drove his car into the automobile of Wayne Tooman, a special agent in Muscatine, Iowa, Tooman used the encounter to open a series of conversations which ended with his selling a $10,000 policy on the other driver's life and health insurance coverage on his mother. Cy Seltman, a special agent in Pittsburgh, having failed to persuade a prospect, was leaving when he slipped on the ice; "It wouldn't make any difference if I were hurt," he called out to the client, "because I've got the kind of insurance you should have"—and the householder finally gave in and bought the policy Seltman had recommended. As a tornado wrecked much of Fargo, North Dakota, special agent Calvin J. Dargan, huddling in a basement with a young couple and their baby, got their signature on a health insurance policy; at that moment, all the young husband wanted to know was, "Where do I sign?" In Oklahoma an agent even sold a policy to a policeman who had stopped him for speeding.

Almost anything can happen to an insurance agent. Tom Watanabe, of Bakersfield, California, called on a policyholder to urge him not to let his insurance policy lapse. After agreeing to keep the policy in force, the policyholder brought out his pet, an alligator, and Watanabe, trying to show his friendliness, reached out to see if the alligator would open its mouth. It did, and the next day Watanabe had the embarrassment of explaining to his doctor and his manager how he happened to get bitten on the arm by an alligator.

Because of the frequency of their calls to collect weekly or monthly premiums, many District agents become trusted advisers to their policyholders. After the death of an elderly woman, a note was found in her handwriting. "Please see my insurance man," it said. "He will take care of everything and knows exactly what to do." The note also asked that he speak at the woman's funeral. He did as she had asked. As a result, her daughter decided to buy a mortgage insurance policy from him on her home, as well as a policy on the life of each of her four children.

In St. Petersburg, Florida, agent Stan Brezic, calling on two elderly sisters who were barely able to subsist, heard one of them mention some "old, worthless" stock they'd had for years. When he checked with a stockbroker, the agent found the stock was actually worth $46,000. Understandably, they chose to invest it in Prudential annuities.

Special agent Jim Chandler wrote a $20,000 policy on a young man. When the client named his fiancée as beneficiary and mentioned that they had not yet decided who would perform the wedding ceremony, Chandler pointed out that as a notary public he was authorized under the laws of their state to administer the marriage vows. Two days later Chandler officiated at the ceremony.

When Robert H. Wlecke began as an agent in 1936 on his father's debit, "old No. 7," in Mount Vernon, Illinois, "I can recall a Mrs. Rose saying when I was collecting in her home at noontime, 'Well, Bob, this is your Dad's day to have luncheon with me, so sit down.' " Because Wlecke's father, Fred C. (Fritz), always had walked his debit in winter and could not get back home for his noon meal, he always lunched with a different policyholder, depending on the day and the date of the month. Young Robert, who later became a manager in Quincy, Illinois, covered his debit by automobile and found "it took a lot of talking without hurting those fine people's feelings" to persuade them to accept his desire to drive home for lunch with his wife, Helen.

As a boy, Robert sometimes rode on the handlebars of the bicycle with which his father had covered the debit in summer. During the gas and tire rationing days of the second World War, when the younger Wlecke couldn't get any tires or enough gasoline, he "bought a bike and rode it for a year on that same old debit No. 7," and he "would take one of my little girls on the handlebars during the nice summer days."

To get to every nook and cranny of the American continent, agents have used virtually every conceivable means of transportation. Years ago, when Canadian agent Fred Smith, like a number of other agents, used snowshoes to reach remote lumber and mining camps, he still managed to win the President's Trophy as the top agent in the dominion. Today several agents in the U.S. as well as Canada cover their debits by snowmobile. Horses have been used, and so have boats. Kelleys Island, a 2,900-acre spot in the western part of Lake Erie, ten miles north of Sandusky, is part of John J. Hildebrand's debit; of the 60 or so year-round families, 46 are Prudential clients, and Hildebrand reaches them by ferry in summer and airplane in winter.

To an outsider's eye, there is no discernible pattern to successful agents. Robert A. Beck, who became president of Prudential, second only to MacNaughton, in 1974, was the first agent to rise to the highest rank of management since Dryden himself. He recalled a former opera singer who became "a great agent." Then, too, "teacher-coaches are usually good." For a time, Henry Aaron, the baseball immortal who broke Babe Ruth's home-run record, was a Prudential agent during off-season. Kenneth Witt—who fell ill with osteomyelitis, a bone disease, in 1929 at the age of eight and suffered the amputation of most of his right leg in 1938, when he was 17—flunked a Prudential aptitude test for agents in 1952, but nevertheless persuaded Bill Reis of Pru's Lincoln, Nebraska, agency to take him on, first as a part-time special agent, and within months as a full-time person. In his first full year he was the leading special agent in the North Central Home Office's territory, earned membership in the President's Club of Pru for at least 10 consecutive years, and was awarded life membership in the Million Dollar Round Table.

Many of the best agents never intended to go into the insurance business. Ron Sempetrean of Chicago wanted to be a teacher and "took Pru's job only because they hired me." However, his parents were Prudential policyholders, and he had noticed that "the agents [who came to the house] dressed well and apparently did well." Like many other novice agents, "for the first couple of years [he] felt like a huckster." Then a 180-degree change occurred. The reason: "I started paying claims." In Sempetrean's view, "You really become an agent when you pay a claim that enables a family to maintain its standard of living." He remembered the indescribable expression of warmth and relief on the face of a widow when he delivered a check that made it possible for her to pay off the mortgage on her own. On the other hand, he was haunted by his failures in salesmanship, like a barber he tried to sell "who was painting the wrought iron railings on the steps of his shop; he had two kids and only $500 in insurance, but he said, 'I ain't gonna die'—and the following Sunday he dropped dead after Mass." Despite his initial lack of commitment, Sempetrean sold $1 million worth of life insurance during his first year as an agent and duplicated that feat his second year. But it was not until his first wife died at the age of 31 that he fully realized that "everyone is subject to the hazards of living." Ever afterward he told his associates, "I can hang in there longer because of what I've gone through."

An increasing number of agents, as Pru's centennial approached, were women and members of ethnic minority groups. In fact, as a 1975 Ordinary Agencies memo pointed out, "Long before the feminist movement became the 'in' thing, women were making significant contributions to the Ordinary Agencies' growth." The memo listed these examples:

Laura Benham of Buffalo, who ranked among the top producers as early as 1945 and was a consistent leader in a club whose goal was to turn in at least one policy application each week. She was the first Prudential woman agent to reach the Million Dollar Round Table.

Mary C. McKeon of Newark, who was an excellent insurance saleswoman. She became "one of the first women to enter agency management" when she accepted appointment as an assistant manager in 1952.

Moo Kit Tsui of the New York Agency, who was still active at the time of the company's centennial. "A perennial million dollar producer since 1952," she was the first Prudential woman to become a qualifying and life member of the Million Dollar Round Table.

Felina Saguil, "a multimillion-dollar personal producer and an outstanding division manager," became Pru's first woman agency manager when she was named head of the Knickerbocker Agency in Manhattan in 1973.

Two retired women agents who were still selling insurance made the list. They were Jennie L. McNulty, who was 80 in 1975, an outstanding agent from the time she joined the Miami Agency in 1942 until her "retirement" in 1965, and Anna V. Connor, who became an Ordinary agent in the Tampa Agency in 1932. Although she "retired" in 1965, Anna Connor nevertheless managed to sell over $1 million worth of insurance for the year in 1970, 1973, and 1974, although she was then almost 80.

The proportion of blacks was growing steadily in both the District and the Ordinary agency forces. A leading District agent, for example, was

Donald A. Lusk of the Marquette (Wisconsin) District. In his first year of service, 1964, he became a million-dollar producer. In the first half of the 1970's Lusk won a President's Citation as an outstanding agent every year and, beginning in 1971, qualified each year to be a member of the Million Dollar Round Table.

Another was Larry W. Clark, who also became a million-dollar producer in his first year as an agent, 1965. That was in the Chicago Heights District, where he was promoted to sales manager at the beginning of 1967. In his first year as sales manager, his staff won the President's Trophy and also averaged over a million dollars per agent—a first in the District Agencies. Four years later Clark was promoted to manager of the Calumet Gateway District.

Still a third who wrote a million dollars' worth of insurance in his first year as an agent was John Lassiter. That was in the same organization as Lusk—the Marquette District—and in the same year that Lusk first reached a million, 1964. An alumnus of the University of Illinois, Lassiter was named sales manager in that district in 1966, and two years later his staff won the President's Trophy. In 1969 he became manager of the district, and beginning the following year his district won four consecutive President's Citations.

On the Ordinary side, the field forces included such extraordinary blacks as Booker Rice, who had been offered scholarships from 60 colleges when he graduated from high school. He chose Notre Dame University, from which he graduated in 1959 with a bachelor's degree in finance and economics. By May 1970 he had been given the assignment of starting a new agency in Chicago, beginning operations with five agents. Little more than a year and a half later, the agency had grown to 20 agents who produced close to $20 million of new business. In January 1973 he was promoted to director of agencies in the North Central Home Office, which at the time made him the highest ranking black in Prudential's field organization.

Then there was Albert W. Thompson, who, although he was nearly 50 years old when he entered the insurance field as a special agent for Pru, quickly earned his CLU (Chartered Life Underwriter) degree. In 1968—the year after he went to work for Prudential—Thompson qualified for the Million Dollar Round Table, and he kept on achieving that goal every year thereafter, earning seven President's Citations from the company along the way. Eventually he became the first black qualifying and life member of the Million Dollar Round Table. Thompson was with the Cleveland Central Agency.

Charles L. Brown, in the words of a company memorandum, "earned considerable renown among his peers by selling a Group case on the largest department store in Baltimore simply by walking in off the street and asking to see the personnel manager." A Pru special agent since 1963, Brown was named manager of its Center City Agency in Baltimore in 1971.

Still another notable black special agent was Andrew Langston of Rochester, New York. Besides being a sales leader whose business had an unusually low lapse rate, Langston was also prominent in civic activities. He was chairman of the Rochester Chamber of Commerce's transportation committee, treasurer of the local council of the Boy Scouts of America, first vice president of the Rochester Business Opportunities Corporation, one of the founders of the first black radio station in Rochester, and chairman of the board of Action for a Better Community, which, among other achievements, was instrumental in establishing the first full-service minority bank in the city. Besides winning a place with the Million Dollar Round Table and various Prudential sales honors, Langston twice won the company's Community Service Award. In Pru's centennial, his long-standing commitment to his community was to be recognized with a Prudential Century Award.

Among all Pru agents—male and female, black and white—probably the most unusual and controversial was Gary Fink, of Minneapolis. Fink, a transplanted New Yorker who became an enthusiastic resident of Minneapolis, had fairly long, curly hair, long sideburns, a mustache that compared with Groucho Marx's, and clothing that was once described by the Minneapolis *Tribune* as "considerably beyond businessman-mod." His office in the Pillsbury Building, where he had incorporated his operations as Phinque, Inc., looked more like an elegant crash pad than a business center: there were few conventional desks, big floor pillows abounded, a small but very active dog enlivened things, several young women of exceptional beauty moved about, and mural-sized photographs and posters of people like the Beatles, Janis Joplin, and Lenny Bruce covered the walls.

But Fink, despite his somewhat counterculture appearance, was thoroughly business-like in his approach to insurance, and Minneapolis businessmen had come to appreciate that fact. More than half his business was with corporations, and the proportion rose each year. In his first 15 years with Prudential as a special agent, he qualified for the President's Club, an honor for top salesmen, 13 times and won the President's Trophy for leading the entire company three times. In 1971 he set company records for both volume and premiums.

"An outlandish success," as the Chicago *Daily News* once described him in its business and financial section, Fink contrasted sharply with his agency manager, Burton Bauernfeind, of whom he was very fond. "I'm kind of conservative," Bauernfeind once said, in a monumental understatement, "and at first I thought [Fink's unconventional appearance and life-style were] kind of cockeyed. But he's the leading agent in our office, and why should I care how he looks as long as he does the job. Anyway, I can't control my own kid and I guess I can't control him."

But there were others in the company and the industry who were less tolerant of Fink's ways, probably because of a combination of envy, inhibitions, and distrust of new mores. Fink didn't help matters, either, with some of his public pronouncements. Once, for example, he told a reporter for a national features service, "The insurance business today is conservative, sometimes reactionary, and appallingly humorless. Being an insurance salesman under these conditions is like eating Rice Krispies dry."

Of course, the same could be said for almost any other line of work. In fact, a strong case can be made for the argument that the selling of life insurance offers more satisfactions than most other fields. Ray Chin, of Worcester, Massachusetts, could attest to that. On the last day of 1967 he received this letter from a client, William R. Beyer:

Hi, Ray:
This is the holiday season. It means, among other things, a breather for me in my quite busy schedule. Furthermore, it is a time for reflection; and, as out-of-place as it may seem, you, Ray, are in my thoughts.
Stated simply: thank you for being of service to me that fortuitous day last August when we met on Commonwealth Avenue at Boston University. By God, you're right! Life insurance, even for a person like me with no direct dependents, *does* give one a satisfied mind. And Ray, listen to this to bring it into focus:

Last October 28 I was involved in a traffic accident, my first in eight years of driving. My car, hit broadside at an intersection, was demolished and went to the scrap pile. I, by the grace of God, escaped unscathed. But Ray! Oh, so close, so close!

You, Ray, take people's money from them. But, barring rampant inflation, it is a purely equity situation. I am saving for no one's end other than my own (or my future wife's) and I am receiving manifold protection in and for myself at the same time.

Idealistic thoughts are nice, but don't kid yourself: boiled down, we are living in a cold, impersonal, and very materialistic society. How many friends have you if you can't pay your bills —even for the essentials of food, clothing, shelter? Within reason, due in no small part to you, I have very little worry here.

Ray—you have a role as important as any doctor, lawyer, minister, or rabbi. You help people to protect and preserve themselves. My appreciation I extend to you for serving me.

During the decades following the second World War, both the District Agencies and the Ordinary Agencies underwent sweeping changes. By far the most dramatic reshaping took place in the District Agencies. In part, it was stimulated by the union activity but some of the reforms instituted during the Shanks administration occurred before collective bargaining, and most of the improvements, refinements, modernization were inevitable, given the nature of Carrol Shanks's revolutionary resculpturing of the company and the business.

Before the war, agents were recruited for the District Agencies in hit-or-miss fashion, were underpaid, had little or no hope of advancement through management jobs (which were usually given to persons who had started as clerks in the Home Office), worked a six-day week, and were subjected to intense pressure and harassment—even to humiliation, as in "The Report," a week's end meeting of each District Agency, where agents were given tongue-lashings in front of their colleagues if they had not achieved their goal for the week, and the agent making the worst showing, in some agencies, was actually forced to sit in a corner with a dunce cap on his head. Even the most productive of agents hated "The Report."

During Shanks's administration all of that changed, but for once the credit must be given, not to that business giant, Shanks, but to another man, his executive vice president for field operations, Harold M.

Stewart. Although Stewart was widely disliked for what many people regarded as sadistic practices toward his peers and the higher levels of management under him, he apparently was capable of empathy with, and compassion for, the men in the field—possibly because his own father had been a field man. At conferences of field men, Stewart usually was able to address every man by name, although he might only have met him once.

"A half century ago," recalled L. LaVern Wilkinson, who retired as vice president for sales of the Southwestern Home Office in 1974, "few of our agents were really salesmen who knew their products. Most of them were simply premium-collectors. It used to be said that streetcar conductors made the best recruits, because they made change real good."

One of the most important changes initiated by Stewart was the announcement of a new policy: hereafter, men could not expect to rise to executive positions in the District Agencies Department unless they had had field experience—and Stewart made it plain that he preferred the field work to be the selling of insurance as an agent.

Tests were devised to help identify those persons with the maximum aptitude for life insurance selling, and recruiting was put on an organized basis. So was training. Stan Gagner, who started as a Prudential agent in 1939, said, "At the beginning I received six small manuals about which I had to complete questionnaires, and that was about the extent of my training." Beginning under Stewart, an elaborate system of manuals, audio-visual aids, and other training materials was developed. For a time, the company even experimented with sending new agents to a school operated at the Corporate Home Office in Newark, but that proved no better than carefully prepared instructional materials sent to the man in the field and the field training he received from his sales manager.

James E. Rutherford had succeeded Orville Beal as head of District Agencies, but after one year he was sent out to Chicago to head the Mid-America Home Office there, and Paul Palmer took his place. After six years as the head of District Agencies, Palmer gave way to William P. Lynch in 1959, and Lynch had directed that organization for 16 years by the time of the company's centennial—years of the greatest growth in the history of the District Agencies.

In the opinion of Lynch, who started as an agent when he was given "the rate book and a pat on the back," Stewart's reforms in the District Agencies—although of relatively little interest to Shanks, who did not profess to be an insurance expert, interested in the intricacies of agency work—formed the spearhead for Shanks's demolition of the elite complex of executives, practices, and modes of thought which had dominated the company for six decades.

The years after World War II saw some remarkable achievements by District agents. For example, William L. Joiner, Jr., working out of Cedartown, Georgia (population: about 10,000) repeatedly outsold agents from richer and more populous areas. He won the President's Trophy for Agents four times—1960, 1962, 1963, and 1966—and qualified 15 times for Pru's International Business Conference because of the huge volume of insurance he sold.

Joiner's record was almost equaled by Donald D. Slovin of Chicago's Jefferson Park District. Slovin, who began working as an agent in 1963, qualified for the International Business Conference every year after his appointment, and he won the President's Trophy twice, in 1965 and 1969. In the years when he didn't win the trophy, he won the President's Citation.

Ronald P. Sempetrean, like Slovin, qualified for the International Business Conference his first year with Pru and every year after that—16 years in all, by the spring of 1975. (Besides Slovin and Sempetrean, only one other District agent—John C. McChesney, of the Mid-America Home Office's Northwest Suburban District—qualified during every year after his appointment.) Sempetrean of Chicago's Lake View District also won the President's Trophy in 1972.

Another unusual President's Trophy winner was Peter C. Zimmer, who won it in the Oshkosh, Wisconsin, District in 1946 and 1948. Zimmer came from a Prudential family, many of his relatives having worked for the company in and around Milwaukee. Although he started as an agent, Zimmer was a District manager when he won the trophy. In 1949 he became a director of agencies.

Another Prudential family was composed of the Hurst brothers of California. Glenn N. Hurst was manager in Pasadena, and his brother, Edgar J. Hurst—who won the President's Trophy three times (1947, 1950, and 1951)—was manager in San Diego.

One Prudential family decided to start their own insurance company. They were J. C. Kendall, manager of a Los Angeles District, and A. W.

Kendall, manager in South Bend. Eventually they left Pru to launch the Washington National Insurance Company of Evanston, Illinois.

In the 1970's one of the District Agencies' star performers was Michael Xifaras, an agent in the Fall River District in Massachusetts. He won the President's Trophy in 1971, 1973, and 1974, and in 1974 he set an all-time record for the total amount of life insurance sold in one year by a single District agent—$8,665,190 in face value.

Because of such pace-setting agents, the character of Pru's District business was dramatically transformed during the three postwar decades. While the Weekly Premium policies on which the company had been founded kept declining as a factor in income (until, in the early 1970's, they were down to about 30 per cent of all in-force premiums), the sales of Ordinary insurance by the District agents soared until in 1973 about 75 per cent of all the new, paid-for, Ordinary life insurance was being sold through the District Agencies.

By that time the Metropolitan had decided to phase out its District Agencies by not recruiting any more District agents; ultimately, the Met would operate strictly as an Ordinary company. Starting in the 1960's, the Met's debit operations had been conducted on a different principle from the Pru's. For example, there were District and Ordinary agents in the Met's field offices, while Pru had separate agencies and field offices for its two major sales organizations. After the Met announced its decision, Prudential re-examined its own set-up and decided that it wanted to remain a "combination" company, maintaining both sales organizations. Whether the Met's decision was the wiser, or Pru's, only the future could tell.

One thing was sure: if private enterprise failed to meet the needs of the poor, the blue-collar workers, and the lower-income ranks of the middle class, government would step in to fill the social and economic vacuum. By providing insurance to people at every level of society, Prudential felt that it was helping to prove that private enterprise could, in fact, accommodate the need for protection on the part of all who earned a living, and their dependents.

In the Ordinary Agencies Department, too, far-reaching changes took place during the three decades after the end of the second World War. George H. Chace—a man with a Home Office background who had headed that branch since 1940—retired in 1946 and was succeeded by Sayre (Pat) MacLeod, who started as a special agent in Philadelphia.

MacLeod's administration lasted for 21 years. In 1967 he retired, and Robert A. Beck, a former agent who was now well on his way to the top rank of management, became senior vice president in charge of the department. After three years Beck was chosen to be executive vice president in charge of all marketing activities. Subsequently E. William Nash, Jr., was named to head the Ordinary Agencies Department.

Perhaps even more than their colleagues in the District Agencies, the men and women of the Ordinary Agencies were sensitive to the manner in which they were regarded by the public. In the 1940's, the life insurance agent was considered the epitome of the obnoxious, rudely persistent, assertive salesman; comic strips and cartoons in the daily press lampooned insurance agents, and every comedian had a joke or two—or 15—about them. "Even the Home Office people used to look on us as hucksters," one high-ranking company official, who once served as an Ordinary special agent, remembered with some bitterness.

Over the years that image of the insurance agent faded into oblivion for a number of reasons. One underlying cause was that the public had a new understanding of the value and importance of insurance. "Imagine," Nash said, "when I went into the Army in the second World War, my father had $8,500 in insurance on his life. Then, suddenly, I had $10,000 insurance on my life, because of the National Service Life Insurance that was available to GIs after 1940."

Another reason was the thrust toward "creative selling" that rose to the surface during the postwar years. Eventually, in the 1960's, this would be manifest in the Estate Conservation Program and the Business Valuation Program, both intended to help the agent present the client with computerized but personalized insurance plans that averaged about $100,000 per sale in 1972. But the first, exciting new instrument for "creative selling" available to Pru's agents emerged from the Field Training Division, which was responsible, at that time, for training both District and Ordinary field forces of the company. In October 1946 William P. Lynch was transferred to the division and assigned to work with a consultant on the development of a programming aid to help in the sales effort. Lynch represented the District Agencies during the work on the project; in the beginning, his opposite number from the Ordinary Agencies was Roy Whitelaw, but he was later succeeded by Donald Bishop. Their labors resulted in the Dollar Guide, which was used by both District and Ordinary agents.

In a reminiscent memorandum written in 1974, John G. Lytle recalled the new aid's impact:

"The Dollar Guide . . . was introduced at the Ordinary Agencies
Business Conference at the Rice Hotel in Houston, Texas, on the
afternoon of November 20, 1947, by Kenneth L. Brooks. Mr. Brooks
gave an electrifying presentation of the Dollar Guide and it immediately
caught fire. . . . [The Dollar Guide was] still in existence and usage
over a quarter of a century later. Although many changes have taken
place in [it], the basic concept of covering the seven economic needs of
the family are the same: Last Expenses, Emergency Fund, Educational
Fund, Mortgage Cancellation, Critical Period Income (while the children are growing up), Lifetime Income for widow (after the children
reach maturity), and Retirement Income for the life of the husband and
wife."

Fueled by such sales tools, the Ordinary agents roared into high gear
in the postwar years. (Even while the war was raging, in 1943 Fuller W.
Fooshe of the Atlanta Agency became the first Prudential agent to write
one million dollars or more [in face value] in one year—the first, that is,
since the turn of the century, when Prudential general agent Edward A.
Reilly of Philadelphia sold a $1,000,000 policy to L. Rodman Wana-
maker. But Reilly was a general agent, the head of a big agency, so he
doesn't really count in the competition among agents.) During the year
in which the war ended, 1945, Leslie R. Hummel of Charlotte sold $2
million in insurance.

Not until 13 more years had passed was another milestone reached,
when Jesse D. Jones of Jacksonville sold $3 million in insurance in one
year. But the Ordinary agents, like pole vaulters, kept lifting their goals.
In 1966 Fred A. Gottesman of New Orleans sold $5 million worth of
insurance. Five years later Gary Fink in Minneapolis doubled that,
selling $10 million. The next mark—$13.5 million worth of insurance
sold in one year—was set by James A. Mueller of Oklahoma in 1973.

One of the most remarkable of Prudential's Ordinary agents was
George Morris of Amarillo, Texas. Although his city ranked only 111th
among all U.S. cities in population, Morris sold so much insurance that
he was the first Pru agent to achieve a production of $9 million sold in
one year. But he was more than a great salesman—he became an elder
statesman whose opinion and leadership were so respected that any
room where he was scheduled to speak at a regional or national sales

conference was certain to be jammed with other agents, eager to hear him. "As far as I know," president Robert Beck said, "George Morris is unique among all the agents in Prudential's history."

The agents of the Ordinary Department—along with their colleagues in the District Agencies—rose in the public's opinion during the three decades after the second World War in large measure because of their increasing professionalism. "The world is much more complicated these days than it was before the war," said Pru president Beck, "and people are more sophisticated. Furthermore, there are many more varieties of insurance protection available today. Now an agent has to be a real professional if he's going to meet the needs of his clients."

There are several forms that professionalism takes in insurance. In the property and casualty field—of concern to Pru agents after the company began writing automobile, homeowner's and other liability insurance in the 1970's—there is the CPCU degree (the letters stand for Chartered Property and Casualty Underwriter), granted by the American Institute for Property and Liability Underwriters after intensive study and examinations. It dates back to 1942.

In the administrative area, there are courses offered by the Life Office Management Association (LOMA). Its graduates are known as Fellows, Life Management Institute, or FLMIs. There were 311 FLMIs at Prudential in 1974.

For insurance sales operations, there are two principal degrees which can be earned by intensive study and exhaustive tests. The intermediate, or sales skills, degree is the LUTC, granted since 1947 by the Life Underwriters Training Council; it was conceived a few years earlier by several top officers of the National Association of Life Underwriters (NALU), including James E. Rutherford—then executive vice president of the organization and its managing head, and later top man in Pru's District Agencies Department and finally its Mid-America Home Office in Chicago.

The most prestigious life insurance designation is CLU (Chartered Life Underwriter), awarded since the late 1920's by the American College of Life Underwriters. In 1974 alone, 161 Pru employees completed their work for the CLU degree, compared with 119 for the company's closest rival, Metropolitan. Throughout Prudential there were some 2,025 CLU's in 1974. "For many years," a company statement said, "Prudential has led the industry in the number of CLU and LUTC graduates."

The growth of professionalism within the ranks of Prudential's agents, both District and Ordinary, was indicated in one statistic cited by Nash: in 1962, about eight per cent of the company's staff consisted of CLUs; 10 years later, the proportion was 15 per cent.

Prudential's contribution to the growth of professionalism in the insurance industry was indicated by the top level roles played by a number of Pru people. Charles W. Campbell—superb agent, developer of talent, foremost agency manager, and finally, senior vice president of the South Central Home Office until his retirement—was elected the first president of the General Agents and Managers Conference (GAMC).

Lewis C. Yount, manager of Pru's Seattle Agency, was elected president of the National Association of Life Underwriters (NALU). In 1975 he was serving in high posts with GAMC; in keeping with that organization's custom, it was expected that he would soon be its president. If so, he would be the first person in the insurance industry's history to have headed both the NALU and the GAMC.

Louis J. Toia, a special agent in New Jersey, served as president of the American Society of Chartered Life Underwriters. A consistent multimillion-dollar producer and a Life and Qualifying member of the Million Dollar Round Table, Toia set an all-time Prudential record in 1972 for combined net premium credits of over $477,000 on sales of $8,806,000 worth of life insurance.

Because of men like these, the high-pressure, foot-in-the-door insurance salesman of the old cartoons and comic strips had gradually given way to the low-key, thoroughly trained agent who could serve equally well as a counselor on family security matters or on business protection problems.

But the fervor, the crusading spirit of the early days was still there, unchanged. As *Fortune* once said, "Life insurance was a belief before it was a business; it is a missionary effort. . . ." And Prudential's evangelists were the best.

22 / Priming the Pump

It is not clear whether Caleb (Pete) Stone knew that he had been Colonel Franklin D'Olier's first choice to succeed the colonel as president of Prudential—only a heart attack kept him out of the running for the job, which eventually went to Carrol M. Shanks—but Stone's attitude toward Shanks made a number of people in the company wonder whether he felt some antagonism toward the man who did become head of the company during World War II.

Beyond personalities, however, was a genuine disagreement over policy between the two men. Shanks believed that Prudential could safely liberalize its portfolio and engage in prudently selected, risk-taking investments. As the Regional Home Offices came into existence, they also began to report a need for capital on the part of many companies scattered across the country, companies which could grow and prosper if they were able to get financial backing.

On every one of these points, Shanks and Stone clashed. Stone insisted that anything less than an AAA bond threatened Pru with disaster. Although railroad bonds, for example—considered the safest of investments in the 1920's—had inflicted the worst investment losses on the insurance industry during the Depression, Stone clung to the idea that only blue chips could be completely trusted. As for investing in companies in other parts of the country, Stone, in the words of one of his assistants, "hated to make a loan to a company he wasn't personally acquainted with, so most of his loans on behalf of Prudential were made to large, New York-based companies."

As head of Pru's Bond Department, Stone's cooperation was vital to the success of Shanks's plan for a more aggressive, flexible investment program, but "Stone fought everything," Shanks later recalled. Many of the investments that Shanks thought Pru ought to be making were approved by Stone, but not enough to satisfy Shanks. There was resistance every step of the way.

The first public clue to the friction behind the scenes came in January 1956, when Prudential issued an announcement—innocuous on its face—that it was setting up a new Commercial and Industrial Loan Department to handle small and medium-sized loans. It was Shanks's first move against Stone, an idea that had occurred to Shanks while he was shaving one morning.

To head the new department Shanks chose Ernest S. (Jack) Allsopp, the No. 2 man in the South Central Home Office at Jacksonville and a man with long experience in the mortgage loan business. Square-jawed and heavy-set, Allsopp had the air of never having been uncertain in his life. Irreverent colleagues called him "Jarrin' Jack," but they liked him.

In a statement announcing the creation of the new department, Shanks said, "We are confident that this new organization will facilitate the providing of capital needed for expansion in [the] field [of moderate-sized loans]."

Already the largest private financier of home and farm ownership in the U.S., Prudential quickly became a major element in loans to moderate-sized companies—business establishments which were happy to pay a slightly higher interest for the capital they needed on which to grow. "Until then, our bond buying had been essentially passive," Shanks said. "Now we were able to adopt a more aggressive investment policy in at least one significant segment of the economy."

But Stone still opposed Shanks at every opportunity. With any president that would have been hazardous, but with Shanks it was suicidal; he was proud, strong, impatient, and hot-tempered, and it must have been difficult for him to have restrained himself up to that point. Finally Shanks decided there had to be a showdown. A week or two after the new Commercial and Industrial Loan Department was established, Shanks discussed with the board his difficulties with Stone.

On February 1, 1956, a statement was issued which said:

"In order to give vice president Caleb Stone relief from the administrative responsibilities of the Bond Department, second vice president Monroe Chappelaer has been placed in charge of that department, president Carrol M. Shanks of the Prudential Insurance Company announced today. Mr. Stone will continue his activities in the investment work of the Bond Department, Mr. Shanks said.

"Mr. Chappelaer joined the Prudential in 1935 after an impressive background in engineering, utility, and investment fields. He rose rapidly in the Bond Department and was elected a second vice president in 1949.

"Mr. Stone has been associated with Prudential's Bond Department since 1931, and was elected vice president in 1943."

In fact, Stone had been stripped of all authority. He was left with his salary, his office, and a secretary who had little or nothing to do. Five months later he resigned to become a general partner in the Wall Street investment banking firm of Smith, Barney and Company. He retired from Smith, Barney in 1960 and died seven years later.

During the period between Stone's fall from power and his departure from Prudential, life must have been painful for his successor, Chappelaer, as well as for Stone himself, for Chappelaer and Stone were friends, caught in an impossibly embarrassing situation.

The year in which the clash between Shanks and Stone came to a head was a memorable time for another reason: it was the year in which Prudential introduced one of the most popular policies it had ever offered—the Family Policy, which covered the life of the husband, the wife, and every child under the age of 18, each child being covered automatically at birth with no increase in premium. In the first four months after the Family Policy went on the market, a quarter of a million families signed up for $1.5 billion worth of the new insurance, making it Pru's best-selling policy by a wide margin.

Fueled by the Family Policy, Prudential finally passed the Metropolitan that year, 1956, as the biggest seller of life insurance in the world. For the rest of Pru's first century it would retain that lead, and gradually overtake the Met in other measures of size and strength, too.

As the cash flow increased, so did the need to find additional, profitable investments. As *Time* pointed out in a cover story on Shanks and Prudential, "U.S. insurance companies are the nation's greatest reservoir of private capital, the dispensers of investments that have an incalculable impact on the U.S. economy."

The article went on to say:

> Almost anyone, big businessman or little, can qualify for a Prudential loan or mortgage. At the top of the Pru's list of borrowers is the *Who's Who* of U.S. industry: International Business Machines [IBM] . . . General Motors, Chrysler Corporation,

Union Carbide and Carbon Corporation, International Harvester, Goodyear Tire and Rubber.

The giants are only a fraction of the Pru's business. At president Shanks's direction, the company pours an even bigger chunk of its treasure into mortgages and loans to individuals and small businessmen. . . . In every U.S. activity there is Pru money, from cattle and cotton to guided-missile factories, race tracks, and country clubs.

Among the smaller loans made by Pru through its new Commercial and Industrial Loan Department, the magazine found "$200,000 to help reforest a Florida tree farm, $750,000 to a Nashville religious-book company, $54,000 to Kansas City's Papec Machine Company, makers of agricultural appliances, another $120,000 to six El Dorado (Arkansas) doctors who convinced the Pru that their town needed a medical center."

In the latter part of the 1950's, the Bond Department—always the biggest of Pru's investment operations—came increasingly under the influence of Frank J. Hoenemeyer, who was chosen the department's No. 2 man in 1958. A native of Cincinnati, Ohio, and a graduate of Xavier University there, Hoenemeyer had earned a master's degree in business administration at the University of Pennsylvania's Wharton School after service in the Air Force in the second World War. A Prudential recruiter induced him to visit the Newark headquarters, and Caleb Stone sold him on the advantages of working for the company.

Besides, Hoenemeyer decided there was more of a challenge in working for an insurance company than in working for a Wall Street investment banking house. As Stone told him, back in 1947, "On Wall Street, if you've sold a bond, you're all right if the company [issuing the bond] doesn't go bankrupt in six months. But at Prudential, when we buy a 20-year bond, we have to live with that for 20 years."

If anything, Stone was understating the case. At the time of Pru's centennial, its portfolio still included four per cent general mortgage bonds, with a principal amount of $2,507,000, issued by the Cleveland, Cincinnati, Chicago and St. Louis Railway in 1893 for a period of 100 years. The railroad was part of the Penn Central system and the bonds were in default.

Hoenemeyer began building a strong organization in the investment area of Pru. One of his first steps was to get in touch with a former Pru investment man, Raymond A. Charles. A Phi Beta Kappa alumnus of Knox College in Illinois, Charles had seen service in the war also and had an MBA from the University of Chicago, after earlier study at the Massachusetts Institute of Technology. He had gone to work for Pru in 1947, the same year that Hoenemeyer joined the company.

For a number of reasons, Charles left Prudential in 1950 to go to work for the Ford Motor Company as an assistant manager on the finance staff. Coincidentally, his desk was only two feet away from one occupied by Robert A. Beck, one of the young men engaged by Ford as part of its famous "Whiz Kids" program to attract unusually talented and intelligent people. In later years, Charles could not recall whether he had ever discussed Prudential with Beck, "although I'd guess we must have talked about it." But a couple of months after Charles arrived at Ford, Beck quit his job there and joined Prudential, where he eventually rose to be president.

In 1956 Charles accepted a position with the Equitable Life Assurance Society as assistant manager of its industrial securities division. Two years later Hoenemeyer telephoned him and suggested that they get together for a drink. That led to an invitation to Charles to return to Pru. By 1965 Charles was head of the company's Bond Department, where he increased the company's yield markedly by a willingness to undertake certain risks. For example, Charles frowned on buying bonds with a high (Aaa) rating, preferring to invest in sound, high-yield bonds of somewhat lower rating (Baa from Moody's or BBB from Standard and Poor's). "On a company-wide scale," he said, "this means that our income is $90 million higher than it would be if we bought the high-rated bonds. But our losses, under this investment program, have been less than two basis points"—a basis point being .01 of one per cent.

The second major investment area for Prudential is the Real Estate Investment Department. In 1970 Donald R. Knab was named to head it. Like Hoenemeyer, Knab was a native of Cincinnati, and it was there that he joined Pru's local real estate investment field office after he graduated from the University of Cincinnati and passed his bar examinations in 1947. During the next two decades, Pru moved him all over the map—to Newark, then to the South Central Home Office at Jacksonville, back to Newark, out to the Southwestern Home Office at Houston, and finally back to Newark again. When the Commercial and

Industrial Loan Department was founded, Knab was one of the first assigned to it, and he wrote its first operating manual. A decade later he helped design the financial models which management and the board of directors studied in trying to determine whether the company should enter the property and casualty insurance business.

Because rates in the residential mortgage field had been driven down by competition from savings and loan associations, Pru, under Knab, found itself involved in ever more important commercial and industrial mortgages and even long-term real estate ownership. The largest privately owned office building in the U.S.—55 Water Street, in Manhattan, with 3,250,000 square feet of office space—was financed by Prudential. So was the Empire State Building. And the Merchandise Mart in Chicago. Some of the most famous hotels in America were owned, at least in part, by Prudential and operated by experienced hotel-management companies. Part of the California crop of wine grapes was planted and harvested with Prudential money. Indeed, in 1975 Knab was able to say, "We are probably one of the biggest real estate developers in the U.S. today."

One of the reasons for Prudential's strength in real estate investment, of course, was the network of field offices set up by Roger Rogers early in the Depression and maintained ever since. As *Fortune* once commented about Pru's mortgages, "There are not, as is the case with most large lending agencies, mortgages bought blindly in bulk, or supplied by independent correspondents. They are directly secured, appraised, and serviced by Prudential's own national network of 58 mortgage-loan offices."

A third element in Prudential's investment activities is its investments in common stocks. In this area, as in so many others, Pru led the industry because of Shanks's unconventional, but usually sound, approach to business problems.

Like many private investors, he reasoned that a prudent proportion of funds invested in common stocks might help to offset some of the pressure from inflation. But there were legal limits on the proportion of life insurance assets which could be invested in common stocks. Shanks had two answers to that problem: first, he put as much pressure as he could on the regulatory authorities to lift the limits slightly; and, second, he established separate accounts for pension funds, which would not be subject to the insurance-law limitations.

Thus, Prudential began investing in common stocks in 1950, before most other large life insurance companies. "Moreover," according to Edgar F. Bunce, Jr., the head of the Common Stock Department, "it has led the industry in the absolute size of its common stock investments. As a result, Prudential had both experience and expertise when the first separate account was established for equity investments of qualified pension and profit-sharing plans. . . ."

The company's common stock portfolios, the largest in the life insurance industry, were valued at more than $4 billion at the end of 1974—at a time when the prices of shares were depressed.

One of Prudential's few Ph.D.'s, Bunce came from a scholarly background. His father was president of Glassboro College in New Jersey. After earning his bachelor's degree from Duke University and two master's degrees and a doctorate from the University of Wisconsin, he joined the staff of E. I. du Pont de Nemours and Company, where he became manager of the securities section. He also lectured on economics at Duke and at the universities of Florida and Delaware. At a dinner in New York City in 1963, Bunce found himself sitting next to Robert C. Oley, who had been directing Pru's common stock operations from the time they began. Oley was then close to retirement age, and Hoenemeyer and Ray Charles had been looking for someone who could head the common stock activities after he left. Oley's dinner conversation with Bunce led, in a short time, to the latter's being chosen for that responsibility. Four years after Bunce joined Pru it was announced that his operations would be designated as a full department, with Bunce heading it as senior vice president. He celebrated by going on vacation to Florida, where he broke a leg.

Only stocks of companies on a list approved by Prudential's board of directors could be bought by the Common Stock Department, but there were usually some 250 companies on that list. Indeed, the list was so broad that in 1973 Pru had about $200 million invested in Japanese companies—enough to justify the engagement of a consultant, Shigeru Shimizu, who specialized in the securities of that country.

The immense size of Prudential's investments never fails to awe new members of the board of directors, no matter how experienced and sophisticated they may be in the ways of business. One board member used to tell about his first Finance Committee meeting.

"As we strolled into the meeting room," he said, "one of the other board members said to me, 'Nothing important is coming up today.'

"But when I sat down at my place, there—on the first page of the material prepared for me—it said, 'There will be the usual resolution to commit $100 million.' "

The rigid, lengthy, and minutely detailed Policy Statement on Conflicts of Interest and Business Ethics adopted by the board sharply limits the financial activities of all directors and employees, especially those of middle-management rank and above. One rule, for example, prohibits such persons from having "any position with or a substantial interest in any other business enterprise operated for profit, the existence of which would conflict or might reasonably be supposed to conflict with the proper performance of his company duties or responsibilities, or which might tend to affect his independence of judgment with respect to transactions between the company and such other business enterprise."

Another rule forbids the acceptance of "gifts, gratuities, or favors."

Rule 2 says that "during negotiations and for a period of six months following the signing of the agreement or termination of such negotiations" no director or employee of significant rank—nor any member of his or her family living in the same household—may buy or sell "directly or indirectly" any stock in a business which has made "application for a direct placement investment (loan or stock), a mortgage loan, or a real estate investment."

One of the more interesting rules flatly prohibits "reciprocity and tie-in sales." To reinforce this bar, the rule even forbids the exchange of information within Prudential on the company's "lending, investing, banking, or purchasing" activities.

Despite such rules—or, perhaps, because of them—Prudential has consistently out-performed most of its competitors in its major fields of operation: insurance, pensions, and investments. At the end of 1974, MacNaughton was able to report:

"Prudential's 1974 net investment income rate, after investment expenses but before federal income taxes, was 6.44 per cent, an increase of 28 basis points over the previous historic high of 1973."

In 1974 the company's board of directors demonstrated their appreciation of Pru's consistent record of superior performance in what was, perhaps, the most dramatic way open to them at the time: Frank

Hoenemeyer, who had been executive vice president in charge of all investment activities since 1965, was elected to the board.

It was a tribute well earned by the man who, more than anyone else—except for Shanks, who had been long gone from Pru—was responsible for the extraordinary investment achievements of what *Fortune* once called "that mighty pump, Prudential." In that article in 1964, the magazine described Prudential in a vivid metaphor that was still true:

"It's a kind of universal power plant, vast of maw and spout, breathing in and breathing out. Its function is the collection and redistribution of the people's savings. As the giant mechanism pumps away, there are few U.S. businesses—or few U.S. citizens, in fact—that escape the effect of either its updraft or its downdraft."

23 / An Exposé by the *Journal*

The first sense that Prudential was about to be shaken by great changes might have been aroused in 1957, although the volcanic eruption was still three years off. But looking back from the perspective of 18 years, the early signs, the subtle cracks in the structure, were evident.

In the summer of 1957 Harold Stewart went on disability leave, never to return. The following year he retired and eight years after that he died.

As Stewart left on leave, Louis Menagh and Orville Beal—as disparate as two men could ever be—were elected executive vice presidents. There were now three executive vice presidents, the third being Valentine Howell, who would retire at the end of 1961.

The dynamic, scrappy head of the Western Home Office, Harry J. Volk, was summoned back to Newark, amid rumors that envious rivals at the highest ranks in the company had finally persuaded Carrol Shanks to clip the wings of that game cock, who had waged such a long and tireless fight for all the autonomy he could get. Instead of returning, Volk announced that he was resigning—to accept a position as head of the Union Bank in Los Angeles. Over the next 15 years under his leadership, the bank grew to 13 times its 1957 size, "close to the best record among the nation's top 25 banks," according to *Fortune*. Moreover, 10 years after he joined the bank Volk "started American banking on a new road" by diversifying under the one-bank holding-company rule. And in the process he made himself rich, which would not have been possible at Prudential which, as a mutual company, has no stock options or other goodies to offer its executives—the kind of benefits which enable a stock company officer to start building a fortune.

Associate general counsel J. Edward Day was sent out to head the Western Home Office in Volk's place. After the election of John F. Kennedy as U.S. President in 1960, Day would leave Pru to become Postmaster General of the United States.

Alexander Query was sent out to Minneapolis to take Beal's place as head of the North Central Home Office and William Chodorcoff was elected comptroller to succeed Menagh.

Plans for the Northeastern Home Office (NEHO) in Boston were made public, and Shanks said that Harold E. Dow would be its head.

A new generation was rising to the top: Donald S. MacNaughton. Kenneth C. Foster. Frank J. Hoenemeyer. Fredrick E. Rathgeber. William P. Lynch. Jack T. Kvernland. Raymond A. Charles. Donald R. Knab. Kenneth C. Nichols. Thomas Allsopp. Eugene J. Conroy. John B. Stoddart, Jr.

Men like Alfred C. Linkletter, who had been performing gargantuan feats in connection with the construction of Pru's Regional Home Offices and its other buildings.

And Robert W. Harvey, who was destined for tragedy.

By the end of 1958 Stewart had retired. Edmund Whittaker was dead. Other familiar faces were passing from the scene.

A whole generation was on the move.

A decade died—the 1950's.

A decade was born, with hope—the 1960's.

It began auspiciously enough. Prudential announced that it had made a $100 million loan to a Mexican government agency, an act which resulted in solemn editorials in newspapers across the country, all of them favorable. In the spring there were more kind newspaper references to Pru because of its sponsorship of one of the most distinguished series of television programs, *The Twentieth Century*.

Then, on Friday, June 3, 1960, the *Wall Street Journal* carried an article under the general heading, "Business Milestones." The specific headline said, "Georgia-Pacific Unit Buys Timberland; Cost Estimated at $10 Million." The report said that Georgia-Pacific, through a wholly owned subsidiary, Coos Bay Timber Company, had purchased as much as 13,000 acres of timberland, valued at up to $10 million. It said the land had been purchased from Carrol M. Shanks, president of Prudential and a Georgia-Pacific director. The article said that Shanks had just acquired the land from another company. According to the article, a year earlier Pru had bought timberland from the Georgia-Pacific subsidiary and had "entered into an agreement with Georgia-Pacific providing for management and logging of these timberlands and for selling logs to Georgia-Pacific." It was also pointed out Prudential had made several loans to Georgia-Pacific, including nine mortgage loans.

The news item, which was probably carried on the Dow-Jones news wire (Dow-Jones owns the *Wall Street Journal*) also appeared in other newspapers ranging from the *Humboldt Standard* of Eureka, California, to *The New York Times*. But that appeared to be the end of the matter.

Until August 15, nearly two and a half months later.

On that date the *Wall Street Journal* went into the transaction again. But this time the article started on the front page and jumped to page 15, running for 47 inches in all. There were several "decks," or sections, to the front page headline, but the biggest deck said: "It Shows How Some Boards Let Top Men Trade with Own Firms."

The article, by Ed Cony—it subsequently won the Pulitzer Prize for national reporting—began with this paragraph:

"Is it wrong for a corporation officer or director to profit personally from sideline transactions with the company he serves?"

The newspaper offered Shanks's deal with Georgia-Pacific "as a case study of one company where officers and directors have had personal dealings with the corporation with the approval of the directors." The corporation it referred to was Georgia-Pacific, but the principal casualty was Prudential, as it turned out.

What had happened was this: Shanks was on the board of directors of Georgia-Pacific, and Owen Cheatham, Georgia-Pacific's board chairman, was on Prudential's board. One day Shanks, whose salary of $250,000 was not inordinate when compared with the compensation of other chief executives of comparable companies, was talking with Cheatham about the difficulty of putting aside money for his estate because he was in a very high tax bracket and most of his income was in the form of taxable salary. Cheatham suggested that Shanks take part in one of the complicated, third-party, timber-buying deals which were rather common in the lumber industry. That would shelter a substantial part of Shanks's money from full taxation.

So, using $100,000 of his own money and several million dollars in loans from the Bank of America, Shanks bought the Timber Conservation Company in Oregon. About 30 minutes later, Shanks sold the 13,000 acres of Oregon timber to a subsidiary of Georgia-Pacific. The Georgia-Pacific subsidiary, as part of the purchase agreement with

Shanks, agreed to cut and sell the timber over a period of five years, pacing its harvest so as to enable Shanks to recover his $100,000 and to make it possible for him to pay both the principal and interest on his loan from the bank. The advantage for Shanks was this: the deductions for interest payments, combined with depletion allowances and capital gains, would allow him to save about $400,000 in income taxes. There was also a plum for Georgia-Pacific in the deal: it could acquire the timber it needed without adding debt to its balance sheet. Moreover, the arrangement protected Georgia-Pacific against the possibility of an antitrust prosecution for gobbling up a smaller timber company.

But once the transaction was exposed to public view, there were a number of ticklish aspects to the deal. There was Shanks, on Georgia-Pacific's board. There was Cheatham, on Prudential's board. There were those Prudential loans to Georgia-Pacific—loans totaling some $65 million. And there had been other, perfectly proper, transactions between Prudential and Georgia-Pacific, all of which were set forth in considerable detail in the *Wall Street Journal* report. The fat was in the fire.

Before the end of the week, the New Jersey Commissioner of Banking and Insurance announced that he was going to investigate the matter. He did, and subsequently found nothing illegal about the transaction.

The commissioner's announcement came shortly after Shanks, in a letter to him, declared that he was ridding himself of the timberland investment because he felt that there was a widespread misunderstanding of the transaction which he could never dispel.

However, Shanks's letter of renunciation and the commissioner's bill of health were too late. There had been other prominent conflict-of-interest cases in major U.S. companies over the previous few months, and business as a whole was highly sensitive to the subject.

Besides, Shanks was not simply the head of a business enterprise—he was the most responsible person in a mutual insurance company, and that is a position of special trust. A mutual company exists solely for the benefit of its policyholders (although its employees, of course, enjoy the fruits of faithful service and—more important—the national economy is strengthened by the mutual company's contribution to capital accumulation). Ever since the Armstrong investigation, more than half a century earlier, life insurance executives had taken great care to act—and to be perceived by the public as acting—like Caesar's wife, above reproach in their business dealings.

Despite the commissioner's announcement, Prudential's board of directors established a committee to look into the affair. Strangely enough, Shanks apparently had not realized how damaging the story could be when it first appeared, but the appointment of the board committee made him acutely aware of the danger in which he stood. Several of his close associates in the company urged him to engage his own legal counsel, arguing that it would not be proper for Pru's Law Department to represent him, and he agreed.

In later years, Shanks tended to believe that hostile elements on the board had worked for his downfall. (Similarly, some Prudential people deluded themselves that all the publicity had been secretly generated by envious rivals in the insurance industry.)

In the end, the board, in effect, forced Shanks to resign, which he did with dignity and composure. In a letter to the insurance commissioner, Shanks argued that the kind of transaction for which he was being criticized was "frequently" entered into by high-salaried men as a means of gaining "a reasonable amount of financial independence." Then he added a most revealing sentence. "Apparently," he said, "as president of a mutual insurance company, I am not entitled to make the same kind of arrangement that is available to other executives. I think this is unreasonable."

That was the heart of the matter. For many years there had been a consensus among insurance executives, regulators, legislators, legal authorities, and others that the executives of mutual insurance companies did *not* have the freedom of action that other businessmen enjoyed.

In December of 1960 Shanks submitted his resignation. After he left Prudential, it was more than a decade before he returned for a visit. By that time, the one unfortunate episode at the very end of his career with the company could be seen in perspective against the vast canvas of his contributions, not only to Prudential, but also to the entire life insurance industry and to the people of the U.S. and Canada. As scores of Pru employees—most of whom had never met him—wrote to him after his resignation, he was, in all truth, one of the giants of American business.

Inevitably, there were ugly rumors, but for nearly two years after

Shanks left Prudential, officials of New Jersey, with New York state authorities sitting in as observers, scrutinized his activities while president. Nothing illegal was ever uncovered.

One aftermath of the affair was the passage by the board of minutely detailed conflict-of-interest rules to govern the directors themselves, as well as the people in management.

The astonishing business genius of Shanks, which had meant so much to Prudential, tended to obscure the fact that he was, after all, as fallible as other mortals. He had made mistakes, some of them major errors. For example, the overnight success of the Family Policy, introduced by Pru in 1956, led Shanks to decree a massive expansion of the agency field forces. The Regional Home Offices even had quotas which had to be met—quotas specifying the number of new agencies and agents to be in operation by a given date. The result of this program was an over-expansion that drove up administrative expenses. After Shanks's departure from Pru, an across-the-board cut in expenses had to be ordered to bring matters back into balance.

Another curious failure of Shanks became apparent at the time of his resignation: he had done nothing to groom a successor. (Perhaps the reason was his excellent health, which he maintained by daily exercises, including jogging around his neighborhood before dawn every day. That practice caused the Montclair, New Jersey, police to pick him up one morning as a burglary suspect—on the not unreasonable grounds that a man running through the streets in the dark of night has probably committed a crime.)

To fill the vacancy caused by his resignation, the board selected Louis Menagh, then 68 years old. Menagh always insisted that he was not an "interim president," but directors who were on Pru's board at the time said that he was. Nevertheless, he had already been serving, in effect, as acting head of the company during most of 1960, while Shanks was busy defending himself against the insinuations of misconduct. Menagh's conduct, then and during his presidency, contributed immeasurably to Prudential's success in emerging from the crisis with its reputation for probity unstained.

During the period of his presidency, which lasted about 21 months, Menagh acted very much like a politician who's caught Potomac fever. He visited every department, toured Regional Home Offices and even field offices, and regaled employees with tales of his early days as a lingerie salesman. Grandfatherly in manner and clearly anxious to be popular with Pru employees, he obviously enjoyed his new status, as well he might. As people always will, some told nasty jokes about him behind his back, but there were others who saw the shrewd businessman behind the aging façade.

Jack Armstrong of the North Central Home Office, for example, recalled how Menagh would sit with both feet on a bottom drawer of his desk.

"You'd swear he wasn't listening to a word you said," Armstrong once said, "but two days later he could quote you word for word."

Alan Thaler always admired Menagh for his role in holding the company and its employees to the straight and narrow path.

"During a period of rapid growth, such as Pru enjoyed during the 1950's," Thaler said, "there are always a myriad of opportunities for unethical practices. But Menagh kept Pru clean during that time."

During his relatively brief span as president, Menagh also took two personnel steps of considerable importance to the company. On his recommendation, the board of directors promoted associate general counsel Donald S. MacNaughton to vice president and made him a special assistant to the president, and designated William Chodorcoff, the comptroller, whom Menagh had been grooming for years, as an executive vice president.

In January 1962, a year after Menagh became president, a committee of the board of directors told executive vice president Orville Beal that they had decided he should be Menagh's successor. After thanking them, Beal warned them that he and his wife had determined that he would retire when he was 60 years old. That would be in 1969, and he felt the board might not want to choose a president who would only serve for a half dozen years. Nevertheless, the board clung to its decision. According to Sydney G. Stevens, a board member who was on the committee at the time (and was the board's most senior member at the time of the company's centennial), the directors were certain that Beal, having once tasted the power of the presidency, would not relinquish it prematurely.

But they were wrong. Beal did, indeed, retire at 60.

In order to let the company—and the industry—know that Beal was the heir-designate, the board immediately elected him senior executive vice president, a title which had never existed before.

After succeeding to the presidency itself, on October 1, 1962, Beal lowered the average age of the senior executive group drastically by encouraging the retirement of men who had been permitted to remain on the job past the usual retirement age. He accomplished the same result with the directors: when he assumed the top office, the average age of the members of the board was 72; by the time Beal retired, it was down to about 58.

As the older executives retired, vacancies occurred at the higher levels of the company, and they were filled by bright, younger men: Robert W. Harvey was promoted to executive vice president in 1962, and Raymond A. Charles, Thomas Allsopp, and John D. Buchanan, Jr., were also among those who took another step up the ladder. In 1963 Eugene J. Conroy was made general counsel and Duncan Macfarlan and Robert C. Oley became vice presidents. The following year important promotions went to Frank J. Hoenemeyer, E. Carroll Gerathy, Irving S. Schupper, and Joseph M. Savage, among others. Donald S. MacNaughton became an executive vice president in 1965, Hoenemeyer was elected to a newly created position, executive vice president for investments, and significant step-ups went to Buchanan, Charles, Jack T. Kvernland, Kenneth C. Nichols, Robert A. Beck, Floyd K. Bennett, Floyd H. Bragg, John K. Kittredge, Donald R. Knab, Edwin E. Lineberry, John J. Marcus, A. Douglas Murch, John B. Stoddart, Jr., and William T. Wachenfeld, as well as a number of others. During the next year, Fredrick E. Rathgeber and Kenneth C. Foster were elected executive vice presidents, and Beck, Macfarlan, Meyer Melnikoff, and Frederick A. Schnell rose to senior vice president. And so it went—the company was opening up to younger men.

24/Tragedy and Triumph

From the first, Orville Beal had conceived his mission as head of Prudential to be the re-shaping of the organization into an integrated, smooth-working team. During Shanks's administration, the company had gradually evolved into a host of duchies, each headed by a feudal lord jealous of his prerogatives. Factionalism had become a way of life. There was a tendency to put labels on everyone; this man was "one of Menagh's fellows," that one was "a Howell man." Where there is factionalism, there is friction which usually results in bad feeling. As Beal saw it, the need was for healing, conciliation, the restoration of comradely feelings—and the destruction of departmental barriers.

Because of his honestly benign temperament, the establishment of an atmosphere conducive to good feelings was not difficult for Beal. But that was not enough for him to do if he was to re-make the company into a coordinated, effective, united organization. A suggestion advanced by some of the officers at the 1963 spring session of the Vice Presidents' Council gave Beal the lever he needed. The proposal was that the Eastern Regional operations be divorced from the Corporate Home Office, thus carrying decentralization to its logical conclusion. Beal countered with a proposal incorporating that idea but going much further: why not have a comprehensive study of the entire company?

Thus was born the Special Committee on Home Office Organization (usually called the SCHOO Study), appointed in May 1963. The chairman was Donald S. MacNaughton, who was promoted to executive vice president in January 1965, a month after the committee submitted its final report. Others on the committee were Fredrick E. Rathgeber, who would later be elected an executive vice president; Alan Thaler, ultimately a senior vice president; and senior vice president Francis Quillan. A management-consultant organization was engaged to assist the committee.

"Within the broad charter given it by the president," the SCHOO

261

report, which was never made public in its entirety, said, "the committee imposed certain standards upon itself. First, it agreed to look no further than 10 years ahead in formulating its recommendations. A longer period would be much too speculative. A second principle decided upon was to avoid recommending change simply for the sake of change. Finally, the committee agreed that it would weigh its recommendations carefully against the impact they would have on the Prudential's performance and Prudential people."

When it began fact-finding—the first such "comprehensive examination of the company's organization" ever undertaken—"the committee culled historical files for background information. Little was discovered. In fact," the report commented, "it is remarkable that dramatic and expensive organizational shifts such as decentralization have occurred in the Prudential without the retention of a complete historical record of the events leading to the changes."

The SCHOO study examined the structure of other companies in and out of the insurance industry, interviewed 340 Prudential executives and 150 supervisors at lower levels, and prepared questionnaires which were filled out by all senior officers. The committee also examined in depth 10 different Prudential decisions which had been made within the past five years to gain insight into the decision-making process within the company.

As a result of the SCHOO study, the company began a major reorganization in 1965. The most obvious step was the establishment of an Eastern Home Office, of which Charles Laing became the head. Laing, who had been in charge of Planning and Development under Shanks, had been shipped out to Los Angeles to be in charge of the Western Home Office after Menagh was elected president. Now he was back in Newark in charge of an Eastern Home Office whose territory included New York City, Long Island, New Jersey, and those territories—Pennsylvania, Delaware, Maryland, and the District of Columbia—which would be broken off to make up the Central Atlantic Home Office region in 1969.

A second major proposal in the SCHOO report was the re-structuring of the Corporate Home Office in Newark into four specific areas of responsibility, each under an executive vice president: Corporate Services, Insurance, Investments, and Planning and Control. As Beal reported to the board, "Under the new arrangements, Prudential will have a Corporate Home Office whose primary responsibility will be forward planning. It will no longer be burdened with the usual responsibilities and problems connected with the day-to-day sale and servicing of our products. Rather, Corporate personnel will be able to devote most of their attention to planning, policy-making, coordination, evaluation, and control. Too often in the past, these important functions have had to succumb to the pressures of daily production requirements.''

The changes also would make it far more difficult—although Beal did not say so—for any senior executive to build his own little domain within the company.

While the changes recommended by the SCHOO report were beginning to be made, another epochal event for Prudential was taking place in 1965. The Northeastern Home Office in Boston was opened.

NEHO, as it was usually called within the company, had been announced in 1957, but unusually difficult political, legal, and tax problems had severely delayed the project. Moreover, there had been a strange internal division of responsibility: although Harold E. Dow was the head of NEHO, the various complications involved in getting on with the building of the project had been entrusted to Fred Smith, who seemed to have inherited Admiral Eubank's job as free-lance troubleshooter for Shanks. Smith, who had been brought into the company and given the title of vice president, apparently proved effective in his efforts on behalf of Pru, but he did not remain with the company long after Shanks's departure.

In 1962 Dow was called back to Newark, and Thomas Allsopp was appointed head of NEHO. There he remained until 1974, when he was asked to return to Newark to organize the new Public Affairs Department. Articulate and intellectual, Allsopp was the perfect choice for the Boston post. As one of the Boston newspapers put it, he was one of the ''new Boston breed.''

But he was a Prudential man—and a showman. The dedication ceremonies for the $150 million Prudential Center included parades, bands, a 100-voice chorus, a symphony orchestra, teen-age girl bagpipers, marathon runners, a charity ball, an opera performance, and a world forum headed by Anthony Eden, former British prime minister, and Adlai E. Stevenson, then U.S. Ambassador to the United Nations, with television anchor man Walter Cronkite as moderator.

Located on 31 acres in the Back Bay area, Prudential Center had, in the words of Beal, turned "an old blighted freight yard . . . into the largest unified civic, business, and residential complex in the world." There were a 52-story office building, another high-rise office building, three soaring apartment houses, a hotel, and a shopping mall with two major department stores and 30 smaller stores. It was, and is, a staggering achievement.

Unfortunately, those who were most staggered by it were the nation's leading architectural critics. For example, Ada Louise Huxtable, in *The New York Times,* called it "a textbook example of urban character assassination," which seemed to be a somewhat extreme statement of disapproval. But *Architectural Forum* was on firmer ground when it pointed out that "the city's economic health" had dictated the form this redevelopment would take. For many years there had been no new building in Boston. Now, even though "few of Boston's numerous purists like the sleek coldness of the Pru," the magazine said, "even fewer would argue against [the plan under which Prudential] will hand over 20 per cent of the gross rental income . . . to the city, with a guarantee of $3 million per year." Furthermore, most of the critics knew that Prudential Center would stimulate a general redevelopment boom essential to the city's economic well-being, and so it did.

In the spring of 1966 it seemed that fortune was truly smiling on Prudential. The SCHOO recommendations were being implemented with good effect, an era of good feeling was developing under the leadership of Orville Beal, the company was close to catching up with, or surpassing, the Metropolitan in terms of assets, and at the top of the organization were four men who worked well together and with Beal —the four executive vice presidents: Donald S. MacNaughton, Robert W. Harvey, William Chodorcoff, and Frank J. Hoenemeyer.

On April 5, 1966, Harvey dropped by MacNaughton's office to chat for a moment on his way out of the building. In the course of some inconsequential conversation, he mentioned that he and Harold Dow were on their way to a Harvard alumni meeting, traveling in Dow's car. That evening, in Madison, New Jersey, their car was struck by another vehicle containing four young men, some of whom had been drinking. Harvey and Dow were both critically injured. Six weeks later Dow was released from the hospital, but Harvey, who lay in a coma for a long time, was hospitalized for 122 days. Although he remained on disability leave for a year and efforts were made to help him return to his work, the accident had made it impossible for Harvey to function fully as an executive vice president again.

At Beal's request, MacNaughton and Chodorcoff met a day or two after the accident to discuss how they could divide Harvey's responsibilities between themselves until his return to work. It was agreed that they would go into the matter in more detail after Chodorcoff returned from New Orleans, where he was to give a speech on April 18.

On the afternoon of the 18th, MacNaughton received a message that Beal wanted to see him immediately.

"As I walked into Orville's office," MacNaughton recalled, "he was looking out that window, with his back to me. I knew something was wrong. I was afraid that Bob [Harvey] had died. Then Orville turned around and told me that Bill had died. It was a hard day. Bill and I were very close."

Chodorcoff's death had come just a few minutes after he had finished delivering a speech to delegates to the company's Canadian National Business Conference, which was being held at New Orleans that year. A Canadian by birth—he had also married a Canadian girl, Rita Raphael, who was in the front row listening to his address—Chodorcoff enjoyed getting together again with Canadians and hearing the friendly accents of his youth. But he did not enjoy speaking. A perfectionist, he agonized over speeches. Indeed, he had suffered a slight heart attack a few years before just after giving a speech.

In retrospect, Chodorcoff's speech at New Orleans seemed to be a perfect valedictory for the man.

"I have been in this business for 35 years," he said, "and with each passing year it has become increasingly meaningful to me. I know of no business that can give greater personal satisfactions than the job of protecting families. . . .

"The life insurance contract is one of the most effective financial instruments ever devised. It is a vehicle for thrift. It offers an efficient method of assuring the continuity of a business. It is invaluable in estate planning. In its Group form, it has done much to increase harmony among employers and employees. . . .

"Yes, the jobs performed by the life contract grow more numerous all the time. But none of them is more important than the original goal of life insurance—the protection of the family against the hazard of death or disability of the breadwinner. This need for family protection was the reason for the development of the earliest forms of life insurance, and family security is still today the heart of our great business.

"I ask you, what could be more important? In my mind, there is no business on earth that has a more essential job. Our industry provides a means whereby millions of people can make certain that a roof will remain over their heads and food on their tables. The members of this audience know the real effect of insurance better than anyone else, for you have seen what insurance means to families that have lost a husband and father. You have seen it lighten a widow's burden. You have seen it fulfill a man's hopes and fondest dreams. . . . I am sure that each of you men feel, as I do, a sense of pride and security in the knowledge that through our own insurance programs we have provided for our loved ones. . . .

"The life insurance business is a business like no other. It covers the entire spectrum of human relationships and human needs. It binds the family together, it protects the young, it educates youth, it guards the old against unforeseen reversals. It asks the best of a man, based on the premise that he is basically good, capable of understanding, of long-range planning, and of unselfishness. It is based on the belief that, in a free society, economic security is the foundation for all our cherished freedoms. . . ."

Toward the end of his speech, he said:

". . . If we are going to identify with insurance, why not identify with the best company in the industry, the Prudential? . . .

"The Prudential is outstanding because it is an organization of outstanding individuals—individuals who have identified themselves with the best company in the best industry in the world.

"The Prudential is not a record, or an achievement, or even a long history of records and achievements. The Prudential is, in the final analysis, an organization of dedicated people. People like you and me who are proud to be identified with their company and who are proud to serve its great goals."

A moment later Chodorcoff stepped down, amid applause, and sat down in an empty seat next to John B. Maver, an old friend from Toronto, as a woman speaker, who was next on the program, began her remarks. Suddenly Chodorcoff gagged, and fell over into Maver's arms. He was carried out of the hall at once, and a doctor appeared—it is Prudential policy to have a physician present at all of its conferences.

An agent tried to give the fallen man artificial respiration, but the doctor indicated that nothing could bring Chodorcoff back.

In his eulogy during the funeral services at Temple B'nai Jeshurun, Rabbi Ely E. Pilchik said, among other things, "In our perplexing time we can hardly afford to lose this quiet, modest giant. . . ."

As he listened, Beal felt those words with special poignancy, for he had now lost two of his executive vice presidents.

"It was a very heavy blow," Beal said later, "because both of those men had great ability. They both were actuaries. Bob Harvey had moved out of the Actuarial Department into Administration. Then I chose him to succeed me as head of the sales operations for Prudential. That's quite unusual—to have an actuary as head of sales—but he was that kind of man—highly respected by everybody. He was doing an excellent job when that unfortunate accident occurred.

"And then, Bill Chodorcoff. He had moved from the Actuarial Department into the Comptroller's Department. He succeeded Louis Menagh as comptroller, and he was probably one of the most knowledgeable men—from the point of view of Prudential's total financial operations—that we have ever had. He also had great promise. If he had only lived. . . ."

With Harvey and Chodorcoff both gone, MacNaughton was executive vice president in charge of everything but investments, which were Hoenemeyer's territory. Now MacNaughton's work on the SCHOO study paid off handsomely to the company, for in the course of that inquiry he had learned a great deal about almost every operation in Prudential. Another assignment MacNaughton had been given during Menagh's administration was the responsibility for controlling expenses. "You can't get into expense control," said Beal, "without learning something about every operation that lies behind the expense sheet and the columns in the ledgers."

In May Beal decided that Rathgeber, the senior vice president and actuary who had worked on the SCHOO study with MacNaughton, should be elected executive vice president to relieve the strain on MacNaughton. In December of that year, 1966, Kenneth C. Foster, who had been out in Los Angeles heading the Western Home Office, was elected an executive vice president to fill the gap in marketing left by the continuing disability of Harvey.

No man had ever been more qualified to head Pru's marketing

operations than Foster. He had worked in an agency, in the field. It seems unlikely than anyone else had ever held responsible assignments at or near the top in all three branches of the business—District Agencies, Ordinary Agencies, and Group. Furthermore, he'd had an opportunity to see the company's operations from the viewpoint of a Regional Home Office head, for he had been in charge of the Western Home Office from 1965 to 1967. On any insurance subject his comments were always trenchant, for he was not only as well-informed as probably any other man in the industry, but he was also a reflective man who had thought his way through the rhetoric that confused so many problems of social legislation.

When agents in Wisconsin had expressed concern in 1960 that Group sales might affect them adversely, Foster had resolved the controversy with a closely reasoned letter in which there was not a single unnecessary word. First he had restated Prudential's dedication to the agency system. Then he pointed out that political, social, and economic factors, not creative selling, had been responsible for the very rapid growth of Group coverages during the previous 15 years. More than 99 per cent of Pru's Group cases were sold by agents or brokers, and commissions were paid to them, he said. But he flatly rejected the idea that commissions should be paid to agents even for those cases which were not sold through them. "It is our opinion," he said, "that in a private enterprise system any franchise concept which requires payment for service not rendered will not long survive."

Beal needed all the help he could get, for those were hard times to be the head of a great insurance company. In the halls of Congress, for example, the insurance industry was under attack by a coalition that demanded some form of national health insurance, even if it was restricted to the aged. Prudential did not agree with the industry's opposition to Medicare, as it came to be called, but it did not publicize its own position. In 1965 Congress finally enacted Medicare, but the clamor for a national health program which would cover everyone continued.

Then the cities became battlegrounds—to the bewilderment of almost everyone, including those engaged in the battle on both sides. One of the first cities to explode was Newark. On July 13, 1967, rioting began in the ghettos, starting as a protest against the alleged mistreatment of a black taxicab driver. There were numerous incidents of arson and vandalism, and the police used live ammunition. Emotions escalated, and so did the fighting. Five persons were killed before the National Guard was called in. During the days that followed, 20 more persons were shot to death.

A number of books have been written about the Newark tragedy, and about the disorders that wracked many another U.S. city during the 1960's. There is not the space here to go into the background of the troubles in Newark, nor the details of the city's problems.

But those days of violence and fear left their mark on everyone in Newark, including all who worked for Prudential. For a time its Newark offices could not be fully staffed, but with the return of some degree of order to Newark, work at Prudential began to get back to normal—more or less. Nevertheless, for a long time there would remain suspicion and distrust—and, above all, fear—on the part of many employees, white and black.

When Newark elected its first black mayor, Kenneth A. Gibson, in 1970, he asked MacNaughton, then the head of Prudential, and other business leaders for help. The business community contributed a team of four seasoned executives to assist Gibson. The team was headed by Pru vice president Robert W. Smith, who was sworn in as the city's business administrator. C. Robert Wieselthier, another Prudential vice president, also worked with Smith at City Hall, and so did Smith's secretary, Inez Iuzzolino.

Four years later, when Los Angeles elected its first black mayor, Thomas Bradley, he, too, asked Prudential for help—an indication of how Pru's Western Home Office had established the company's local identity. MacNaughton, with the approval of the board of directors, authorized Frederick A. Schnell, then senior vice president in charge of WHO, to spend the calendar year 1974—his last before retirement—working with Mayor Bradley as his Executive Consultant for Economic Development.

In Newark, the immediate response to the 1967 rioting at Prudential was a re-examination by Beal, MacNaughton, and their associates of the company's philosophy and practices in the area of social responsibility. Just a few months before the disorders, a company publication, *Prudential People,* had devoted a substantial amount of space to the company's pledge of equality of opportunity in employment for all, regardless of age, sex, race, creed, color, or national origin. The periodical gave examples of Pru's work on behalf of minority groups and other underprivileged persons throughout the country.

But now Beal and MacNaughton were determined to re-double Pru's efforts. As one newspaper account said, a few months after the rioting, "Negro leaders have access to Mr. Beal. If ghetto leaders have a grievance to discuss, Prudential executives are available, day or night."

The Institute of Life Insurance, an industry organization which happened to be headed by Beal at the time, responded to the civil disorders by pledging the life insurance industry to commit $2 billion in investment aid to the cities. According to *Business Week,* "Beal . . . was a driving force behind the idea." By the summer of 1972, Pru was able to report that its commitments under that program had reached more than $333 million, well above its alloted share.

Most of all, Prudential was opening up new employment opportunities to members of minority groups. Just in the period from December 1965 to December 1971, Pru's minority staff rose by about 230 per cent, although the total company employment went up less than 11 per cent.

The women's movement, too, made company officials take a new look at accepted practices. One result was that the percentage of women employed at the associate manager level and above grew from 4.4 in 1969 to 10.8 in the summer of 1974. In 1971 the company elected a woman lawyer, Mrs. Isabelle Kirchner, as vice president and secretary, and two years later Ms. Margery S. Foster, president of Douglass College, was elected to Pru's board of directors.

In order to ensure a continuing, strong effort in areas of social responsibility, MacNaughton in 1974 established a new Public Affairs Department reporting directly to the chairman and chief executive officer. To head it, he persuaded Thomas Allsopp, the head of Pru's Northeastern Home Office in Boston, to move to Newark. In his new role Allsopp, who had recently spent some time as Businessman in Residence at Tufts University, was responsible for policyholder relations, consumer issues, employee relations, the public affairs aspects of investments, government relations, academic relations, contributions, community affairs, industry associations, and public relations and advertising.

Announcing the creation of the new department, MacNaughton said, "We have been convinced for a long time now that it is of paramount importance for Prudential to strengthen its role in American society by making the conduct of our business as responsive as possible to the needs of our policyholders, our employees, and society as a whole.''

At a conference of senior vice presidents, MacNaughton spoke of criticisms being made by public interest and consumer groups.

"These criticisms cannot be rejected out of hand," he said. "They need to be faced up to—item by item, issue by issue. Where the criticism is justified, we must change our practices; where the criticism is unjustified, we must do a better job of explaining our position."

As important as its role in society might be, however, Prudential was still a business organization. Although Beal had his hands full of social problems during his administration, there were also business satisfactions.

For a lifelong Prudential man, the son of a Prudential agent, Beal was able to rejoice in the best of all news—in 1966 the Pru moved into first place, ahead of the Met, in assets.

In its annual listing of companies, *Fortune* noted the change in status in an item entitled, "The Rock at the Top." The last paragraph of the article said:

"Prudential is treating its new distinction with modesty. In its press release summarizing 1966's results, the company took no note at all of its asset position relative to the rest of the insurance industry, saying simply that 'the Prudential Insurance Company recorded 1966 as one of its finest years.' Actually, it was also one of Metropolitan's finest years."

But Metropolitan was no longer No. 1 in assets.

25/A Surprise for the Board

On April 9, 1968, five and a half years after he had become president of Prudential, Orville E. Beal startled the board of directors by announcing his intention to retire in April of the following year. When several members protested and urged him to reconsider, Beal reminded them gently that he had told them, before accepting the presidency, that he would quit when he reached the age of 60. On April 1, 1969, he pointed out, he would have reached his 60th birthday "and have completed over 42 years of continuous service with the company." Those board members who had expected him to become infected with the fever of power during his presidency had not known their man.

As Beal later said in a conversation, "It really came down to a question of values. I had never desired to be rich. I had never desired to be powerful. Staying on five more years at top salary, building up a pension—it would have cost too much in personal terms. Mrs. Beal and I agreed that we were willing to trade less income for more freedom to do the things we would like to do.

"I had always had to work hard. I got my college at night after I came to the company. I got my master's degree at night. I got my CLU at night. Because of my studying, and the burdens of work, including a great deal of travel, I did not have very much freedom for the 42 years of my active career. I don't think I showed strain or stress, but inwardly I knew that my values needed to be balanced out a little bit."

In later years, he said, he never regretted his decision to retire five years earlier than the mandatory age.

"I think I might have regretted it if the young men that I was counting on hadn't come through so quickly. If things had turned out badly here, I might have said, 'Well, Orville, you didn't do right by good old Prudential.' But they have done well—they have done amazingly well. That makes me happy and enables me to really enjoy my retirement."

In a letter to company employees distributed the day Beal made his

272

announcement to the board, he said, "The time has arrived when I should relinquish leadership to younger hands. My early announcement will make it possible for the board to work out an orderly, smooth transition."

Instead of making a single recommendation to the selection committee of the board, Beal had prepared a chart listing several possible candidates for the post he would be leaving. For each man on the chart there was an analysis of his strong points and his weaknesses. The chart indicated the personality of each man, his general background, his experience with the company, his special interests, his individual talents. It was clear to the committee that Beal believed Donald S. MacNaughton was the person best qualified to be the next president.

Before the board meeting was over on the day that Beal announced his forthcoming retirement, the directors elected MacNaughton senior executive vice president, effective immediately. That designation followed the pattern set when the board chose Beal to succeed Louis Menagh. It was tantamount to an announcement that MacNaughton would be the next president.

Like Shanks's, MacNaughton's primary background was in law, but few men in the company could rival his overall knowledge of Prudential's operations. His work with regulatory agencies had made him familiar with all the technicalities of insurance activities, from the licensing and training of agents to the actuarial basis for rates and coverages. Under two company presidents he had served as special assistant to the president, handling all manner of assignments relating to various parts of the business. As executive vice president in charge of corporate services, he had been responsible for public relations, advertising, and other activities closely related to the marketing of insurance. After the loss of Harvey and Chodorcoff, he had proved himself a strong, forceful, adaptable executive who could be relied upon when the pressure was on.

Under MacNaughton's leadership, Prudential, which had never lost the momentum developed in the long effort to overcome the Metropolitan, would use the unity, strength of purpose, and cooperative spirit which had been fostered in the Beal administration as a springboard from which to make a new quantum jump to higher levels of achievement in life insurance, as well as diversified activities which could serve the policyholders' interests in different and better ways.

Officially, MacNaughton was to assume the presidency on April 1, 1969; in fact, Beal left office in February, to all intents and purposes, to go on vacation (although he remained a member of the board of directors for years afterward), and MacNaughton was in charge from that time on. On February 19 he expressed his "thoughts as to the company's purposes, principles, objectives, and organization" at a meeting of the Prudential President's Council, which included senior management of the Corporate Office and of the Regional Home Offices. MacNaughton's statement came to be called "the Pumpkin Papers" by everyone—even by MacNaughton—because of the color of the paper on which it was later printed for distribution as a brochure to employees.

He began with a tribute to Beal, who was not present at the meeting. Recalling a tribute President Kennedy once paid to Robert Frost, MacNaughton said, "When I first ran across it, it made me think of Orville Beal and Prudential." The encomium was this:

"We honor a man whose contribution was not to our size, but to our spirit; not to our political beliefs, but to our insight; not to our self-esteem, but to our self-comprehension."

Then, plunging into a discussion of the nature of the company, MacNaughton delighted the marketing people and those close to the agents with a blunt statement:

"The company was created to *sell* and today, nearly 100 years later, that is still our primary function—to *sell*. Too often we get so involved in the complexities of the enterprise or in our own particular responsibility that we lose sight of what we are really trying to do—which is to *sell*. Also, we get so impressed with the power, strength, and importance of Prudential that we assume people know us, love us, and will come to us. In fact, often this is not the case. They still must be persuaded. They must be sold. Today, as in the beginning, our primary function is to *sell*. And no matter what a person's job is in Prudential, he should consider it his responsibility to further the sale of our products."

As in the past, MacNaughton said, life and health insurance—and annuities—would continue to be "the backbone of our business." On the other hand, he made it clear that Prudential was willing to try other approaches to financial security, including "an equity base for our products." (Pru was just introducing its Financial Security Program, which permitted combinations of insurance, annuities, and equity purchases, the latter being managed through a newly established Gibraltar Fund. Many agents were trained and licensed to sell the Financial Security Program.)

Reiterating his faith in the individual agent as the basis of the business, the new president said, "It is our intention to remain first in individual life insurance sales and [life insurance] in-force, as measured by premium income"—despite the impact of Group coverages, "government-provided benefits, and the multiplicity of mass merchandising techniques." Given the importance of the agent, he said, the company's most serious problem would be "to compete successfully for good men"—"to attract and retain an adequate sales force."

The District and Ordinary Agencies, in MacNaughton's view, should "continue to remain separate organizations at the field level." (This differed from the practice at the Metropolitan, which had agents from both branches in each field office. Many Prudential marketing people believed that the undesirable effects of this merging helped to bring about the Met's decision in the early 1970's to phase out its debit system, so that the Met eventually would be using only Ordinary agents.)

Next, MacNaughton raised the possibility of Pru's entry on a large scale into international insurance. The company had made foreign investments from time to time, and "recently we completed an arrangement with several foreign insurers to handle the foreign business of our American and Canadian Group Insurance clients." Most of Pru's large commercial clients were already operating as multinational organizations, he pointed out, and even the company's domestic business might eventually suffer if Prudential did not, "some day, learn the language, customs, and mores of the international business community." Four years later Pru was at the point of plunging into the insurance market in Great Britain, but held back because of political and economic uncertainties that emerged at the last moment.

Then MacNaughton took up the question of the company's relationship with its policyholders. Emphasizing that "we are a mutual company," he said, "our relationship with our policyholders is almost a fiduciary one, and carries with it the high degree of accountability exacted from a fiduciary under the law. I stress this relationship because we have begun to expand our sphere of operations. In the years ahead, we are likely to embark upon new ventures. Our traditional products will remain our main preoccupation but new products and new approaches will be tried. This new scheme of things will cause us to think and behave differently in many respects; it will tend to confuse some of our traditional beliefs and behavior. Through it all, we must never forget that we are different from the ordinary business corporation whose stockholders can, in relative terms, walk in or back out of the enterprise at will. We are a mutual company with a high degree of accountability to our policyholders. Whatever we try, whatever we do, there must always be a reasonable expectation of value to Prudential's policyholders.''

As the largest insurance company, Prudential also carried some moral burdens, he said. ''With stature comes responsibility,'' he argued. ''If ever it was proper to say our sole task is to make a profit, it is no longer. If ever it was proper to say our sole concern is Prudential and its people, it is no longer. If ever it was proper to say we are solely a business institution, not a social one, it is no longer.''

He talked about the social responsibility of the company; about the need for cooperation, rather than antagonism, between business and government in the solution of social problems.

Some of his thinking implied major changes in the organization. He said he intended to explore Pru's entry into the field of property and casualty insurance. He went on: ''We will also expand in areas that are not directly customer-oriented in the traditional life insurance sense. However, these activities will be related to our business or our customers, either directly or because of the promise of increased investment returns. An example is joint ventures in real estate, two of which we have already embarked upon. . . . I think our minds should not be closed to the possibility of any service which may be related to our traditional lines of business.''

One of the top priorities MacNaughton set for his administration was the development of a work environment that should encourage every Pru man and woman to work creatively.

Finally, he asserted that ''management's most important function is to reproduce itself.'' By that he meant, ''Encourage the young people. Challenge them, train them, and give them responsibility. As someone said, 'Youth demands fervor.' Give it to them.''

Then he closed with these words:

''Prudential is a marvelous organization. It is a complicated, complex, intricate piece of machinery. It is an organization of human beings with a purpose—a noble purpose. It is more than a business. It is a great social force. We are all part of it and dependent upon it. And it is dependent upon us. This is our machine, yet we are a part of it. When it works well, it performs miracles, and work well it will, if we tend it properly. I will work as hard as necessary to do that job and will expect the same of you."

Over the following six years MacNaughton lived up to the guidelines and goals he had set in that speech. Only time would tell how successful or wise his ventures were, but he did, as he had promised, lead Prudential into new endeavors, and most business observers approved of his judgment.

By October 1971 Prudential was so immersed in new activities, or in planning for them—for it was about to enter, or broaden its interest in, such diverse areas as property and casualty insurance, reinsurance, the marketing of equity-based individual annuities, and medical laboratory work—that it seemed only prudent when MacNaughton announced that he had asked Richard G. Merrill, then a vice president in Group Pension and later senior vice president in charge of the Southwestern Home Office, to undertake a re-examination of the company's organizational structure. MacNaughton told Merrill that it was time for an in-depth study to determine whether any changes should be made by Prudential to help the company adjust to the rapidly shifting social and economic conditions of the past few years. With Robert P. Hill as his chief lieutenant, Merrill started to work on the project, which was called the "Organization Plan for the Seventies."

About a month later, senior vice president E. Carroll Gerathy and his wife, Julia (who was always called 'Julie') spent the weekend with the MacNaughtons, as they often did. The MacNaughtons had a home on Cape Cod near Chatham. On Monday, November 22, when it was time to fly back to New Jersey, the two couples arrived at the Chatham airport where their chartered airplane, a twin-engine Aero Commander, awaited them. It was a "bleak" morning, as Gerathy recalled it, raining, with strong gusts of wind. Although the two couples were not aware of it, the National Weather Service was forecasting low ceilings, snow, and snow showers, with occasional moderate icing on airplane surfaces in precipitation areas.

At 8:27 A.M. the plane, designated N87K, took off, with a pilot and co-pilot at the controls, on an instrument flight plan for Newark. At 2,500 feet the plane entered the clouds. A minute or two later it was flying through snow showers. The pilot leveled off for cruise at 10,000 feet, still in snow showers.

Back in the cabin, the two couples sipped coffee and commented on how smooth the air had been once the plane was off the ground. But Don MacNaughton felt cold. He asked the co-pilot to turn on the cabin heat, but she said she couldn't get any more heat. MacNaughton felt the air inlet near his seat. Only cold air was coming in. He turned it off to prevent the cabin from getting colder.

After a few minutes, the passengers noticed an irregularity in the sound of the engines. MacNaughton thought to himself that it sounded as though the left engine was losing power. But none of the passengers mentioned their uneasiness. As Gerathy later said, they wanted "to avoid upsetting one another."

Leaning forward to talk to the pilot, MacNaughton said in a low voice. "It sounds rough."

The pilot agreed. He said he thought the propeller was icing.

"Let's get down," MacNaughton said.

"That's what I'm going to do," the pilot replied.

A short time later the co-pilot said the plane had been cleared for a direct approach to T. F. Green State Airport at Providence, Rhode Island.

As the plane began its descent, it lurched violently. Perhaps for the first time, the passengers were now truly frightened.

At the pilot's request, Approach Control—the radar air traffic controller on the ground—cleared the plane for an ILS (instrument landing system) approach to Runway 5. Although the pilot had been told to level off at 1,800 feet, he found he was unable to stop the plane from continuing its slow descent. He feathered the left propeller—that is, altered the pitch so the blade chords were parallel with the line of flight.

The plane was now below the clouds, which were only 400 feet from the ground. The people in the plane could see trees just below them.

MacNaughton, who was seated facing his wife, leaned across and kissed her, saying, "It was great while it lasted, Winnie."

An instant later, the plane crashed in boggy woods about nine miles southwest of the Providence airport. Fortunately for those who survived the crash, at least two persons on the ground knew at once that there had been an aircraft accident.

One was a self-employed travel agent who lived on Shady Hill Drive in East Greenwich. He heard a plane approaching his house so low and fast that he got up and went to his office door to take a look at it. He saw the plane "hit or brush the top of the trees in my yard" but stagger on through the air, finally disappearing into some nearby woods. The man immediately called the East Greenwich Police Department and the control tower at the airport.

Another witness was a special officer in the East Greenwich Police Department who lived on South Road. He heard a plane approaching with such a roar that it seemed it might fly right into the house. The engine noise was "loud enough to cause alarm" to himself and his 11-year-old daughter. "Suddenly the engine noise stopped," he later reported, "and I knew that the aircraft had crashed. I waited for an explosion, but there wasn't any, nor did I hear any impact." He called the police department, then rushed to Shady Hill Drive to join a rescue party and search team that was already forming there, about to set forth into the knee-deep mud and water.

Meanwhile, in the wreckage, MacNaughton was recovering consciousness.

"Can anybody hear me?" he called out.

"Yes," Gerathy answered. "I'm here. I think I'm all right."

"Are we on fire?" MacNaughton asked.

"No," Gerathy told him.

Mrs. MacNaughton was found unconscious under a wing. The pilot and co-pilot were both terribly injured.

Julie Gerathy was dead.

For many of those at Prudential who knew MacNaughton and Gerathy, it was a fearful reminder of the dreadful fortnight a few years earlier when Robert Harvey and William Chodorcoff had been snatched away by fate.

But this time there was a new organization at the top of the company. In the spring of 1970 the board of directors created a new post, chairman of the board and chief executive officer, and MacNaughton had been named to fill it.

Kenneth C. Foster, who had been executive vice president in charge of marketing, was elected to succeed MacNaughton as president. In turn, the vacancy created by the promotion of Foster was filled by the election of Robert A. Beck as executive vice president.

At the same time, MacNaughton established an Executive Office, consisting of the chairman and chief executive officer, the president, and the three executive vice presidents. Those five men would pool their talent, knowledge, and experience to formulate corporate policy and strategy and to oversee operations, although each would have his own area of primary responsibility. In this way, MacNaughton felt, a large corporation could keep growing without losing its operational agility.

MacNaughton wanted Foster in the president's chair because, in years of working with Foster in a variety of circumstances, he had found that "his counsel was always sound."

In the 1950's and the first half of the 1960's, MacNaughton had seen the significant contributions that Foster had made as head of Group Insurance. It was no coincidence that such talented younger men as Kenneth C. Nichols, James B. Jacobson, and John K. Kittredge had risen from the ranks under Foster.

From 1967 on, when Foster was executive vice president in charge of marketing, MacNaughton's respect for his abilities had grown.

"Ken did damned good work in that demanding job," MacNaughton said. "I learned to appreciate the man's experience and intelligence even more than before. He caught on to other people's ideas at once —you didn't have to draw pictures for him. And any idea he worked on was developed very well."

When Prudential decided to set up a property and casualty subsidiary, Foster had handled the intricate negotiations with the Kemper Insurance Group, which led to Kemper's agreement to help Pru get the new operation started.

Above all, Foster had the perspective that age and experience can give an intelligent, thoughtful person. In a 1970 speech, deprecating the doom-sayers in the insurance industry, Foster said:

"When I entered the business over 30 years ago, old-timers told me that I came too late because the recently enacted Social Security law would ruin the life insurance business. By the time I became assured that it would not, I learned that Group insurance would ruin us. After I learned that not to be so, I heard that expansion of Social Security, extension of Group arrangements, and some form of national health insurance would soon eliminate the need for individualized financial security services. . . . However, year after year, those who went on . . . keeping their techniques up-to-date appeared not to know that they had been ruined."

Then he put into one sentence the essence of Prudential's philosophy of business:

"Undue effort and attention—often emotional in nature—is given to preserving existing products, markets, and distribution systems, and not enough to the development of new ways of improving our effectiveness in existing markets and advance recognition of new ones."

Earlier in that speech Foster had expressed his faith—and Prudential's belief—that there would still be an important role for insurance companies even if government-provided protection were to be expanded. The public would still want "individually provided financial security services, including and emphasizing cash value life insurance," he said, for six reasons:

> Men will continue to seek economic security.
> There are limits to the capability and appropriateness of government arrangements.
> There are limits to the capability and appropriateness of Group arrangements.
> The remaining market will continue to be large and can never be fully covered because its size is determined in part by the salesman.
> There are supplements to but no substitutes for cash value life insurance.
> There are supplements to but no substitutes for individual service.

With a man of Foster's intellectual dimensions as president, Prudential was in a strong position during MacNaughton's convalescence.

During those years of the MacNaughton administration, Prudential's decentralization—or regionalization—program, which had been started 20 years earlier, finally reached completion with the creation of the Central Atlantic Home Office (CAHO), and the development of the Eastern Home Office (EHO) as a distinct entity with a personality and a flavor all its own.

This concluding movement began with the recommendations of the Special Committee on Home Office Organization (the SCHOO study), which MacNaughton had headed. That report urged that a Corporate Office be established which would have no line responsibilities. At that time, Newark still handled insurance and investment operations throughout the mid-Atlantic states, in addition to serving as headquarters for the entire company. The SCHOO study said that a new Corporate Office should be set up, retaining responsibility for broad policy-making, planning, coordination, control, product development, and other broad administrative duties. It would also direct major investment activities, particularly bond and common stock transactions.

The line duties would be assumed by a new Eastern Regional Home Office, along with those staff support functions necessary for effective line operations. EHO would be by far the largest Regional Home Office, with a population about double that of any of the others, including, as it did, the five boroughs of New York City, all of Long Island, Westchester, and Rockland counties in New York state, and all of four other states—New Jersey, Pennsylvania, Delaware, and Maryland—as well as the District of Columbia.

When he announced that move, in 1965, Orville E. Beal had pointed out that the new Corporate Office would "be unencumbered with many of the administrative responsibilities directly associated with the sales and service of our products." He added, "For the most part, the Corporate Office will devote its attention to staff responsibilities —planning, policy-making, product development, coordination, evaluation, and control. . . . A Corporate headquarters devoted primarily [to those responsibilities] should provide the means to meet our rapidly changing needs."

As for EHO, Beal said, "Consistent with corporate policies and controls, it will be responsible, within its territory, for planning, directing, and controlling the sale and service of our products, the placement of investment funds, and the administration of certain community and public relations activities." Because of the separation of Corporate functions from those of EHO, lines of authority would be clarified, and there would be "simpler administrative routines, shortened lines of communication, and a heightened sense of identification and purpose among personnel engaged in regional work."

"The fine *esprit de corps* in our Regional Home Offices is well known to all of us," he said pointedly.

Corporate Office would be in the Prudential Plaza Building in Newark. EHO would have its headquarters in the company's Washington Street Building two blocks away, but linked to the Plaza Building by a tunnel. The block between the two buildings was occupied by Pru's Gibraltar Building, which would be used, as needed, by the Corporate Office and by EHO.

To head EHO, Beal chose Charles B. Laing, who had been running the Western Home Office in Los Angeles for four years. Laing's place there was taken by Kenneth C. Foster, who was ready to leave the Group Insurance Department at that time. The resulting vacancy at the head of Group Insurance was filled by the promotion of Kenneth C. Nichols.

By February 1968, less than three years later, Beal was ready to tell the board of directors that he had "reached the conclusion that the Eastern Home Office [was] too large for a most efficient operation and that we should consider a further step in our decentralization program."

The Eastern Home Office, Beal pointed out, had five vice presidents; all of the other Regional Home Offices operated with one or, at the most, two vice presidents. The staff of EHO, not counting field personnel, was about 4,800 persons, including 188 executives; the Western Home Office, the next largest, had about 2,000, with 88 in the management force. "Our experience has shown," Beal said, "that even with high quality personnel in all of the key jobs, it is difficult to weld such a large management group into an effective operating organization." In EHO territory there were some 200 District and Ordinary agencies, with a total of 6,600 agents and 1,700 field clerks; the next biggest Regional Home Office from that standpoint was South-Central, which had 3,650 agents and 1,000 field clerks working in 122 agencies.

As a result of Beal's presentation, a study was initiated into the desirability and the problems of establishing another Regional Home Office. A year later—by which time MacNaughton was senior executive vice president and heir-designate (indeed, he had enjoyed that status for almost a year, and within a matter of weeks he would be the head of Pru)—the company announced that it was going to build a new Central Atlantic Home Office in Upper Dublin Township, Pennsylvania, to cover Pru's operations in Pennsylvania, Delaware, Maryland, and the District of Columbia. The CAHO site was on the Pennsylvania Turnpike 15 miles north of the center of Philadelphia. The head of CAHO would be Raymond W. Cobb, who was senior vice president in charge of the company's operations analysis and research at the Corporate Office. Before that he had been head of the Mid-America Home Office, so he was familiar with Regional Home Office operations.

The plans for CAHO, beyond any doubt, reflected MacNaughton's interest in aesthetics. Prudential had chosen as its architect Vincent G. Kling of Philadelphia, who had established a reputation as a designer who was able to combine style and flair with functionalism. The low-silhouette structure he conceived occupied only five of the site's 82 acres, and the natural beauty of the rolling, wooded land was preserved by the plan. The building, which provided 500,000 square feet of working space, consisted of two units connected by a three-story, 70-foot-long, glass-enclosed bridge and by a 150-foot tunnel. Between the two units was an outdoor court with benches and trees, and not far from the building was a one-acre pond and a helipad. Inside the building were a cafeteria, a dining room, an assembly hall, library and television lounges, a recreation room, and a medical suite. The building was dedicated in June 1973. As Cobb said, "Our four-story building without right angles is unique among home offices from a design, layout, and decoration standpoint. The reaction of our many visitors has been overwhelmingly enthusiastic and favorable."

Meanwhile, the Eastern Home Office had found itself confronted with some problems that were quite unexpected. In the beginning, EHO's head, Laing, had said, "Our Newark location next to Corporate headquarters has given us one big and unusual advantage: a ready-made, highly trained staff with which to begin operations—not just a nucleus of management personnel, as in other new Regional Home Offices, but a whole staff of trained specialists. Other RHO people built a building, then staffed it. We're doing just the opposite."

But before long the EHO people, working literally in the shadow of the Corporate Office, found that theirs was not a Regional Home Office like the others. Naturally enough, people at the Corporate Office tended to get more involved with EHO operations than they would have if EHO had been, say, a thousand miles away. In the community, too, EHO had made little impression—to outsiders, Prudential was Prudential, and Newarkers thought of it in terms of the Corporate Office. Even among its own employees, EHO had difficulty establishing its own identity. Laing did his best—and Laing's best was always very good —but EHO never quite shook off its "kid brother" relationship to the Corporate Office, although it had made great strides forward by the time Laing retired in February 1970, being succeeded by Nichols, who moved over to EHO from heading the Group Insurance Department at the Corporate Office.

For Nichols, the new assignment had a special challenge. During his first six months, he tried to visit everyone at the associate manager level and above throughout the EHO territory. He walked into some offices which had never seen a high-level officer before. At lunch time he frequently sat down and ate with a table full of clerks, asking them about their work. Surprisingly, many of them felt free to air their complaints—about procedures, bosses, and many other things—and many of their gripes turned out, on examination, to be well-founded. Those contacts with clerical employees proved so fruitful that they became a part of Nichols's management style.

During one visit to EHO's Woodbridge office, one of the employees, Shirley Thompson, said she had a question to ask him: could she have a ride in the helicopter by which he had traveled there? To the surprise of her fellow workers, Nichols said, "Yes," so that afternoon she flew back to Newark in the helicopter with him and was then sent home in a company car.

To some extent, Nichols's management style reflected his service under Orville Beal when the latter was head of the North Central Home Office in Minneapolis. "At all levels Beal got through to people," Nichols said. "His door was open to everybody, at all levels. Agents would come in from the field to talk with him. Orville was so people-oriented—he took the time to listen to people." Much the same could be said about Nichols at EHO.

In 1972 Prudential announced that—although its Corporate Office would remain in Newark—its Eastern Home Office was moving out. In order to solve a number of problems, including the identity confusion caused by its proximity to the Corporate Office, EHO would move into three satellite offices in nearby areas of northern New Jersey. A Raritan Valley Office, to be designed by Vincent Kling for construction on a site in South Plainfield, would be "home base," housing Home Office services, central coordination and control functions, and the Ordinary Agencies administration. The Woodbridge Office, on the Garden State Parkway just north of Woodbridge (and near the Metro Park station of the Penn Central/Amtrak rail lines), would contain the District Agencies operation. Group sales and service would be centered in a building at Willowbrook. MacNaughton characterized EHO's development of satellites as "one of the most dramatic experiments ever made by Prudential."

In the first half of the 1970's, a number of other Regional Home Offices built satellites to house specific operations, and two Corporate

Office functions moved to satellites in northern New Jersey: the Group Pension Department to Florham Park, and computer operations to a new center at Roseland.

While construction of many of the satellite offices was under way, MacNaughton announced the outcome of the study of Pru's organizational structure which he had asked Richard G. Merrill to begin in October 1971, not long before the fateful airplane trip which nearly cost the company its chief executive. In a letter to all "Field and Home Office Management Staff," dated August 3, 1973, MacNaughton said the report, called "Organization Plan for the Seventies" (OPS), had been discussed by top management, and that some of its recommendations had been reviewed "with the various executives whose assignments would be affected by the proposals." Several recommendations were rejected.

Among the recommendations which were accepted and implemented was a proposal that the Real Estate Investment and the Bond and Commercial Loan officers in each region report directly to their respective Corporate Office departments, rather than through their Regional Home Office heads. Some people throughout the company feared that this might signal a retreat from decentralization, but those fears appeared to be groundless. As MacNaughton said, there had been "a decided shift in the nature of our investments" which no longer made the old reporting pattern logical.

Similarly, Group Insurance sales, underwriting, and claim functions were left as they had been functioning within the Regional Home Office structure, but administrative operations were consolidated for handling in only four RHOs: Eastern, Central Atlantic, North Central, and Western.

The size of the Western Home Office territory was reduced slightly by the transfer of Montana and Wyoming to the North Central Home Office and Colorado and New Mexico to the Southwestern Home Office.

In a presentation to the board of directors, Fredrick E. Rathgeber, Pru's executive vice president for administration, said:

"Another recommendation of the report was that an official company statement of objectives be developed and communicated throughout the organization. This certainly seems like a most sensible suggestion and we have considered similar ones in the past. However, when we have tried to develop such a statement, it turns out to be a series of platitudes that can be interpreted to support any currently preferred course of action.''

Platitudes were not the style of the modern Prudential. The skeptical, self-critical tone of that phrase, ''any *currently preferred* course of action,'' caught the flavor of Pru in the administration of MacNaughton and Foster.

26/Number One – All the Way

On December 13, 1973, a luncheon was held at the Corporate Office, celebrating the completion, less than a fortnight before, of the company's "Advanced Ordinary System" (AOS), a highly sophisticated computerization operation which had taken more than 10 years to plan, design, install, test, and put into operation. According to company sources, AOS was one of the "five largest and most complex computer application systems ever developed . . . comparable in size and scope to the government's SAC [Strategic Air Command] and space programs." By the time the system was in operation, nearly 11 million policies had been recorded in its computer memory banks.

In a sense, the stimulus for developing AOS came from the computer controversy of the late 1950's. By the early 1960's the company had come to realize, in the words of an internal memorandum, "that the existence of three different major systems was costly in terms of human resources and that it imposed serious restraints on Prudential's ability to respond quickly to demands for new products, for variations in compensation plans, for change of all kinds." Executive vice president Robert W. Harvey called the Pru computer experts together in February 1963 and told them:

"We share two general objectives. These are to advance—that is, to make each of our systems better than it is—and to reach a reasonable state of company-wide systems uniformity, unity, or compatibility. . . . The manner in which we have decided to proceed is to describe and agree on an improved and advanced mode of operation which will be a company-wide mode of operation, utilizing equipment which will be compatible company-wide, and then move our various systems and equipment configurations to that uniform or compatible position."

After Harvey's disabling accident, Fredrick E. Rathgeber, who became executive vice president for administration, had the responsibility for carrying forward the research and implementation involved in the program. A quiet, unassuming man, Rathgeber had made Phi Beta Kappa at Williams before joining Pru as an actuarial student. During World War II he had served with the Navy in the Pacific. After his return to the company he was one of the first group of executives who set up the Western Home Office. He was the sort of man who did nothing flamboyantly—but everything he did, he did well.

By the time the entire company had been converted to AOS, the system was handling about 550,000 transactions each night. Paper work in the field had been reduced, and productivity had been increased by 12 per cent. Moreover, more information could be obtained, and at faster speeds, than ever before, and routine transactions were being recorded in much less time. In addition, the system was so designed that some 2,000 program changes were fed into AOS three or four times each year, assuring ample potential for growth. As A. Douglas Murch, senior vice president in charge of the Computer Systems and Services Office, put it, "In a sense, we have a new version of AOS almost every quarter, and that is a powerful advantage."

About the time that AOS was completed, Kenneth C. Foster retired. For a year or two there had been rumors that he would retire then, when he was 60—a birthday which he had just passed, with 35 years of Pru service—so the news of the retirement did not come as a surprise.

His successor was Robert A. Beck, who had been executive vice president for marketing. Beck was the first man to rise from agent to president in Prudential history—at least, the first since John F. Dryden himself. In the course of his rise through the ranks, Beck had worked at many jobs in many places for Pru. "We moved 14 times in 20 years and we enjoyed every place we ever stayed and dreaded leaving it," he once said. An old friend said, "We used to joke that he was still paying for his Cincinnati draperies two moves later."

A dynamic marketing man—he not only could talk with agents about his own experiences as an agent, but also had an unusual ability to inspire other men to extraordinary levels of performance—Beck had long been marked by his associates as a future leader of the company. When his election as president was announced, one old friend sent a message, "What took you so long?" (At 47, Beck was one of the youngest men to hold the second highest post in a corporation of Prudential's size.)

A *summa cum laude* graduate of Syracuse University, Beck had had his first taste of selling insurance as an officer in his paratroop outfit in

World War II; at that time he was persuading the GI's to take advantage of the National Service Life Insurance available to them at low cost. Although he worked part-time as an agent for Prudential while attending college, Beck spent a year after graduation working for the Ford Motor Company as one of a group of 60 who were called the "Whiz Kids."

"But I wanted to sell," Beck said, "and I kept thinking of insurance. Of all the products, I liked life insurance best. So I called Prudential and told them I wanted to be an agent for them."

His feeling about life insurance always had an undercurrent of missionary zeal about it. Indeed, in many ways he gave many friends and acquaintances a sense of a crusading zeal burning within him. To one successful agent who had been asked to become a part of Prudential management—where he would make less money than he had been earning as an agent—Beck said, "Take the job. You can affect the lives of more people in that job."

Beck was part of a new generation of senior executives, of men who had been trained academically and in the business world to emphasize planning very strongly. One of his first moves as president was to strengthen the planning process throughout Prudential.

In the same way, his relative youthfulness put him in closer touch than older executives might have been with the strong currents of the time —like consumerism. "I don't think it's a fad and I don't think it's going to pass away," Beck said. "There are a sufficient number of very serious, dedicated, purposeful people who are raising the kinds of questions that need to be answered better by businesses. And the questions aren't going to go away until they get answers. Moreover, I think it's good for us because it will require everyone in business to be more responsive to the needs of the consumers. They may be a silent majority, but their purchasing power speaks very articulately and forcefully to me. The Prudential is listening."

Beck's election to the presidency left his old job vacant. It was filled by Duncan Macfarlan, when he became executive vice president for marketing. Like Beck, Macfarlan had started with Pru as an agent. And—again like Beck—he was one of the many men whose mentor was Charles W. Campbell. Macfarlan had served in the South Central Home Office at Jacksonville, the North Central at Minneapolis, and the Southwestern (which he headed) at Houston, before he was summoned to the Corporate Office.

The year 1975—Prudential's centennial—was also MacNaughton's

20th anniversary with the company, his "POG," as Prudential always put it, for the Prudential Old Guard, which Dryden had established, had proved to be a durable institution. For MacNaughton, it should have been a year of considerable satisfaction—Pru, after six years of his leadership, had never been stronger, as the figures showed.

In 1968, the last year before he took over the helm, Prudential sold $13.9 billion worth of life insurance; in 1974, the last year before the centennial, $30.5 billion. During the same period, life insurance in force shot from $137.5 billion to $218.3 billion, and assets went from $26.6 billion to $35.8 billion. In the three categories by which life insurance companies are judged competitively—sales, insurance in force, and assets—Pru ranked first in the industry in 1974. And 1974 was the *first* year in which it had beaten the Metropolitan in the category of life insurance in force. Pru had long held the No. 1 spot in assets and sales.

It seemed appropriate that 1974 should also be the year in which Pru settled a disagreement which had arisen between it and Prudential Assurance of Great Britain—the company which had not only inspired, but even given friendly advice to, John F. Dryden a century earlier. When the British company attempted to do business in the U.S. under its own name, the American Pru had taken legal action to stop it, arguing that the public would be confused by two companies with almost identical names. But in March 1974 MacNaughton was in London, where he was to deliver a major address to the World Insurance Conference of the *Financial Times* of London. With one or two of his associates, MacNaughton was invited, while in London, to lunch with the senior management of the British Prudential. It was an unusually pleasant moment in the busy lives of a number of leading insurance men—so pleasant, in fact, that MacNaughton and his British counterpart decided to take a stab at working out a settlement of their legal dispute.

In short order, they came up with a formula: in Great Britain and any other country in which it was already doing business, the British company would continue to operate under its own name. Similarly, the American Pru would do business under its own name in the U.S. and any other countries where it was already established. (This meant, for example, that both companies would continue to function under the Prudential name in Canada.) Neither company could use the Prudential name in any country where the other company was already at work and it was not; thus, the U.S. company would have to employ a different corporate name in the United Kingdom, and the British company would be barred from calling itself Prudential in the U.S. In countries where neither company was presently doing business, the name Prudential would be available only to the first company on the scene.

As gratifying as the resolution of the dispute might be, MacNaughton had better reasons to feel pleased as he looked over the world of Prudential. For example, there was the board of directors, a strong and active group, selected for their talents, but suggesting by their diversity the breadth of Pru's constituency. There was a woman on the board—a woman who was an economist, dean of a large college, and a mountain climber in her spare time. There was a black lawyer—a man who had won election to Phi Beta Kappa at Cornell while playing halfback on its football team, who was a former Judge of the Court of General Sessions in New York, who had been on the faculty of New York University Law School for 17 years. There were other lawyers, including two former Governors of New Jersey and a Queen's Counsel in Montréal. The board included bankers, food processors, manufacturers of pharmaceuticals and of heavy machinery, public utility executives, an economist famed for his observations of Wall Street trends, an outstanding physician and medical educator, a dairy farmer, and the head of New York City's public transportation system. Geographically, they were scattered from California to Minnesota to Québec, but they faithfully attended monthly board meetings, as well as meetings of committees, three of which—the Executive Committee, the Finance Committee, and the Special Committee on Review of Company Operations—met every two weeks (some places on the Executive and the Finance Committees were on a rotating basis, so that every board member had an opportunity to participate).

The board was the ultimate source of the authority with which MacNaughton presided over an increasingly complex organization, but one which could give him a sense of accomplishment.

Prupac—Prudential Property and Casualty Insurance Company —was headed by David J. Sherwood, who, though a relative newcomer to the ranks of Prudential people, had already earned the respect of his peers. At the end of 1974 Prupac was operating in 30 states which accounted for about 80 per cent of the U.S. population, and it expected to begin doing business in 15 more states before the centennial year ended. Prupac was offering only personal lines protection—

homeowner's policies and automobile insurance—but there was talk of its moving into commercial insurance in the near future.

Prupac was a subsidiary of Prudential's "downstream" holding company, Pruco, Inc.—which, indeed, was the parent of most of the Pru subsidiaries.

A major subsidiary was PIC Realty Corporation, which owned, developed, and managed real estate, especially in partnership arrangements. This was a major investment area for Pru.

Prudential Reinsurance Company, which was also headed by Sherwood, was also earning money which would ultimately help Pru's policyholders. After its first full year of operation as a separate corporation, it was already a significant factor in the reinsurance field, for it reported that premiums written in 1974 reached $73.1 million. Reinsurance is a procedure by which primary insurance companies—those which sold more insurance than they wish to carry as risks alone—resell to another insurance company (the reinsurer) part of the policies they have issued.

PruLease, Inc., had just been acquired in January 1974. That transaction was the first acquisition of an existing concern in Prudential's history. A company specializing in leasing nuclear fuel cores, vehicles, and other equipment to utilities, industrial companies, and banks, PruLease was profitable in its first year under Prudential ownership.

Pruco Securities Corporation, founded in 1971 to act as a broker for securities transactions for the account of investment portfolios managed by Prudential, was a member of the PBW Exchange (the Philadelphia-Baltimore-Washington stock market) and the National Association of Securities Dealers, and it was an associate member of the Boston Stock Exchange. It also had preferred rate access to the New York Stock Exchange and the Pacific Coast Stock Exchange. Approximately nine per cent of Prudential's transactions in 1974 were handled through Pruco Securities.

GIB Laboratories, Inc., marketed chemical analyses and other laboratory services. Although its profits were small in absolute terms, its return on investment was handsome.

There were also two Canadian subsidiaries, one for real estate investment and the other for management of a Prudential-developed mutual fund.

In executive personnel, Prudential was—as it had long been—rich beyond belief. Some insurance commissioners were said to have remarked that Pru had such depth in management that "you could staff 100 insurance companies from Prudential's people." There were few in the insurance industry who would argue with that.

In the Executive Office, working most closely with him, MacNaughton had Beck, president; Frank J. Hoenemeyer, executive vice president for investments; Macfarlan, executive vice president for marketing; and Rathgeber, executive vice president for administration.

Reporting to Macfarlan were Jack T. Kvernland, big, gangling, likable as a puppy, by nature a peacemaker but also the executive most given to speaking his mind bluntly. He headed the Actuarial Department. The others under Macfarlan were William P. Lynch, District Agencies; E. William Nash, Jr., Ordinary Agencies; John K. Kittredge, Group Insurance; Meyer Melnikoff, Group Pension; John J. Marcus, Planning and Analysis; and Martin D. Vogt, Financial Security Program Office.

Hoenemeyer's investments area included Raymond A. Charles, Bond and Commercial Loan; Donald R. Knab, Real Estate Investment; Edgar F. Bunce, Common Stock; Bryan Wilson, Treasurer (he was responsible for transactions in short-term paper, in addition to his other duties); and J. Robert Ferrari, Chief Economist.

The administration area, under Rathgeber, consisted of departments which are vital to any organization, but usually get insufficient attention—except when things go wrong. They included Alfred C. Linkletter, Buildings; Clifford H. Whitcomb, Comptroller, a man who had lent new strength and vigor to a function sometimes viewed with suspicion; A. Douglas Murch, Computer Systems and Services, a man of quiet competence in one of Pru's most demanding fields; E. Carroll Gerathy, Corporate Services; William C. White, Jr., Governmental Health Programs, the man responsible for running Medicare operations in three states and Medicaid in one state, all of the operations administered by Pru for the government in a new kind of relationship that seemed to be developing; John B. Stoddart, Jr., General Counsel, a lawyer who had established a reputation for integrity and legal skill before he came to Prudential; Robert W. Smith, Personnel; Isabelle L. Kirchner, Secretary, a lawyer; and Alan M. Thaler.

The heads of the Regional Home Offices were Raymond W. Cobb, Central Atlantic (during 1975 he retired, and Robert C. Winters took his place); Kenneth C. Nichols, Eastern; William Ingram, Mid-America; Floyd H. Bragg, North Central; Julius Vogel, long a stalwart of the Actuarial Department, Northeastern; John D. Buchanan, South Central; Richard G. Merrill, Southwestern; James B. Jacobson, Western; and W. James D. Lewis, Canadian Operations.

They were a remarkably diverse aggregation of men and women. One quality they all shared: they had made it on their own. Because of Pru's strict antinepotism rule, executives often brag about the careers of their sons or daughters—but they're always employed by another company. The ladder of promotion for talented young people at Pru is not blocked by anyone whose principal qualification for a job is a blood relationship. For that reason, most Prudential executives, it seems, are persons who were brought up in modest circumstances, worked their way through college, and made their way up the company ladder without the benefit of special influence.

Many of those men were involved in one way or another with the development of Prudential's "Centennial" series of policies, named to coincide with the company's 100th birthday, of course. The series, it was asserted, was the result of "the most extensive portfolio revision in the company's history" and reflected the fruits of a five-year development program. Designed to take advantage of recent developments in computer technology and actuarial techniques, the series also was intended to meet a number of consumer requirements. These included a 10-day "free look" at no cost to the buyer, liberalized benefits, simplified and easier-to-understand policy language and forms, and, in most instances, lower premium rates.

The emphasis on being responsive to the consumer was part of the same trend of thought at Prudential that had created the Public Affairs Department, whose head, senior vice president Thomas Allsopp, reported directly to the chairman and chief executive officer. MacNaughton and Beck were aware that an increasing proportion of the problems of Prudential—and of all businesses—involved public opinion in one way or another. But the life insurance industry had been working hard for a long time to earn the public's trust, and apparently the industry had succeeded to a considerable extent. According to a Conference Board study, life insurance ranked sixth in a list of 45 basic products and services on which consumers were asked to express their views regarding value received for money spent.

Then, too, the response to Pru's advertising campaign early in the centennial year—a campaign underlining the fact that more than half of all new Prudential policies were sold to people who already had at least one Pru policy—indicated that the public was impressed by a company which had apparently been judged to be trustworthy by people who had already done business with it.

The centennial year, 1975, began with the country—and most of the world—in an economic slump, much as it had been in 1875, when Dryden began building Prudential. For the managers of the biggest life insurance company in the U.S. (and, undoubtedly, in the world), the responsibilities borne at such a time are even greater than in relatively normal periods. Pru's response was planning.

"Prudential has long engaged in planning the future," MacNaughton said in a speech to an industry group in January 1975, "but current events have caused us to institute a more comprehensive, formal, company-wide, long-range planning system. One of the major features of our planning approach is what the textbooks would refer to as contingency planning and what we in our less esoteric moments refer to as 'what if' planning. What if two-digit inflation persists? What if production does not grow sufficiently to support the expense levels that are increasing due to inflationary pressures? What if agents' incomes do not keep pace with the cost of living? What if mandatory price-wage controls are re-established and extended to life insurance investment operations?"

The future was clouded as the company celebrated its first century. The free market system of the U.S., Canada, and the rest of the non-Communist world, on the one hand, and the totalitarian, closed-market societies, on the other, seemed to be continually drifting toward each other, he said to another industry group a month earlier. He believed that such a drift threatened political and social, as well as economic, freedoms. If that drift were to be stopped, he said, business would have to regain the trust of the public. But that would not be easy to do—in large measure, because of the attitudes of businessmen themselves.

"A common misconception [among businessmen], probably dating back to early entrepreneurial days," he said, "is that business exists for its own ends—that its primary purpose is to provide a return to its owners. But business is not an end in itself. Instead, it is a means to an end, and the end, of course, is to improve society. . . .

"It is the public's view that the opportunity for owners, managers, and employees to gain from business enterprise is a privilege to be earned by a commensurate service to the public. And it is a privilege the public can give or take away. The public is right."

On the eve of the centennial year, MacNaughton said, "We look upon Prudential as an organization which belongs, not to us, but to the people. It was they who granted us permission to function. And to function, not for our benefit, but for theirs."

After a hundred years of service to the public—a century of travail of one kind or another for almost every generation of the company's leadership—Prudential was the admitted leader in its field, a goal John F. Dryden surely never dreamed to be possible. As a mutual life insurance company, it was a rather strange sort of creature, neither fish nor fowl. It was one of the fiercest competitors in a hotly contended field—and yet it was not a true representative of private enterprise in the usual sense, for it did not exist to earn a profit for its owners, but to provide a service at the lowest reasonable price. And yet, peculiar nature and all, the company was one of the country's most valuable resources, as an instrument of capital accumulation—capital which could go toward building, improving, strengthening the nation.

As Prudential completed its first century, nothing could be more pertinent than a statement that MacNaughton made in his first report as president to Prudential's board of directors, in 1969:

"Perhaps the decade of the 1960's marked the beginning of the end of many of our traditional ways of doing things. The period was one of unrest, of protest and demand. We are not so sure, as we once were, that our institutions can absorb the shock of the social upheaval which began in the 1960's. . . . Of one thing we can be sure, that these are changing times, and, to survive, our institutions must change with them. This, then, as I see it, is the big challenge of the new decade. We must resist the temptation to count and add up our past accomplishments; and concentrate on trying to accurately measure what is going on in the world, and adjust our way of life accordingly. If we do this well, we will continue to prosper."

Author's Note

This book presents an outsider's perception of Prudential, today and over the past century. For that reason, many persons inside the company are likely to disagree with the author's emphasis in various places and his interpretation of one or another incident or development. The author is certain that he has devoted too much space, here or there, to some person or event that he found of interest, when an insider might think otherwise. By the same token, some persons who made major contributions to Pru have been given short shrift—indeed, one or two have been barely mentioned.

The author's sole criteria for the inclusion of material were: Is it important to the mainstream of the story? Will it be of interest to the general reader, as opposed to the insurance expert? Does it reveal anything about the company or any of its people?

After more than two years of work, including interviews with about 600 persons at all levels in the company and endless hours spent in wading through documents, files, and other material, the author's only regret is that he did not have time to interview all whom he wished to see, nor to go after all the records he wanted—although no person or record was withheld from him at any time.

Because this is a history, it is a most imprecise record of what actually happened. It is a truism among trial lawyers that an eyewitness is the least reliable evidence. If there are 10 eyewitnesses, there will be 10 differing accounts of what transpired. That is even more true with history, which must make do with memories blurred by the years and records which all too often are found to be incomplete.

For these reasons, anyone who reads a history expecting to find a cinematic replay of the past will be disappointed. A history is closer to a mosaic than to a photograph. At best, a history will only be able to present an indistinct image of the past. There are always too many contradictions, too many gaps in the evidence.

After what has just been said, it should not be necessary to add that only the author is responsible for whatever has been said in these pages. The author has been the only judge of what ought to go into this book, so no meaning should be read into the treatment—whether lavish or sparse—given to any person who figures in this narrative.

So many persons have helped with this book in so many ways that they cannot all be thanked individually. Nevertheless—and with apologies in advance to those who may be omitted inadvertently—the author would like to acknowledge his special debt of gratitude to a number of persons.

The first of these is Donald S. MacNaughton, chairman of the board and chief executive officer. If most company histories—especially authorized accounts, as this one is—are bland and dull, it is because few executives have the courage to permit an uncensored look at themselves, their operations, and their organization's history. It is easier to stand behind a work that will be offensive to no one. MacNaughton agreed with the author from the very beginning that this book should be uncompromisingly honest. He felt that his company was sufficiently strong, honorable, and scrupulous in most of its policies and actions to withstand the exposure of its occasional blemishes and falls from grace. Throughout the many months of work by the author, MacNaughton never faltered in his attitude—indeed, he communicated his feelings so emphatically to his subordinates that they were almost to a man willing to speak with remarkable candor to the author.

The members of the Board of Directors proved equally open and free in their comments. At Prudential, the board is an active, vital part of the organization—setting policy, keeping a close watch on the execution of policy, and generally overseeing the operations of the company. This book benefitted substantially from the observations of board members.

When the author began his research, Kenneth C. Foster was president of the company; he retired during the course of the research, but served as technical adviser after his retirement up to the moment that the last polishing of the manuscript took place. No author could ever wish for a better counselor—incredibly well-informed about his company and his industry, he was also wise, witty, unflinching in his intellectual integrity, and steadfast in his support.

His successor as president, Robert A. Beck, had backed the history project from the very first, and continued to do so when he became chief operating officer. He contributed valuable insights, particularly into the peculiar characteristics of the world of the agent.

The other members of the Executive Office—Frank J. Hoenemeyer, Duncan Macfarlan, and Fredrick E. Rathgeber—were also very helpful, as were their assistants. It is the author's opinion that he has not adequately portrayed the contributions of Macfarlan and Rathgeber to the company, and certainly the book does not reflect the immense help they gave him during his research.

Carrol M. Shanks, Orville E. Beal, and Louis R. Menagh—all retired presidents —were generous of their time and recollections, and so were many other retired Prudential people all over the country. The author is grateful also for the graciousness of Harry J. Volk in drawing on so many of his memories for this work.

In the various Regional Home Offices, the executives responsible for public relations and advertising have a variety of titles (and, in some instances, differing responsibilities). All of them made the work of the author much easier. Unfortunately, it is not possible to list their staffs, who gave so much time to the author and his strange requests; but he would like, at least, to name those who assigned staff to carry out assignments connected with this book: Daniel F. Becker, Charles L. Bochert, Peter J. Bruton, C. Robert Hart, James N. Kelleher, Roderick H. MacDonald, Leonard Nelson, Robert A. Olson, Bozeman O. Pratt and William S. Weier.

Henry E. Arnsdorf, vice president for public relations and advertising, worked most closely with the author from the very beginning. His advice and assistance was invaluable. His entire staff pitched in to help. Although all cannot be named, some should be singled out for mention: Ann Coleman, Margaret A. Flanagan, Barbara Kent,

Ann D. Koelsch, Eugene J. LoCascio, James A. Longo, David I. MacArthur, William W. Meelheim, Howard H. Van Lenten, C. Speed Veal, Joseph A. Vecchione, and Philip R. Warth.

Charles N. Haugen also lightened the author's load in too many ways to enumerate.

The men and women who worked in the District Agencies Department near the author's temporary office on the 13th floor of the Prudential Plaza Building in Newark also contributed to this book without realizing how much they were doing. Two of the veteran employees in that area, Anna Rose and George Kolb, Jr., did much to ease some logistical problems.

No manuscript emerges flawlessly from a writer's typewriter. The task of taking pages hacked and mutilated by the author's corrections, revisions, and endless word changes and turning them into clean copy was handled in downright heroic fashion by Dorothy R. Scott, Don Oshima, and Marilyn Kull—and by the following: Marion Capuzzo, Dorothy Evans, Betty Gilmour, Brooke Haley, Jean Horvath, Lee Ogrodnik, Joan Ongaro, Martha Payseur, Carol Philhower, Mabel Rhodes, Nancy Treloar, Gail Wiebel, and Christine White.

The author's research assistant was Judith Dittus, who performed phenomenal feats in finding obscure materials.

The archives at the Museum were under the general charge of Florence Higgins, and she and her assistants—Patricia Brighton, Marie Caskey, Jean Coleman, and Mary Edmiston—were always ready to do anything they could to further the project; and the demands on them were many.

It is doubtful that this book would ever have seen the light without the intelligent, cool-headed assistance of Joanne Gandolfo. Mary Ann Baliewich, Gina Mendes, and Alyce Martin also were helpful on many occasions.

Others whose help must be gratefully acknowledged include George E. Bridle (of Toronto), M. McC. Kilargis, Maxine James, and Irving S. Schupper. Chapter 21 was strengthened by information provided by Albert R. Snitzer and Charles J. Tiensch.

Finally, the author would like to express his immeasurable gratitude to Rose and Edward Radel for the special kind of help they provided throughout the long period of work on this book. Both have been friends for many years; coincidentally, Rose has been a Prudential employee for a good many years. She helped to introduce the author to company gatherings and to personnel at all levels. Because of the Radels, it was much easier for the author to keep at his task over a period of many months in Newark.

Of course, neither the Radels, nor anyone else mentioned in this note, have the slightest responsibility for any of the text. That responsibility rests, as it should, solely with the author.

Sources and Bibliography

By far the greatest source of information for this book has come from the minds, memories, and files of the men and women who have worked for Prudential or for other companies and professional organizations in the insurance industry. Company records also were made available without restriction, including the minute books of the Board of Directors. The printed reports of examinations of the company made by regulatory authorities also proved helpful. Of the documentary materials, however, the most helpful were the annual reports of the vice presidents to the president of Prudential and the president's annual reports to the Board of Directors—which are, understandably, more detailed than the reports published for the public.

In the company's News Service files and in its Museum archives repose many documents of great interest to anyone who wishes to study Prudential in depth. The files of many departments—and of the Regional Home Offices—also yielded far too many documents to be listed here.

Both the insurance trade press and the general newspapers carried a good deal of information about Prudential over the years. The files of the *Wall Street Journal* were especially helpful, as one might expect. The Newark *Star-Ledger* generously made its files available. The Newark *News* ceased publication in 1972, but its files of clippings up to that time were given to the Newark Public Library, which makes them available to researchers.

For intimate glimpses into the lives of Prudential men and women in every period of the company's history, the author was able to glean valuable material not only from the reminiscences of veteran employees and their families, but also from company publications of all sorts.

Among the books, pamphlets, monographs, speeches, and statements which proved most useful in the preparation of this book are the following:

Baker, Roscoe, *The American Legion and American Foreign Policy*. New York: Bookman Associates, 1954.

Barnard, R.W., *A Century of Service: The Story of the Prudential [of Great Britain], 1848–1948*. London: privately printed, 1948.

Bartleson, Edwin L., et al., *Health Insurance Provided Through Individual Policies*. Chicago: Society of Actuaries, 1968.

Bendiner, Robert, "The Governor Who Couldn't Stop Stealing," *Real Magazine*, 1956.

Bird, Caroline, *The Invisible Scar*. New York: David McKay, 1966.

Boorstin, Daniel J., *The Americans: The Democratic Experience*. New York: Random House, 1973.

Buley, R. Carlyle, *The Equitable*. New York: Appleton-Century-Crofts, 1959.

Bureau of the Census, U.S. Department of Commerce, *Historical Statistics of the United States from Colonial Times to 1957*. Washington, D.C.: Government Printing Office, 1960.

———, *Statistical Abstract of the United States, 1975*. Washington, D.C.: Government Printing Office, 1975.

Campbell, James S., et al., *Law and Order Reconsidered: A Staff Report to the National Commission on the Causes and Prevention of Violence*. New York: Bantam Books, 1970.

Canada 1973. Ottawa: The Ministry of Industry, Trade, and Commerce, 1972.

Canadian Pocket Encyclopedia (28th ed.). Toronto: Quick Canadian Facts, 1972.

Carrick, A.W., "The Origin of the Rock of Gibraltar Service Mark as Gleaned from the Company Archives." Internal memorandum, Prudential Insurance Company of America, 1965.

Carruth, Eleanor, "The Growth-Producing Fission at Unionamerica," *Fortune*, March 1974.

Cochran, Thomas C., and William Miller, *The Age of Enterprise*. New York: Harper, 1961.

Collins, Varnum Lansing, *Princeton, Past and Present*. Princeton, N.J.: Princeton University Press, 1931.

Condit, Carl W., *Chicago, 1930–70*. Chicago: University of Chicago Press, 1974.

Consumer Credit Industry: Hearings before the Subcommittee on Antitrust and Monopoly of the Senate Judiciary Committee, Part 3, 90th Cong., 1st sess., November 27–30 and December 18, 1967.

Creighton, Donald, *The Story of Canada*. Toronto: Macmillan of Canada, 1971.

Cunningham, John T., *Newark*. Newark, N.J.: New Jersey Historical Society, 1966.

Davis, Gordon B., *An Introduction to Electronic Computers*. New York: McGraw-Hill, 1965.

Dawson, Miles M., "Mutualization of Life Insurance Companies," *Annals of the American Academy of Political and Social Science*. Philadelphia, 1917.

Denenberg, Herbert S., et al., *Risk and Insurance*. Englewood Cliffs, N.J.: Prentice-Hall, 1964.

Desmonde, William H., *Computers and Their Uses*. Englewood Cliffs, N.J.: Prentice-Hall, 1964.

Diebold, John, *Man and the Computer*. New York: Frederick A. Praeger, 1969.

Douglas, William O., *Go East, Young Man*. New York: Random House, 1974.

——— and Carroll M. Shanks, *Cases and Materials on Business Units, Losses, Liabilities, and Assets*.

——— and Carroll M. Shanks, *Cases and Materials on Business Units, Losses, Liabilities, and Assets*. Chicago: Callaghan, 1932.

——— and Carroll M. Shanks, *Cases and Materials on the Law of Corporate Reorganization*. St. Paul, Minn.: West Publishing, 1931.

——— and Carroll M. Shanks, *Cases and Materials on the Law of Financing Business Units*. Chicago: Callaghan, 1931.

_____ and Carroll M. Shanks, *Cases and Materials on the Law of Management of Business Units*. Chicago: Callaghan, 1931.

Dryden, John F., "The Inception and Early Problems of Industrial Insurance," *The Insurance Monitor*, 1905.

_____, *Statement to the Republican Members of the Legislature of the State of New Jersey, February 4, 1907*.

Eames, Office of Charles and Ray, *A Computer Perspective*. Cambridge, Mass.: Harvard University Press, 1973.

Edge, Walter E., *A Jerseyman's Journal: 50 Years of American Business and Politics*. Princeton, N.J.: Princeton University Press, 1948.

Ellis, Edward Robb, *A Nation in Torment: The Great American Depression, 1929–1939*. New York: Capricorn Books, 1971.

Fletcher, Linda Pickthorne, "Motivations Underlying the Mutualization of Stock Life Insurance Companies," *The Journal of Risk and Insurance*, March 1966.

Foster, Kenneth C., "Credit Life and Health Insurance," *Life and Health Insurance Handbook* (2nd ed.), ed. Davis W. Gregg. Homewood, Ill.: Dow Jones-Irwin, 1964.

Geschwender, James A., ed., *The Black Revolt*. Englewood Cliffs, N.J.: Prentice-Hall, 1971.

Graham, Hugh Davis and Ted Robert Gurr, *The History of Violence in America: A Report to the National Commission on the Causes and Prevention of Violence*. New York: Bantam Books, 1969.

Gregg, Davis W., *Group Life Insurance* (3rd ed.). Homewood, Ill.: Irwin, 1964.

_____, ed., *Life and Health Insurance Handbook* (2nd ed.). Homewood, Ill.: Dow Jones-Irwin, 1964.

Harris, Richard, *A Sacred Trust*. Baltimore, Md.: Penguin, 1969.

Harriss, C. Lowell, *The American Economy*. Homewood, Ill.: Irwin, 1962.

Haynes, George H., *The Election of Senators*. New York: Henry Holt Co., 1906.

Hendrick, Burton J., *The Story of Life Insurance*. N.p., 1907.

Himber, Charlotte, *Famous in Their Twenties*. New York: Association Press, 1942.

History of the Prudential Assurance Company. London: privately printed, 1880.

Hoffman, Frederick L., *History of Prudential Insurance Company of America, 1875–1900*. Newark, N.J.: Prudential Press, 1900.

Hooker, Richard, *Aetna Life Insurance Company: Its First Hundred Years*. Hartford, Conn.: Aetna Life Insurance Company, 1956.

Huebner, S.S., *The Economics of Health Insurance* (rev. ed.). N.p.: American College of Life Underwriters, 1963.

_____, *The Economics of Life Insurance* (3rd ed.). New York: Appleton-Century-Crofts, 1959.

Jacobson, James B., "An Analysis of Group Creditors Insurance." M.B.A. Thesis, Finance Department, University of Southern California, n.d. N.p.: Prudential Insurance Company of America, 1955.

James, Marquis, *The Metropolitan Life*. New York: Viking, 1947.

Jones, Richard Seelye, *A History of the American Legion*. Indianapolis: Bobbs-Merrill, 1946.

Josephson, Halsey D., *Life Insurance and the Public Interest*. New York: Crown Publishers, 1971.

Kedzie, Daniel P., *Consumer Credit Insurance*. Homewood, Ill.: Irwin, 1957.

Keller, Morton, *The Life Insurance Enterprise, 1885–1910*. Cambridge, Mass.: Belknap Press of the Harvard University Press, 1963.

Knight, Charles Kelley, "The History of Life Insurance in the United States to 1870." Thesis, Wharton Graduate School, University of Pennsylvania, 1920.

Lawson, Thomas, *Frenzied Finance*. New York: Ridgway-Thayer Company, 1905.

Life Insurance Fact Book. New York: Institute of Life Insurance, published annually.

Lynch, David, *The Concentration of Economic Power*. New York: Columbia University Press, 1946.

Maclean, Joseph B., *Life Insurance* (9th ed.). New York: McGraw-Hill, 1962.

MacNaughton, Donald S., *An Address Delivered before the Financial Times World Insurance Conference, London, March 6, 1974*.

―――, *The Family Policy: A Paper Read before the Association of Life Insurance Counsel, White Sulphur Springs, W. Va., May 5, 1958*.

―――, *From Today On: A Speech Delivered before the Annual Meeting of the Life Insurance Marketing and Research Association, Miami Beach, November 13, 1974*.

―――, *Keynote Address to the Allstate Annual Corporate Conference, Pebble Beach, Calif., September 24, 1974*.

―――, *Let Us Help, Not Hurt: Address to the Institute of Life Insurance Annual Meeting, n.p., December 17, 1974*.

―――, *Poverty and Prejudice: An Address to the Canadian Club, Toronto, March 17, 1969*.

―――, *Remarks to the ALIA Executive Round Table, Phoenix, January 5, 1975*.

―――, *A Responsible Business: Keynote Address before the Life Insurance Conference on Corporate Social Responsibility, n.p., October 10, 1971*.

―――, *Statement to the Prudential President's Council, n.p., February 19, 1969*. This is the document usually referred to as "The Pumpkin Papers."

May, Earl Chapin, "Interviews with veteran employees for proposed history of Prudential." Photocopies of Prudential Insurance Company of America private files, c. 1949–1950.

―――, and Will Oursler, *The Prudential: A Story of Human Security*. Garden City, N.Y.: Doubleday, 1950.

McGill, Dan M., *Fundamentals of Private Pensions*. Homewood, Ill.: Irwin, 1964.

Melnikoff, Meyer, "Multiemployer Pension Plans," *Life and Health Insurance Handbook* (2nd ed.), ed. Davis W. Gregg. Homewood, Ill.: Dow Jones-Irwin, 1964.

Melone, Joseph J., *Collectively Bargained Multi-Employer Pension Plans*. Homewood, Ill.: Irwin, 1963.

―――, "Nature and Development of Private Pension Plans," *Life and Health*

Insurance Handbook (2nd ed.), ed. Davis W. Gregg. Homewood, Ill.: Dow Jones-Irwin, 1964.

Morse, Nancy C., *Satisfactions in the White Collar Job.* Ann Arbor, Mich.: University of Michigan Press, 1953.

Myers, Gustavus, *History of the Great American Fortunes.* New York: Modern Library, 1936.

Myers, William Starr, *Fifty Years of the Prudential.* Newark, N.J.: Prudential Insurance Company of America, 1927.

Nadel, Gerry, "Boston's Big Pain in the Glass," *Esquire,* April 1974.

Neu, R.F., and N.T. Hawkins, "Chronology of Major Computers Installations and Systems Changes in the Ordinary System." Internal memorandum, Prudential Insurance Company of America, 1967.

Noble, Ransom E., Jr., *New Jersey Progressivism before Wilson.* Princeton, N.J.: Princeton University Press, 1946.

O'Donnell, Terence, *History of Life Insurance in Its Formative Years.* Chicago: American Conservation Company, 1936.

O'Neill, William L., *Coming Apart: An Informal History of America in the 1960's.* New York: Quadrangle/New York Times, 1971.

Peirce, Neal R., *The Megastates of America.* New York: W.W. Norton, 1972.

Porambo, Ron, *No Cause for Indictment: An Autopsy of Newark.* New York: Holt, Rinehart and Winston, 1971.

Pringle, Henry F., *Big Frogs.* New York: Macy-Masius/Vanguard Press, 1928.

Pusey, Merlo J., *Charles Evans Hughes.* New York: Macmillan, 1951.

Rathgeber, Fredrick E., "Family and Juvenile Policies," *Life and Health Insurance Handbook* (2nd ed.), ed. Davis W. Gregg. Homewood, Ill.: Dow Jones-Irwin, 1964.

Report of the National Advisory Committee on Civil Disorders. Washington, D.C.: Government Printing Office, 1968.

Rigney, Ella Hoffman, "Frederick L. Hoffman." Manuscript of an unpublished biography, 1974.

Rose, Thomas, ed., *Violence in America.* New York: Vintage Books, 1970.

Sackett, William Edgar, *Modern Battles of Trenton,* II. New York: Neale Publishing, 1914.

Shanks, Carrol M., *The Need for Variable Annuities: A Statement before the Business Affairs Committee, State Assembly, Trenton, N.J., May 13, 1955.*

Sheehan, Robert, "Life Insurance: $84 Billion Dilemma," *Fortune,* February 1955.

———, "Life Insurance's Almighty Leap into Equities," *Fortune,* October 1968.

———, "That Mighty Pump, Prudential," *Fortune,* January 1964.

Shepherd, Pearce, and Andrew C. Webster, *Selection of Risks.* N.p.: Society of Actuaries, 1957.

Source Book of Health Insurance Data. New York: Health Insurance Institute, published annually.

Speed, John Gilmer, "Purchase of Votes: How Votes are Bought in New Jersey," *Harper's Weekly,* April 1905.

Spoerl, Charles A., "The Whittaker-Henderson Graduation Formula A," *Transactions of the Actuarial Society of America*. N.p., 1937.

Steffens, Lincoln, "New Jersey: A Traitor State," *McClure's Magazine*, April-May 1905.

Study of Monopoly Power: Hearings before the Subcommittee on Study of Monopoly Power of Committee on the Judiciary, House of Representatives, Serial 14, Parts 1 and 2-B, 81st Cong., 1st sess.

Sullivan, Mark, *Our Times*, I-VI. New York: Charles Scribner's Sons, 1971.

Temporary National Economic Committee: Final Report and Recommendations. Washington, D.C.: Government Printing Office, 1941.

————: *Hearings*, Parts 4, 10, 10-A, 12, 13, 28, 31-A. Washington, D.C.: Government Printing Office, 1939–1940.

————: *Monographs*, Parts 2, 26, 28, 28-A. Washington, D.C.: Government Printing Office, 1941.

————: *Proceedings*. Washington, D.C.: Government Printing Office, 1939.

Testimony Taken before the Select Committee of the Senate of New Jersey, Appointed April 1906 to Inquire into the Business of Life Insurance Companies Doing Business in New Jersey. Paterson, N.J.: Chronicle Printing Company, 1906. [This includes a reprint of John F. Dryden's testimony before New York state's Armstrong Committee, too.]

Thaler, Alan M., "Group Major-Medical Expense Insurance," *Transactions of the Society of Actuaries*. N.p., 1951.

"The Pru Leads Fight to Sell a New Kind of Annuity," *Business Week*, June 28, 1958.

"The Pru's New Objective," *The Institutional Investor*, June 1967.

To Establish Justice, to Insure Domestic Tranquility: The Final Report of the National Commission on the Causes and Prevention of Violence. New York: Bantam Books, 1970.

Transactions of the Society of Actuaries, VII, Nos. 17–19. N.p., 1955.

Tuan, Kailin, ed., *Modern Insurance: Theory and Education*, 3 Vols. Orange, N.J.: Varsity Press, 1972.

Volk, Harry J., and Thomas Allsopp, "Life Insurance Company Organization," *Chartered Life Underwriters Journal*, Winter 1954.

Wesser, Robert F., *Charles Evans Hughes: Politics and Reform in New York, 1905–1910*. Ithaca, N.Y.: Cornell University Press, 1967.

Whittaker, Edmund B., "A Dynamic Group Coverage," *Major Medical Expense Insurance*. Washington, D.C.: Chamber of Commerce of the United States, 1956.

————, "Group Creditor's Life Insurance," *Journal of the American Society of Chartered Life Underwriters*, VII, June 1953.

————, *History of the Group Business in the Prudential*. N.p., 1957.

————, *The Social Responsibility of the Group Insurance Industry*. N.p., 1948.

Wilson, Edmund, Jr., "New Jersey, the Slave of Two Cities," *These United States*, ed. Ernest Gruening. New York: Boni and Liveright, 1923.

Wright, Philip Green and Elizabeth Q. Wright, *Elizur Wright: The Father of Life Insurance*. Chicago: University of Chicago Press, 1937.

Index

307